INDIANA PLACE NAMES

INDIANA PLACE NAMES

Ronald L. Baker

&

Marvin Carmony

INDIANA UNIVERSITY PRESS

BLOOMINGTON & LONDON

Indiana University Press gratefully acknowledges the
financial assistance of the Lilly Endowment, Inc.,
Indianapolis, Indiana, which has helped make the
publication of this work possible. The Endowment's
support was provided so that several publications
relating to the history and life of the State of
Indiana might be published during our Nation's
Bicentennial celebration.

Published in Canada by Fitzhenry & Whiteside Limited,
Don Mills, Ontario

Manufactured in the United States of America

Library of Congress Cataloging in Publication Data
Baker, Ronald L
Indiana place names.
Bibliography
1. Names, Geographical--Indiana. 2. Indiana--History, Local.
3. English language in the United States--Pronunciation.
4. English language in the United States--Dialects--Indiana.
I. Carmony Marvin, joint author. II. Title.
F524.B34   1976   917.72   74-17915
ISBN 0-253-14167-2   1 2 3 4 5 79 78 77 76 75

Contents

Introduction

A place name is the name of any geographic feature, natural or artificial. This study of Indiana place names includes mainly names of
selected artificial features: counties, cities, towns, and villages. A few
names of streams and lakes have been included, but these names amount
to only 155 of 2,271 names in this study. Thus, this is a selective dictionary of Indiana place names, emphasizing settlement names, and is
by no means a gazetteer. A complete survey of Indiana names, now un-
derway as part of the Place-Name Survey of the United States, will take
many years, and the findings will fill many volumes. In the meantime,
this study will serve as a guide to some of the names in the state. Until
publication of *Indiana Place Names,* Indiana was one of about twenty-
seven states without a place-name dictionary.

An adequate place-name dictionary should include four kinds of data:
historical, linguistic, geographic, and folkloristic. An attempt has been
made to treat each of these aspects of place naming, although in some
cases it has been either impossible or irrelevant to include all four kinds
of information. Throughout, the aim has been concision and readability,
and the emphasis has been on current names. Within the entries, however, former names and spellings frequently are given.

The Pronunciation of Indiana Place Names

In this study of Indiana place names, the principal linguistic objective
has been to obtain an accurate local pronunciation of all of the names
under consideration. It has not been assumed that the way a place name
"ought" to be pronounced is the usual way or the only way it actually
is pronounced in the community it signifies. For example, Hoosiers living outside the Martin County city of Loogootee usually pronounce the
name as [lə'gōdē]; but not so the townspeople themselves, who pronounce
it as ['lō'gōdē]. Thus an effort was made to obtain informants in each

county, not merely to ascertain their own pronunciations but to enlist their help in acquiring a good understanding of local pronunciations in general. Though the one hundred or so obliging participants in this phase of the work represent a tiny sample of Indiana residents, there is some justification for the belief that the details of pronunciation presented in the listing are essentially accurate and reasonably full. One's hope is that the pronunciations will prove of interest and value not only to present-day readers but also to those of future generations, doubtless destined to find many relics of old Indiana speech in these pages.

With the details of place-name pronunciations in mind, one can use this linguistic corpus to determine something of the relationship between the pronunciation of place names and pronunciation at large in the state. Such an endeavor embraces both matters of regional dialects and of modifications of place-name pronunciations that have occurred during the habitation of the land by English-speaking peoples.

Inasmuch as Indiana communities were established by settlers who came in varying proportions from all three of the geographical areas of the late eighteenth and the nineteenth century eastern seaboard, the three major dialects that developed in these areas have influenced—indeed, largely determined—the development of Indiana speech. Of the three eastern dialects—Northern, Midland, and Southern—the principal influence has been exerted by the Midland, which grew out of the middle colonies. This fact is evidenced by a number of regional expressions, grammatical patterns, and pronunciation features which have much in common with those of the middle states settlements of the seaboard. Among the pronunciation features characteristic of the Midland are the use of the [ē] sound of beat in the final syllable of such words as sunny and easy rather than the [i] sound of bit; the [ə] sound of cup in the final syllable of such words as wanted and sheriff rather than the [i] of bit; the [e] sound of bet in such words as marry and narrow rather than the [æ] of bat; the [e] sound of bet in Mary rather than the [ā] sound of bait; and the retention of [r] following vowels, as in bard and bird.

Even within the limited phonetic confines of the place-names corpus, there is ample evidence to support observations concerning the minimal listing above. In the case of the final syllable sound of such names as Ari, Mount Healthy, Ockley, Rugby, and many other place names with a 'y' ending, the [ē] sound of beat is used by virtually all of the informants. Similarly, the frequency of occurrence of [ə] as in the usual pronunciation of the final sound of sofa is high in the lightly stressed or unstressed syllables of place names like Ellison, Paris, Wallen, and Williams. Before [k] and less often before [ch] or [sh], however, the [i] of bit may occur, as in Messick. Otherwise, the occurrence of [i] in such unstressed syllables seems to be limited to place names from the southern third of the state, as in Oliver ['alivər] and Solitude ['salitūd], both from Posey County. This feature of Indiana pronunciation reflects the very considerable north to south gradation of Hoosier speech.

The [e] sound of bet seems to occur uniformly in the pronunciation of place names of the -ar- type such as Brushy Prairie, Gary, Harrison, Paragon, and Paris Crossing, in which the [æ] sound of bat is likely to occur in both Northern and Southern pronunciations. Moreover, despite the small sampling, there is little reason to believe that the [ā] of bait occurs more than rarely in the pronunciation of Indiana place names involving Mary, the [e] of bet occurring in the recorded instances. Finally, just as there is no appearance of the [æ] of bat before [r] in the pronunciation materials, there is likewise no instance of the loss of [r] following a vowel. Thus in terms of these phonological features, the pronunciation of place names in Indiana corresponds rather closely to the pronunciation of English generally in the state.

Certain other features of the pronunciation of place names are of interest for reasons less closely connected with regional dialects. These features can be considered under the general heading of modifications, a partial list of which includes additions, losses, transpositions, substitutions, and reshapings reflecting folk etymologies. These modifications of processes have been at work for centuries in the development of the English language and thus are not at all unique to Indiana.

A familiar addition in Indiana speech is the intrusion of [r] in such words as wash and Washington. The latter word does occur in the corpus with [r] and is heard frequently in the state with this pronunciation. A less noticeable but very common intrusion occurs in words such as advance and fence, in which a [t] is articulated between [n] and [s]. Place names in which the intrusive [t] occurs with some frequency include Lawrenceburg, Prince William, and Rensselaer. An added final [s] occurs in at least two instances, the pronunciation of Kellerville as Kellersville and that of Nead as Neads, both offered as the usual pronunciation of the names.

The loss of certain vowel and consonant sounds is a prominent feature of place-names pronunciations, perhaps more prominent than one might expect within a class of words that would seem to be less subject to various erosions than would ordinary parts of speech. In a number of instances the omission is not regular and may be symbolized accordingly by the enclosure of the optional sound within parentheses. The presence or absence of sounds in the category depends in part on the speaker's situation and the style of speech which he uses to respond to it. Thus in the rapid speech of the Hoosier Indianapolis may be pronounced as [ˌindē'næpləs] but in careful speech as [ˌindēə'næpələs]. Other losses which may be said to be optional for local residents as a whole occur in the pronunciation of Elizabethtown [(ə)liz(ə)bəth͵taun] and Morristown ['mor(ə)s͵taun]. The loss of final [t] in the pronunciation of such place names as East Liberty and West Fork is usually optional and is related to the manner of speaking involved. On the other hand, the loss of initial [h] in the pronunciation of White River is more likely to occur in the speech of young Indianans than of members of the older generations.

A special sort of loss occurs when one of two similar sounds is altered or drops out altogether, presumably because the combination is hard to pronounce. Called "dissimilation," the process is well illustrated in the general vocabulary in the pronunciation of library, which sometimes is rendered as libary, and February, which occurs more often than not as ['febyəwerē]. This very old process in the development of languages is reflected in the pronunciation of several Indiana place names. These include Floyds Knobs as Floyd Knobs, Hurlburt as Hurlbut, Merrillville as Merriville, and Surprise as Suprise. All of these citations were offered as the usual pronunciations of the names in the local community.

In the development of English, a reversal of the sounds of a given word has occurred at times. Thus modern bird developed from Old English *brydd* and horse from earlier *hros*. Called "metathesis," the process is still at work in the general vocabulary, as reflected in such pronunciations as *purdy* for pretty and the fairly common *prespiration* for perspiration. In the pronunciation of Indiana place names at least two instances of the process can be cited. Putnamville is often pronounced as Putmanville and Corunna is reported to be pronounced regularly as Curonna.

In the pronunciation of the word creek and of certain place names such as Lafayette, alternative pronunciations occur more or less freely, though with regional, generational, and perhaps social correlations. A related but somewhat different mechanism is involved in the usual case of substitution. For example, before [l] the expected [æ] or [i] may be replaced by the [e] of bet. Thus in the general vocabulary, aleck in the phrase smart aleck is usually pronounced as ['elik] and vanilla is very often pronounced as [və'nelə]. This habit is extended to the pronunciation of some place names. For example, Alexandria is pronounced as [͵elig'zændrēə]. In many instances, however, the expected [æ] usually remains, as in Alto and Talbot. The use of the [e] of bet in place of the expected [i] of bit appears to be regular in the pronunciation of Manilla, which is heard uniformly or nearly so as [mə'nelə]. Likewise, the usual pronunciation of Avilla is [ə'velə] rather than [ə'vilə]. The same sounds, [i] and [e], are shifted about in Indiana speech before a following [m] or [n]. Thus since may be pronounced by some Hoosiers as *sense* and pin may be pronounced as *pen*. This habit apparently does not have much strength among the place-names informants, at least so far as the pronunciation of place names is concerned. The [i] of bit occurs in Kennedy and Hemlock and is heard in the pronunciation of Vincennes; but the expected [e] of bet occurs in many names, including Eminence, Glenwood, Kenneth, and Pennville.

In the examples given above, the vowel sounds seem to have been influenced by following consonants. For the influence of sounds on one another, a widespread phenomenon, the term "assimilation" is used. Two interesting examples of assimilation among consonants can be cited. Trafalgar is sometimes rendered as Trafalver, the expected [g] being replaced by [v], a sound articulated in the same position as the preceding [f]. In the case of Bainbridge, the assimilation works in the opposite direction to produce an added sound, resulting in the pronunciation Brainbridge.

One of the most common substitutions encountered in the study of Indiana speech involves the [ə] of but and the [ē] of beat. In older Indiana, speech words ending in 'a' were frequently pronounced as if they ended in 'y'. Thus banana was pronounced as *banany* and Indiana as *Indiany*. Of the latter pronunciation, the Indiana poet William Herschell attributed the inspiration for his "Ain't God Good to Indiana?" to the question of an old man who looked up from his fishing lines in Blue River east of Knightstown and commented: "Ain't God good to Indiany?" Given the frequency of its occurrence in the Indiana speech of an earlier day, it is hardly surprising that 'y' pronunciations are still heard, especially in the speech of older Hoosiers. Though the use of [ē] in this manner has lost ground, the sound appears in the place-names listing as a local or older pronunciation of such names as Arba ['arbē], Arcadia [ˌar'kādē], Banta [bæntē], Buddha ['būdē], Mecca [mekē], Salamonia [ˌsælə'mōnē] and Sparta ['spartē]. But Paoli is usually [ˌpā'ōlə], perhaps partly in response to the association of the [ē] pronunciation with the Indiana countryside of an earlier, more rustic period.

The modification of the phonetic shape of some place names goes beyond the kinds of changes that have been outlined in the preceding paragraphs. Some pronunciations seem to reflect an effort to make words, especially those of foreign origin, sound more familiar, to have more "sense." Thus the changes are more the result of a psychological process than of a phonetic one. In Indiana speech, and probably in American English generally, one occasionally hears *cold slaw,* a folk etymology for coleslaw, derived from Dutch *koolsla,* in which *kool* signifies cabbage. Among American place names, this kind of reshaping or "folk etymology" is well illustrated by the treatment accorded the French name for a western river, the *Purgatoire,* which the early settlers made sense of as the Picket Wire, one of the current names for the river.

Introduction

Among Indiana place names, Stendal is heard locally as Standale; and Savah occurs as Savoy. Both appear to be instances of the effort to reshape the strange into something more familiar.

From this brief commentary on the pronunciation of Indiana place names, two or three conclusions may be drawn. One is that the pronunciation patterns of the place names are very largely consonant with Indiana pronunciation patterns generally. It is likewise evident that the pronunciation of Indiana place names reflects and confirms the essential Midland nature of Indiana speech, at the same time demonstrating the more Northern-like to more Southern-like gradation of Hoosier speech as one moves from Lake Michigan toward the Ohio River. Finally, the study evidences as well the fairly free operation of linguistic processes among words which by definition have a special place in the general vocabulary.

The Classification of Indiana Place Names

The place names in this collection have been sorted into thirteen main categories and several subcategories. In the following discussion of the major classes of Indiana place names, the percent given refers to the count within each of the three groups of place names covered here— counties, settlements, streams and lakes—and not to total names in the study.

1. NAMES FOR A PERSON

Names embodying personal names, especially surnames of national or state heroes and local pioneer settlers or founders, are among the most common kinds of place names in the United States. Of Indiana's ninety-two counties, seventy-eight (84.78%) were named for personal names. Seventy-three of these counties (79.35%) were named for non-local people, especially military heroes, as fifty-five counties bear the names of heroes of the Revolution, the War of 1812, or Indian wars. Of the latter wars, the Battle of Tippecanoe was especially influential, as ten counties were named for soldiers in that famous Hoosier battle. Only five counties (5.43%)—Bartholomew, Clark, Floyd, Gibson, and Grant—were named for local men.

The largest class of names of cities, towns, and villages also is for personal names, for 740 settlement names in this study (36.58%) are for people. Unlike Hoosier counties, however, most settlement names are for local rather than non-local people. Local citizens, generally early settlers or founders, gave their surnames to 580 cities, towns, and villages (28.67%); and non-local people are honored in the names of 103 populated places (5.09%). Christian, middle, and nicknames were the source of fifty-seven settlement names (2.82%), and all of these save one, Dale, are for local people.

Although the selected names of streams and lakes in this study are too few for a meaningful analysis of either specific or generic names, certain patterns are suggested. In these names of mostly natural features the personal name still is influential, accounting for thirty-three of the 155 names (21.30%); however, only one of these names, Brouillets Creek, honors a non-local person, and there is some doubt about the origin of that name. Likewise, only one name of a watercourse, Nineveh Creek, is for a christian name, unless one accepts the legendary explanation of Jacks Defeat Creek, which also seems to be for a personal name.

2. NAMES FOR OTHER PLACES

A relatively high percent of Hoosier names are transfer names. Ten of the ninety-two county names (10.87%) are for other places. Lagrange and Switzerland counties bear names from foreign countries, while Orange County received its name from a county of the same name in North Carolina. Seven of the borrowed county names (7.61%) are local transfers coming from the names of natural features. Elkhart, Ohio, St. Joseph, Tippecanoe, Vermillion, and Wabash counties were named for nearby streams, while Lake County received its name from Lake Michigan, which forms its northern boundary.

Transfer names constitute the second largest class of settlement names, with 562 settlements (27.78%) receiving their names from other place names. Foreign names account for 147 (7.27%) of borrowed names, while names from other states total 165 (8.16%). Local transfers, however, are the most popular of the borrowed names, as 250 cities, towns, and villages (12.36%) bear names of nearby features.

Just as most stream and lake names embodying personal names are for local people, most transfer names applied to these features are for local places (12.90%). Only one name, Wyalusing Creek, of twenty-one transfer names of streams and lakes is from another state, and the other twenty borrowed names are local transfers.

3. LOCATIONAL NAMES

Locational names, sometimes classified as a subtype of objectively descriptive names in other place-name studies, are those names indicating direction or position. Some of these place names could be classified as local transfers since they bear directional prefixes applied to nearby place names. All such local transfers with directional adjectives, if they are truly descriptive of location relative to the borrowed name, as well as other names descriptive of location, have been included here. These names are not especially common in Indiana, for no county names and only thirty-seven settlement names (1.83%) are locational. Stream names like East Fork Tanners Creek, East Fork White River, Half Way Creek, North Branch Garrison Creek, North Fork Salt Creek, and West Fork White River are fairly common throughout the state, though, and constitute 3.87% of the sample.

4. DESCRIPTIVE NAMES

Descriptive names may be either objective or subjective. Objectively descriptive names identify places by noting some characteristic of the feature or surrounding area. Subjectively descriptive names are those in which personal judgment or taste enters. Only one county in Indiana bears a descriptive name. The French name *LaPorte,* "the door," is objectively descriptive. Apparently a natural opening in the forest here served as a door through which trade between southern and northern Indiana passed.

Objectively descriptive names constitute the third largest class of settlement names, but with only 167 names (8.26%) falling in this category, they rank far behind settlement names borrowed from personal names and other places. Five of these names—Bluecast, Lapel, Long Beech, and two Pinhooks—are descriptive of shape, size, or color, while two others—Badger Grove and Oriole—are for fauna. Local flora has been much more influential than fauna on settlement names, though, as thirty-nine Hoosier cities, towns, and villages bear names like Ash Grove, Beechwood, Cloverdale, Maple Valley, Oaklandon, Pine, Plum Tree, and Sycamore. Some of these names seem commendatory as well as descriptive. The most popular objectively descriptive names of settlements are those inspired by landscape, situation, or association (4.35%). This group consists of eighty-eight place names, including Bridgeton, Canal, Cementville, Edgewood, Five Points, Hillsdale, Milford, Prairieton, Quakertown, River, and Tunnelton. Subjectively descriptive settlement names—such as Aroma, Grandview, Mount Healthy, and Pleasant Ridge—number only twelve (.59%).

A larger percentage (19.97%) of streams and lakes than counties or settlements have objectively descriptive names. Names like Blue Lake, Crooked Creek, Halfmoon Lake, Long Lake, and Silver Creek describe shape, size, or color and constitute 5.80% of the sample. Other names (3.22%)—Beech Creek, Big Pine Creek, Butternut Creek, Caney Fork, and Cedar Lake—are descriptive of flora. Bass Lake, Buck Creek, and Wolf Run were named for local fauna (1.93%). Other names of watercourses—such as Coal Creek, Flint Creek, Richland Creek, Salt Creek, and White Lick Creek—are for minerals or soil (3.22%). Nine names of lakes and streams—including Lake of the Woods, Lost Creek, Mill Creek, and Prairie Creek—were suggested by landscape, situation, or association (5.80%). Only one stream or lake name in the sample, Pretty Lake, is subjectively descriptive.

5. INSPIRATIONAL NAMES

Subjective place names generally are rare in place-name studies, and this collection of Indiana names is no exception. Only one county, Union, has an inspirational name, but even here sources disagree on the origin of the name. Some say that when Union County was organized in 1821 it was so named to discourage fighting between rival towns for the county seat, but more likely the name suggests a more general feeling of patriotism.

Eight settlement names are idealistic (.40%); sixteen are classical (.79%); and thirteen are literary (.64%). Idealistic names include Harmony, Patriot, and Union City. Among the classical names are Argos, Delphi, Mt. Olympus, Rome, and Troy. The literary names suggest that Sir Walter Scott's novels were among the most popular pieces of literature, as they gave Indiana three place names: Waverly, New Waverly, and Rob Roy. Biblical or religious names, numbering twenty-seven (1.33%), are only slightly more popular, with Palestine being one of the most common biblical names, as it was applied to several communities.

Most of the inspirational names may be classified as commendatory names, a term used by George R. Stewart to identify names that just seem to be good names, ones that have pleasant connotations and will attract settlers. Eighty (3.95%) of the settlement names in this study are commendatories, including Acme, Bloomingdale, Emporia, Fairfield, Home Place, Prosperity, and Solitude. Inspirational names, including commendatory names, account for only 7.23% of the settlement names in this sample. Of the stream and lake names, only the religious name St. Joseph may be called inspirational.

6. HUMOROUS NAMES

Hoosier namers apparently were a sober lot because fanciful and humorous names are not at all common in the state. Amusing anecdotes explain names like Gnaw Bone, Pinhook, and Popcorn, but apparently these names were not jocularly applied. Needmore and Pumpkin Center, both applied to more than one Hoosier community, may be humorous derogatories, but their origin is uncertain. In fact, of all the names in this collection, only Santa Claus clearly reflects humorous motivations.

7. INDIAN AND PSEUDO-INDIAN NAMES

The Indian occupation of the area we now call Indiana is scarcely remembered in the names of Hoosier counties, cities, towns, and villages. Counties were created after the native Americans had been forced off the land, so naturally Indians would not have had names for such artificial legal entities. In fact, there seems to have been strong opposition to Indian names in the naming of at least one county. When Howard County was organized in 1844, it was called Richardsville, for the famous Miami chief, but there was so much resentment for the name that it was changed two years later to Howard, for Hoosier statesman Tilghman A. Howard. Two counties, however, were named for Indian tribes. At the time of George Rogers Clark's conquest, the Miami tribes occupied much of the present state, and this fact is recalled in the naming of Miami County. When the Delaware Indians were forced from their eastern homes and moved west, they settled in Miami territory, and this is remembered in another county name, Delaware. The Calumet, a large industrial region in northwestern Indiana—including the cities of East Chicago, Gary, Hammond, and Whiting—is a local transfer name from the Grand Calumet River and preserves an Indian name, too.

Only 1.93% of the settlement names in this sample are Indian or pseudo-Indian—that is, Indian names applied or garbled by people other than native Americans. Some of these, such as Ockley and Toto, have uncertain origins but are thought to be of Indian origin. Others, like Mongo, have been changed considerably from their original forms. Of the Indian names of settlements, the most popular type is for personal names, with twelve of these remaining in Indian languages and ten being either translated or European language names of Indians. Indian tribes, including Miami, Muncie, and Wyandotte, gave their names to seven Hoosier settlements.

The Indian had much more influence on the names of Hoosier streams and lakes than on counties and settlements, for 32.90% of the stream and lake names in this study are Indian names. A few, however, such as Lake Lenape, were applied by non-native Americans, and others, like Baugo Creek, are corruptions of earlier Indian names. Some of the Indian names—including Kankakee River, Muskelonge Lake, Ohio, Tippecanoe River, and Wabash River—are actually descriptive names. Others are for Indian tribes: Big Shawnee Creek, Iroquois River, Kickapoo Creek, Maumee Creek, Patoka River, and Wea Creek. Three lakes—Shipshewana, Wawasee, and Winona—have Indian language names of individual Indians. Ben Davis Fork, Charley Creek, Killbuck Creek, and Squirrel Creek also are from Indian personal names, although, of course, they are English language names or translations. In fact, translated Indian names constitute the largest class of Indian names (14.19%). Descriptive stream names like Cedar Creek, Clifty Creek, Driftwood River, Eel River, Flat Rock River, Sand Creek, Sugar Creek, White River, and Yellow River are all translations from Indian languages.

8. NAMES FROM LANGUAGES OTHER THAN ENGLISH

Place names from European languages other than English are extremely rare in Indiana. The early French exploration and settlement within the present state is reflected in one county name, LaPorte, a descriptive name discussed earlier. Two other county names, Fayette and Lagrange, are for the Marquis de la Fayette and his home near Paris, but since these names honor the famous military officer of the Revolution, they do not reflect the French settlement of the state. Of the settlement names, Terre Haute preserves a French influence, as do Vincennes and St. Croix, although the latter was applied for devotional reasons. Another French name, Amity, apparently is commendatory, as is the Latin Amo.

As the French were traders and explorers, frequently they gave French names to watercourses, or else they translated Indian names of streams. Since they were Catholics, sometimes they named Hoosier streams for saints. Stream names like Aboite Creek, Maria Creek, and the St. Joseph River show a French influence on the naming of Indiana streams.

The influence of other European languages on Indiana place names is minimal and largely indirect. Haubstadt, named for local storekeeper Henry Haub, uses a German generic, -*stadt,* which is rare in Indiana. Greek names like Eureka and Philomath are incident or commendatory names and not direct applications. The Spanish Plano is perhaps a transfer name from a western state. Accordingly, Indiana place names reflect an early settlement history of English-speaking immigrants. Although during the late nineteenth and early twentieth centuries there was considerable foreign immigration from other European countries, these later settlers had virtually no effect on Indiana place naming, as English remained the basic language and most names had been fixed by then.

9. INCIDENT NAMES

Incident names generally arise from local happenings. None of Indiana's counties has an incident name, although five settlements and three streams in the sample bear such names. Still, the percent of these names is low—1.93% of stream and lake names and merely .25% of settlement names. Two incident names were inspired by the Battle of

Tippecanoe. Armiesburg was so named because William Henry Harrison's army camped there on the way to that battle, and Battle Ground received its name because the battle was fought there. Cyclone was named for a cyclone there in 1880. The explanation of one supposedly incident name, Rome City, actually appears to be legendary. Three stream names also are incident names. Hurricane Creek, a small stream in Johnson County, was so named by the evidence left there by a hurricane. Poison Creek was named for milk sickness once in the area, and Treaty Creek recalls a treaty made with Indians near its mouth in 1826.

10. FOLK ETYMOLOGY

Folk etymology occurs when an unfamiliar name is reshaped to make it more familiar. Since most Hoosier place names are of English language origin, folk etymology is not common in Indiana geographical nomenclature, although it has occurred with a few names. Koleen apparently was reshaped from kaolin, a type of clay used in making pottery, and Gnaw Bone apparently is a corruption of Narbonne, a French city. Although Russiaville seems to have been named for the country, actually the name is a corruption of Richardsville, the French name of a Miami chief. Spiker comes from an attempt to make the German personal name Speicher more meaningful. Two stream names in this collection also result from etymology. Weasel Creek derives its name from an attempt to make sense out of the former name of the stream, *Wesaw,* for a Miami chief. Although the name of another stream, Mary Delarme Creek, still suggests its French origin, it has been considerably reshaped from its French name, *Marais de l'Orme,* "Elm Swamp."

11. COINED NAMES

Place names manufactured from other names, coined by reversing letters, or formed from initials offer some of the most interesting names in place naming. All examples of coined names in this study are settlement names, constituting only .94% of the total names of populated areas. Two place names, Kyana and Michiana Shores, resemble boundary names, as the former was coined from the abbreviation for Kentucky and the last three letters of Indiana, while the latter was coined from the first four letters of Michigan and the last four letters of Indiana. Bromer and Elwren are acronyms formed from the names of founders and settlers, and Gimco is another acronym formed from the name of a local company. Five Hoosier place names were formed from parts of two personal names. Broad Park comes from the names of two large landowners, Broadstreet and Parker. Carwood comes from the surnames Carr and Wood. Hanfield was coined from the names of two statesmen,

Hancock and Garfield. Loogootee also comes from two personal names, Lowe and Gootee, as does Wilfred, which honors two local mine operators, Wilford and Fredmon. Both Holton and Woodbury were manufactured from the names of their founders, Holman and Ellingwood. Perhaps the most celebrated coined name in the state, however, is Trevlac, which is the name of one of the founders, Calvert, spelled backwards.

12. MISTAKE NAMES

A few Hoosier settlement names (.25%) have their origin in errors made by the Post Office Department or local clerks. One community applied for a post office as Comet, but a series of misunderstandings changed the name to Correct. Another town formerly was called Moores Mill until a mistake was made when it applied for a post office, so now it is called Moores Hill. Siberia first was called Sabaria, but the Post Office Department hoping to correct an error committed an error and changed the name to Siberia, not an especially commendatory name. Perkinsville was to be named for early settler William Parkins, but an error was made when the plat was recorded. Another clerical error changed Laswell, for the personal name, to Taswell.

13. LEGENDS AND ANECDOTES

The study of place-name legends is still in its infancy in the United States, for folklorists have done little with names, and onomatologists have done even less with folklore. In fact, one aim of some American place-name studies has been to discredit folk accounts of the origin of names and to present the bare facts. In this collection, the emphasis has been on the factual rather than fanciful aspects of Indiana place names, too; however, some local legends have been included here for their cultural value and to stress that such stories about the origin of names are fairly common. For thirty-one names in this study, legends serve as the only available explanations of the names, and for several others— including Galveston, Lorane, Roann, and Waterloo—legends have been included even though other explanations seem more likely. Although legends do not always preserve accurate details of naming, they provide other kinds of information. They give some impression of the people who live in an area, and they reveal what the name means to the people who use it. To a person using a name it makes little difference what the name actually means; the name functions just the same whether the locally held explanation is factual or fanciful. Moreover, for one interested in the cultural value of names, fanciful stories explaining the origin of names often are more revealing than factual explanations, as place-name legends occasionally suggest something about the beliefs, prejudices, values, and humor of the people telling them. In this study, none of the explanations of county names is legendary, and the percent of settlement names (1.43%) and stream and lake names (1.29%) with only legendary origins is small.

Method of Presentation

The entries are arranged alphabetically with cross references provided for current alternate names and local transfers. Whenever possible or relevant, the following kinds of information have been given for each name:

1. PRESENT SPELLING

Although former spellings frequently are given within entries, emphasis has been on current spellings.

2. PRONUNCIATIONS

Since it cannot be assumed that any pronunciation is commonplace, pronunciation has been given for each name. Familiar pronunciation symbols—modifications of those in *Webster's New Collegiate Dictionary*—have been used rather than the more technical International Phonetic Alphabet. The pronunciations given are current ones as spoken by residents of the county in which the name is found. At least one informant from each county was interviewed, and a list of those informants agreeing to have information published about them is appended.

3. ALTERNATE NAMES

Following pronunciations, current alternate names, if any, are given in parentheses.

4. TYPE OF FEATURE LABEL

Only eight feature labels have been used in this study: state, county (given as part of the name), county seat, city, town, village, stream, and lake. Other types of features have been excluded. Following categories established under the general laws of Indiana, cities have been classified according to population. First class cities, of which Indianapolis is the only one in the state, have a population of 250,000 and over. Second class cities are those with a population of 35,000 to 250,000. The population of third class cities ranges from 20,000 to 35,000. Fourth class cities have a population between 10,000 and 20,000. Fifth class cities are those with 1,500 to 10,000 population.

Towns are incorporated settled areas having less than 1,500 population. A few populated places have a population of over 1,500 but still are classified as towns since they have not held the appropriate elections to become cities. All unincorporated populated places have been classified as villages, although some were established as railroad stops, post offices, or resort communities; and some may have a scattered population unlike the usual concept of village.

5. LOCATION

Ideally, geographical coordinates should be used in place-name studies when the place is emphasized rather than the name; however, since latitude and longitude prove difficult to some readers without adequate maps, location is provided in this study by county, when appropriate, and locational symbols as found on the current "Official Highway Map" of Indiana. Readers who desire more precise coordinates may consult *The Times Index-Gazetteer of the World* (Boston, 1966), which gives latitude and longitude for 345,000 geographical locations, including those for many Hoosier settlements.

6. ORIGIN

In an attempt to keep the study concise, the origin of the present name, generally traced back a single step, has been emphasized rather than etymology or a complete history of the naming. For 256 settlement names (12.65%) the origin is unknown or uncertain. Possible origins suggested for some of these are clearly qualified and should not be considered factual. In most cases, the year of founding is given for settled places, although sometimes the name is older than the official establishment. Dates for the naming of natural features have been virtually impossible to find. The namers usually are noted when known, but most of them remain anonymous. Sources of information about the origin of the names are given in the Bibliography.

7. LEGENDS

Even when the actual origin of a name is certain, folk legends and anecdotes sometimes are included in the entries for their cultural value and popular appeal. Occasionally verbatim texts and variant accounts are given, but for economy it has been necessary to give mere abstracts of some of the stories. In all cases, legendary accounts are clearly identified.

Acknowledgments

This book was conceived in the fall of 1968 when the Indiana Place-Name Survey formally was launched. Since then at Indiana State University we have founded a journal, *Indiana Names,* devoted to onomastic theory and methodology as well as to Indiana place names; we have held six annual conferences on Indiana place names; we have taught a summer workshop on place-name research; and we have been cooperating with the Place-Name Survey of the United States, sponsored by the American Name Society. This book owes a great deal to those place-name scholars who have spoken at our conferences and published in our journal: the late Francis Lee Utley, E. C. Ehrensperger, Frederic G. Cassidy, Robert M. Rennick, Byrd H. Granger, W. F. H. Nicolaisen, Donald J. Orth, Wayland D. Hand, Allen Walker Read, and W. Edson Richmond—all of whom we thank for their advice and inspiration. We also thank Paul Koda and Robert L. Carter of the Rare Books and Special Collections Department of the Cunningham Memorial Library at Indiana State University for their excellent cooperation and assistance in making the Indiana collection and W.P.A. manuscript materials available. Graduate student Rex May spent an academic year as research assistant working on the Indiana Place-Name Survey. We also owe much to Mary Ann Boyer, who helped with the preparation of the manuscript.

Marvin Carmony

Indiana State University   Ronald L. Baker, Director
Terre Haute, Indiana   Indiana Place-Name Survey

INDIANA PLACE NAMES

Pronunciation Guide

ə above, banana, collect
  cup, Tipton

ər further, pearl

a father, bother, park

ā say, cape, make

æ mat, map, bat, badge

ai bite, pylon

au now, mountain, loud

b baby, bib

ch church, nature [nāchər]

d did, Adams

d city, Cincinnati, little,
  rider, as pronounced by
  those who have neither
  [t] or [d] in such words

e bet, bed

ē beat, evening

f fifty

g go, big

h. hat, behind

hw while (unlike wile)

i bit

j judge, gem

k keep, make

l level

m mummy

n noon

ŋ sing

ō open, boat

o all, saw

p piper

r rake, park

s see, place

sh ship, machine

t tip, pit

th thin, ether

th then, either

u pull, wood

ū boot, rule

v vivid, river

w walk, awake

y young, year

z zip, wise

zh vision

ˈ primary or strong secondary stress
in following syllable

ˌ secondary or weaker stress in following syllable; used sometimes as
a syllable marker

( ) encloses optional sound

[ ] encloses pronunciation symbols

- stands for all before
or all after, as in
[ˈhemˌlak; ˈhim-]

A

Aberdeen [ˈæbərˌdēn] (Bascom), village in Ohio County (L-10).

First settled in 1814 and named about 1819 for Aberdeen, Scotland, by a Scottish settler, Dr. Robert Gillespie. Bascom, perhaps for a personal name, was a post office name.

Abington [ˈæbiŋˌtən], village in Wayne County (H-10).

Laid out in 1817 and probably named for Abingdon, England, perhaps via New England.

Aboite [əˈboit], village in Allen County (D-9).

Platted in 1889 and commonly thought to be named for an Indian chief; however, the name probably comes from a local stream, Aboite Creek.

Aboite Creek [əˈboit ˈkrēk], stream in Allen County.

Flows southwest to the Little Wabash River. The name is a corruption of the French name, *Rivière à Boitte,* or *à Bouette,* "River of Minnows," especially those minnows used as bait.

Acme [ˈækˌmē], village in Jackson County (L-7).

A post office called Acme was established here in 1884. Apparently a commendatory name meaning "best."

Acton [ˈækˌtən], village in Marion County (H-7).

Platted in 1852 and named Farmersville, but since there was

already a Hoosier town of that name, the name was changed to Acton, for General Acton, who lived here.

Adams [ˈædəmz] County (E-10).

Organized in 1836 and named for John Quincy Adams, sixth President of the U. S.

Adams [ˈædəmz], village in Decatur County (J-8).

Laid out in 1855 and named for President John Quincy Adams, probably via Adams Township, in which it is located.

Adamsboro [ˈædəmzˌbərō; -bərə], village in Cass County (E-6).

Laid out in 1872 by George E. Adams, for whom it was named.

Ade [ād], village in Newton County (D-3).

Laid out in 1906 and named for John Ade, prominent citizen in the county.

Adel [ˌāˈdel], village in Owen County (K-5).

Established in 1859 and originally called Pleasant Valley.

Advance [ˈædˌvænts], town in Boone County (G-5).

Platted in 1820 and first called Osceola, for the Indian chief, but the name was changed to Advance because there was another town named Osceola in Indiana. The present name, apparently commendatory, was applied "in anticipation of the advancement which the com-

1

ing of the Midland railway would bring to the community."

Adyeville ['ādē͟vil], village in Perry County (N-5).

Named in 1861 for Andrew J. Adye, the first postmaster and founder, who platted the town in 1873.

Ainsworth ['ānz͟wərth], village in Lake County (B-4).

Established in 1880 and probably named for a railroad official.

Aix [āks], village in Jasper County (D-4).

Established as a post office in 1892. Apparently named for the French city.

Akron ['ækrən], town in Fulton County (D-7).

Laid out in 1838 and called Newark by settlers from Newark, Ohio. In 1855 the name was changed to Akron, which already was the name of the post office, for the city in Ohio.

Alamo ['ælə͟mō], town in Montgomery County (G-4).

Laid out in 1837 and named for the fort in San Antonio, Texas.

Albany ['olbənē], town in Delaware County (F-9).

Laid out in 1833 and probably named for Albany, New York.

Albion ['ælbē͟ən], county seat, town in Noble County (B-9).

Formerly called The Center before becoming the county seat. Platted in 1846. The present name is from the ancient name of Britain, probably via New York.

Aldine ['ol͟dēn], village in Starke County (C-5).

Established as a railroad station in 1882.

Alert [ə'lərt], village in Decatur County (K-8).

Laid out in 1886. The name probably is commendatory.

Alexandria [͟elig'zændrēə; æl-], fifth class city in Madison County (F-8).

Laid out in 1836 and probably named for the ancient city, although some say for the wife of the founder.

Alford ['olfərd], village in Pike County (M-4).

Formerly called Alfords, it was laid out in 1856 by Elijah, Nathaniel, and Samuel Alfords and named for them.

Alfordsville ['ælfərdz͟vil; 'ol-], town in Daviess County (M-4).

Laid out in 1845 and named for James Alford, an early settler.

Algiers [͟æl'jirz], village in Pike County (M-4).

Laid out in 1868 and called Algiers City, apparently for the city in North Africa. Formerly called Delectable Hill.

Alida [ə'lid(ē)ə; æ-], village in LaPorte County (B-5).

Formerly Alida Station, as it was established as a railroad junction. A post office called Alida was located here in 1876.

Allen ['ælən] County (C-10).

2

Organized in 1824 and named for Col. John Allen, Kentucky lawyer and patriot killed at the Battle of the River Raisin.

Allensville ['ælənzˌvil], village in Switzerland County (L-10).

Laid out in 1816 and named for the Allen family here.

Alliance [əˈlaiˌəns], village in Madison County (G-8).

Probably the name is commendatory.

Allisonville ['æləsənˌvil], village in Marion County (H-7).

Platted in 1833 by John Allison and named for him.

Alpine ['ælˌpain], village in Fayette County (J-10).

Founded about 1832 and formerly called Ashland, for the abundance of ash trees here. When the name was changed, apparently because there is another Ashland, Indiana, Alpine was selected simply for its similarity to Ashland.

Alquina [ˌælˈkwainə], village in Fayette County (J-10).

Founded in 1838 and apparently named for Alquines, France.

Alta ['æltə], village in Vermillion County (H-3).

Platted in 1871. Probably selected as a descriptive name, meaning "elevation."

Alto ['ælˌtō], village in Howard County (F-7).

Platted in 1848 and named for the Battle of Palo Alto in the Mexican War.

Alton ['oltən], town in Crawford County (O-6).

Platted in 1838 and perhaps named for the English town via New England.

Altona [ˌælˈtōnə], town in Dekalb County (B-10).

A post office was established here in 1874. Probably named for the city in Germany.

Alvarado [ˌælvəˈrādō], village in Steuben County (B-11).

Originally called Richland Center. A post office was established here in 1855. Probably named for the Mexican city.

Ambia ['æmbēə], town in Benton County (F-3).

The name was changed from Weaver City to Ambia in 1873, when the town was laid out. Possibly named for Ambialet, France.

Amboy ['æmˌboi], town in Miami County (E-7).

Platted in 1867 and named for Amboy, New Jersey, home of the surveyor.

Americus [əˈmerēkəs], village in Tippecanoe County (F-5).

Laid out in 1832. The name is a masculine form of America, so the name is patriotic.

Amity ['æməˌtē], village in Johnson County (J-7).

Platted in 1855. The name comes from the French word *amitié,* meaning "friendship"; hence, the name is commendatory.

Amo ['āˌmō], town in Hendricks County (H-5).

3

Laid out in 1850 by Joseph Morris and first called Morristown for him. The present name often is said to be a Potawatomi word, *a-mo,* "honeybee," but actually it is the Latin *amo,* "I love."

Anderson ['ændər‚sən], county seat, second class city in Madison County (G-8).

Platted in 1823, its first name was Andersontown, for William Anderson, a Delaware chief, whose Indian name was *Kok-to-wha-nund,* "Making a Cracking Noise." The Delaware name of the town was *Wa-pi-mins-kink,* "Chestnut Tree Place."

Andersonville ['ændərsən‚vil], village in Franklin County (J-9).

Laid out in 1837 and first called Ceylon. In 1849 Thomas Anderson made an addition to the town, and it was renamed for him.

Andrews ['ændrūz], town in Huntington County (D-8).

Surveyed in 1853 and called Antioch until 1881 when the name was changed to Andrews. The present name comes from the name of the railroad yards here, Andrewsia, named for a railroad official.

Angola [‚æn'gōlə], county seat, fifth class city in Steuben County (A-10).

Platted in 1837 and named for Angola, New York, home of settlers.

Annapolis [æn'æp(ə)ləs], village in Parke County (H-4).

Platted in 1837 and probably named for Annapolis, Maryland.

Anoka [ə'nōkə], village in Cass County (E-6).

Sometimes said to be an invented name, but probably it comes from the Sioux adverb meaning "on both sides." It was platted in 1876 by F. Herman Smith and first called Herman City in his honor.

Anthony ['ænthənē], village in Delaware County (F-9).

Probably named for one of the Anthony families who registered land in the county in the 1830's.

Antioch ['æntē‚ak], village in Clinton County (G-6).

First settled in 1828. Named for the biblical city, possibly via a local church.

Antioch ['æntē‚ak], village in Jay County (F-10).

Laid out in 1853 and named by C. H. Clark, one of the founders, for Antioch College in Ohio.

Antioch Junction [- 'jəŋkshən], village in Greene County (K-4).

First settled in 1829 and named for a church that was built here shortly after settlement.

Antiville ['æntə‚vil], village in Jay County (F-10).

According to one anecdote: "In about 1865 a group of people lived in the vicinity of Antiville which were very much opposed to all secret organizations, such as Masons, KKK, Knights of the Golden Circle, etc. Because of this strenuous stand against the secret orders they were given the name of Anti-Masons, Anti-Circles, etc., by surrounding communities. This was changed to Antiville when the blacksmith and sawmill appeared."

4

Arba ['arbē; -ə], village in Randolph County (G-11).

Settled as early as 1815, although not platted until 1855. A post office called Arba, probably for the personal name, was established in 1849.

Arcadia [͵ar'kādē(ə)], town in Hamilton County (G-7).

Founded in 1849 and apparently named for the ancient Greek district noted for its pastoral simplicity and beauty.

Arcana [͵ar'kænə], village in Grant County (F-9).

Platted in 1852. Probably plural of *arcanum,* "hidden," hence commendatory, suggesting "secluded."

Arcola [͵ar'kōlə], village in Allen County (C-9).

Laid out in 1866. The name is found in other states and comes from Arcole or Arcola, a village in Italy where Napoleon won a victory over the Austrians in 1796.

Arda ['ardə], village in Pike County (M-4).

Perhaps named for the Arda River in Bulgaria or Italy.

Ardmore ['ard͵mōr], village in St. Joseph County (A-6).

Named for the town in Ireland, perhaps via Pennsylvania.

Argos ['argəs], town in Marshall County (C-6).

The town was platted in 1851 and originally called Sidney, for Sidney Williams, an early settler. The present name, applied in 1859, is for the Greek city.

Arlington ['arliŋtən], village in Rush County (J-8).

Platted in 1832 and called Burlington, but since there was another town of the same name in the state, the name was changed to Arlington in 1875. The post office here was called Beech Grove. The present name is commendatory, for Arlington, Virginia, site of the national cemetery.

Armiesburg ['armēz͵bərg], village in Parke County (H-3).

Platted in 1833 and so named because Gen. William Henry Harrison's army camped here on the way to what became the Battle of Tippecanoe.

Armstrong ['arm͵stroŋ], village in Vanderburgh County (O-2).

Settled in 1885 and named for Armstrong Township, in which it is located. The township was named for John Armstrong, early settler.

Arney ['arnē], village in Owen County (K-5).

Laid out in 1852 and originally called Middletown.

Arnold Creek ['arnəld ͵krēk], stream in Ohio County.

Flows northeast, then south, to the Ohio River two miles below Rising Sun. Named for Col. Arnold, who was killed by Indians near the stream just after the Revolution.

Aroma [ə'rōmə], village in Hamilton County (G-8).

Founded in 1836. Apparently so named for pleasant odors from flowering trees, new-mown hay, or some other source at the time a name was being selected for a post office.

Artic ['ar̲ik], village in Dekalb County (B-11).

A post office was established here in 1850. A former spelling was Arctic, so apparently it was named for the arctic region.

Ashboro ['æsh̟bərō], village in Clay County (J-4).

Founded in 1858 and named for Asheboro, North Carolina.

Asherville ['æshər̟vil], village in Clay County (J-4).

Laid out in 1873 by John Asher, for whom the village was named.

Ash Grove [̟æsh 'grōv], village in Tippecanoe County (F-5).

The name is descriptive of the ash trees in a wooded area here.

Ashland ['æsh̟lənd], village in Henry County (H-9).

Founded in 1856 and probably named for Ashland, Ohio, home of some settlers.

Ashley ['æsh̟lē], town in Dekalb and Steuben counties (B-10).

Platted in 1892. Perhaps named for the town in Pennsylvania.

Asphaltum ['æsh̟fəltəm], village in Jasper County (D-4).

A post office was established here in 1901. Apparently a descriptive name.

Athens ['æthənz], village in Fulton County (D-7).

A post office was located here in 1896. Originally called Hoover Station, for the Hoover family, first settlers. The present name is for Athens, Greece.

Atherton ['æthər̟tən], village in Vigo County (J-3).

Laid out in 1871 and formerly called Atherton's Island, as the surveyor, a geologist named Atherton, for whom it was named, said the site once had been an island.

Atkinson ['æt̟kə(n)sən], village in Benton County (E-4).

A post office was established here in 1873. Named for W. J. Atkinson, a prominent citizen.

Atkinsonville ['ætkinsən̟vil] village in Owen County (J-5).

Laid out in 1850 and named for the proprietor, Stephen Atkinson.

Atlanta [̟æt'læntə], town in Hamilton County (G-7).

A post office was established here in 1839 and called Shielsville, for landowner James Shiel. In 1854 the name of the town and post office was changed to Buena Vista. Because other towns in the state were already so named, the name was changed again in 1884 to Atlanta, apparently for the city in Georgia.

Attica ['æd̲ikə], fifth class city in Fountain County (F-4).

Platted in 1825. The name is classical, coming from the district in ancient Greece, perhaps via New York.

Atwood ['æt̟wud], village in Kosciusko County (C-7).

Settled in 1856 by John Wood and allegedly named for him.

Auburn ['obərn], county seat, fifth class city in Dekalb County (B-10).

Laid out in 1836 and named for the English village via New York. According to local anecdote, a group of Indians were sitting around a fire when one stuck his finger in the fire and said, "Ah, burn!"

Augusta [ə'gəstə], village in Marion County (H-7).

Founded about 1832. The post office here once was called Eck, for postmaster William Eck. Perhaps named for the other Augusta in Pike County, Indiana.

Augusta [ə'gəstə; ,o-], village in Pike County (N-4).

Established as a post office in 1874. Probably a transfer name from either Georgia or Virginia.

Aurora [ə'rōrə], fifth class city in Dearborn County (K-10).

Founded in 1819, it was named by Judge Jesse Holman of the Indiana Supreme Court for the Roman goddess of dawn.

Austin ['ostən], town in Scott County (M-8).

Platted in 1853 and named for Austin, Texas, by veterans who were stationed there during the Mexican War.

Avery ['āv(ə)rē], village in Clinton County (F-6).

A post office called Avery was established in 1879. Apparently named for a local resident.

Avilla [ə'velə; ə'vilə], town in Noble County (C-9).

A post office was established here in 1846. Apparently named for Avila, the Spanish city.

Avoca [ə'vōkə], village in Lawrence County (L-6).

Platted in 1819 and named for the Irish place name in Thomas Moore's poem.

Avon ['ā,van], village in Hendricks County (H-6).

Settled about 1830. Former names of the post office here were Hampton, White Link, and Smootsdell, for John Smoot. The present name comes from the railroad station here, probably named for Shakespeare's river.

Avonburg ['āvan,bərg], village in Switzerland County (L-10).

Apparently named for the English river associated with Shakespeare.

Aylesworth ['ālz,wərth], village in Fountain County (G-4).

A post office named Aylesworth was established here in 1884. The settlement was named for its founder.

Aylesworth ['ālz,wərth], village in Porter County (C-4).

Named for Giles Aylesworth, local schoolteacher.

Ayrshire ['æshər], village in Pike County (N-4).

A post office was located here in 1886. Probably named for the county in Scotland.

Azalia [ə'zālyə], village in Bartholomew County (K-8).

First laid out in 1831 and named for the flower, although the name is commendatory rather than descriptive.

B

Badger Grove [ˌbæjər 'grōv], village in White County (E-4).

Allegedly so named because badgers were numerous in a grove about 50 yards northwest of the present town site. A post office called Badger was established in 1881.

Bainbridge ['bānˌbrij; 'brān-], town in Putnam County (H-5).

Laid out in 1824 and named for naval hero William Bainbridge by Col. John Osborne.

Bakers Corner [ˌbākərz 'kornər], village in Hamilton County (G-7).

Laid out in 1831. Apparently a local personal name.

Balbec ['bælˌbek], village in Jay County (F-10).

A post office called Balbec was established here in 1865. Apparently named for Baalbec, or Baalbek, the ancient Syrian city, once a Roman colony and famous for its ruins.

Baldwin ['boldwən], village in Allen County (D-11).

For Timothy Baldwin, who platted the town in 1890.

Ballstown ['bolzˌtaun], village in Ripley County (K-9).

Established as a post office in 1844. Named for the first postmaster, Samuel Ball.

Bandon ['bændən], village in Perry County (0-5).

A post office called Bandon was located here in 1905. Probably named for the town in Ireland.

Banquo ['bænˌkwō], village in Huntington County (E-8).

Originally called Priceville, the town was platted in 1906. A local supernatural legend suggested the naming of the town for Shakespeare's ghost.

Banta ['bæntə; 'bæntē], village in Morgan County (J-6).

Probably named for the Banta family, prominent citizens.

Barbers Mills [ˌbarbərz 'milz] (Rockford), village in Wells County (E-9).

See Rockford, Wells County.

Barce [bars], village in Benton County (E-4).

Founded in 1890 and named for Lyman Barce.

Bargersville ['bargərzˌvil], town in Johnson County (J-7).

Founded about 1905 and first called New Bargersville. See Old Bargersville, which formerly was called Bargersville, too.

Barnard ['barnərd], village in Putnam County (H-5).

8

Laid out in 1876 and first called Fort Red, probably for a red schoolhouse here. When a railroad depot was established, it was called Barnard, for Calvin Barnard, on whose farm it was established. In 1880 the post office name was changed to Barnard.

Bartholomew [ˌbarˈthaləˌmyū] County (K-7).

Organized in 1821 and named for Gen. Joseph Bartholomew, who was wounded at the Battle of Tippecanoe and co-sponsor of the county when it was established.

Bartlettsville [ˈbartlətsˌvil], village in Lawrence County (L-6).

For Samuel J. Bartlett, who platted the town in 1860.

Bartonia [ˌbarˈtōnē(ə)], village in Randolph County (G-11).

Platted in 1849 and named for the proprietor, Edward Barton.

Bascom [ˈbæskəm] (Aberdeen), village in Ohio County (L-10).

See Aberdeen.

Bass Lake [ˌbæs ˈlāk], lake in Starke County.

Located 6 miles south of Knox, this 1345-acre lake was named for the large number of black bass in it.

Bass Lake [ˌbæs ˈlāk], village in Starke County (C-5).

A post office was established here in 1892. Named for the adjoining lake of the same name.

Bass Station [ˌbæs ˈstāshən], village in Starke County (C-5).

Established as a railroad station about a mile south of the village of Bass Lake, for which it was named.

Batesville [ˈbātsˌvil], fifth class city in Franklin and Ripley counties (K-10).

Platted in 1852 and named for the local Bates family.

Battle Ground [ˈbætl ˌgraund], town in Tippecanoe County (F-5).

Laid out in 1858. It was the scene of the Battle of Tippecanoe, for which it was named.

Baugo Creek [ˈbogō ˌkrēk], stream.

About 20 miles long, it heads in Elkhart County and flows northwest to the St. Joseph River in St. Joseph County. The name is an abbreviated form of the original name, *Baubaugo,* meaning something like "Devil River," apparently so named for its swift current during a freshet.

Beanblossom [ˈbēnˌblosəm], village in Brown County (K-6).

First named Georgetown around 1833 for the first settler and founder, George Grove. The present name is for nearby Beanblossom Creek.

Beanblossom Creek [ˌbēnˌblosəm ˈkrēk], stream.

About 51 miles long, it heads in Brown County and flows west through Monroe County to its confluence with White River 1.2 miles south of Gosport. A Miami name for the stream was *Ko-chio-ah-se-pe,* which also was the Miami name for the St. Joseph River and means "Bean River"; consequently, the name seems to be a translation of

9

the Indian name. The traditional account of the naming, though, says in 1812 a man by the name of Bean Blossom nearly drowned trying to swim the creek, and General Tipton named the stream for him.

Bear Branch ['ber ˌbrænch] (Freedom), village in Ohio County (L-10).
See Freedom, Ohio County.

Beard [bird], village in Clinton County (F-6).
First settled in 1839 and named for the Beard family, early settlers.

Beardstown ['birdzˌtaun] (Voltz), village in Pulaski County (C-6).
Laid out in 1901 and first named for Beardstown, Illinois. The alternate name, Voltz, for the man on whose farm the town was built, was applied to a post office established in 1915.

Beaver City [ˌbēvər 'sitē], village in Newton County (D-3).
Platted in 1893 and named for its location on Beaver Prairie.

Beaver Dam [ˌbēvər 'dæm], village in Kosciusko County (C-7).
A post office was located here in 1844. Named for the dam here of the same name.

Becks Mill [ˌbeks 'mil], village in Washington County (M-7).
Named for the Beck family who for several generations operated a mill here after 1808 when the village was founded.

Beckville ['bekˌvil], village in Montgomery County (G-5).

Established as a post office in 1860. Named for the local Beck family.

Bedford ['bedfərd], county seat, fourth class city in Lawrence County (L-6).
Platted in 1825 and named by Joseph Rawlins for his home, Bedford County, Tennessee.

Beech Creek ['bēch ˌkrēk], stream in Greene County.
This tributary of West Fork White River in eastern Greene County is about 12 miles long and was named for the numerous beech trees along its course.

Beech Grove [ˌbēch 'grōv], fourth class city in Marion County (H-7).
Platted in 1906 and named for Beech Grove Farm, which was named for a wooded area here.

Beechwood ['bēchˌwud], village in Crawford County (N-6).
A post office was located here in 1875. Named for a large beech grove here.

Beehunter ['bēˌhən(t)ər], village in Greene County (L-4).
Named for a local stream, Beehunter Creek.

Beehunter Creek [ˌbēˌhən(t)ər 'krēk], stream in Greene County.
This small stream in western Greene County was so named because along it was a good place to find honey.

Belknap ['belˌnæp], village in Vanderburgh County (O-2).

Possibly named for the American general and politician William Worth Belknap (1829–90).

Belle Union [ˌbel ˈyūnyən], village in Putnam County (J-5).

Platted in 1873. Apparently the name is commendatory.

Belleview [ˈbelˌvyū], village in Jefferson County (L-9).

A post office called Mud Lick was established in 1855, but the name was changed to the more commendatory Belleview in 1890. "Some of the old citizens got together and decided to name their village Belleview meaning 'beautiful to look upon.' "

Belleville [ˈbelˌvil], village in Hendricks County (H-6).

Laid out in 1829 and a post office was established in 1831. Perhaps from the personal name.

Bellfountain [ˌbelˈfauntn], village in Jay County (F-10).

Platted in 1851. Probably the name was chosen for its commendatory value.

Bellmore [ˈbelˌmōr], village in Parke County (H-4).

Earlier known as Northampton, for the city in Massachusetts, but the name was changed in 1852, allegedly for the daughters of Thomas Moore, whom a visitor, Gen. George K. Steele, admired and suggested the town be named Belle Moore in their honor.

Belshaw [ˈbelˌsho], village in Lake County (C-3).

Once called Belshaw Station, it was named for the Belshaw family who owned land here. George Belshaw settled here in 1842.

Ben Davis [ˌben ˈdāvəs], village in Marion County (H-6).

Named for Benjamin Davis, a railroad superintendent who supervised the building of the railroad station here in 1877.

Ben Davis Fork [ˌben ˌdāvəs ˈfork], stream in Rush County.

This tributary of Flat Rock River received its name from a Delaware chief.

Bengal [ˈbeŋˌgəl; -ˌgōl], village in Shelby County (J-7).

Never platted, it probably was named for the state in India. A post office was established here in 1881.

Benham [ˈbenəm], village in Ripley County (L-9).

Founded in 1857 and formerly called Benham's Station and Benham's Store, for the Benham family here. John Benham, Jr., was the first postmaster.

Bennetts Switch [ˌbenəts ˈswich], village in Miami County (E-7).

Founded about 1854 by Baldwin Bennett and named for him.

Bennettsville [ˈbenətsˌvil], village in Clark County (N-8).

Laid out in 1838. The name was formed from the christian name of the first merchant, Benedict Nugent.

Bennington [ˈbeniŋˌtən], village in Switzerland County (L-10).

Laid out in 1847. The post office formerly was called Slawson. Appar-

11

ently the present name is a transfer from Vermont.

Benton ['bentn] County (E-3).

Organized in 1840 and named for Thomas Hart Benton, U. S. Senator from Missouri.

Benton ['bentn], village in Elkhart County (B-8).

Platted in 1832 and named for Thomas Hart Benton, U. S. Senator from Missouri.

Bentonville ['bentn,vil], village in Fayette County (H-9).

Platted in 1838 and named for Senator Thomas Hart Benton of Missouri.

Berne [bərn], fifth class city in Adams County (E-10).

Platted in 1871 and named for Berne, Switzerland, by Swiss Mennonites who settled here in 1835.

Bethany ['bethənē], town in Morgan County (J-6).

The name comes from the biblical village, perhaps via a local church.

Bethel ['bethəl] (Stout), village in Delaware County (F-9).

See Stout.

Bethel ['bethəl], village in Wayne County (G-11).

Laid out in 1850 and named for a local church.

Bethlehem ['bethlē,hem], village in Clark County (M-9).

Platted in 1812 and probably named for Bethlehem, Pennsylvania.

Beverly Shores [,bevərlē 'shōrz], town in Porter County (A-4).

Perhaps a commendatory name, as it was developed as a fashionable residential and resort village on Lake Michigan.

Bicknell ['bik,nəl], fifth class city in Knox County (L-3).

Laid out in 1869 by John Bicknell and named for him.

Big Pine Creek [,big 'pain ,krik], stream.

Heads in Benton County and flows southwest, then southeast, to the Wabash River at Attica in Warren County. The name is descriptive, as the stream "has high banks covered with pine and cedar."

Big Pipe Creek ['big 'paip ,krēk], stream.

Heads in Grant County and flows northwest through Miami County to the Wabash River in Cass County 7 miles east of Logansport. The name is a literal translation of the Miami name of the stream, *Pwa-ka-na*.

Big Raccoon Creek ['big ,ræ'kūn ,krēk], stream.

About 85 miles long, it heads in Boone County and flows southwest through Montgomery, Putnam, and Parke counties, then northwest to the Wabash River at the Parke-Vermillion county line about 2 miles south of Montezuma. The name is a translation of the Miami name, *A-se-pa-na-si-pi-wi*.

Big Shawnee Creek ['big 'shonē ,krēk], stream.

Heads in Tippecanoe County and flows west through Fountain County to the Wabash River near Williamsport. It was named for the Shawnee tribe, a band of which lived near the stream. *Shawnee* means "Southerners."

Big Vermillion River ['big vər'milyən 'rivər], stream in Vermillion County.

Heads in Illinois and flows to the Wabash River near Eugene. The Algonquian name was *Osanamon,* "yellow-red," meaning vermilion paint. The French name was *Vermillon Jaune,* a literal translation of the Indian name.

Billingsville ['biliŋz‚vil], village in Union County (J-10).

A post office was established here in 1833. Named for the local Billings family.

Bippus ['bifəs], village in Huntington County (D-8).

Platted in 1885 and named for George J. Bippus, who secured the right-of-way for the railroad here.

Birdseye ['bərdz‚ai], town in Dubois County (N-5).

Platted in 1880. According to local tradition, several names were suggested but rejected by the Post Office Department. Finally Bird, for Rev. "Bird" Johnson, postmaster at Worth (now Schnellville), was suggested, and he was invited to help select the post office site. When he decided on the location, he said, "This spot suits Bird's eye to a T-y-tee."

Birmingham ['bərmiŋ‚hæm], village in Miami County (D-7).

A post office was located here in 1869. Probably named for the city in England.

Blackford ['blæk‚fərd] County (F-9).

Organized in 1839 and named for Isaac Blackford, pioneer justice of the Indiana Supreme Court.

Blackhawk ['blæk‚hok] (Mt. Auburn), village in Shelby County (J-7).

See Mt. Auburn.

Blackhawk ['blæk‚hok], village in Vigo County (K-3).

A post office was established in 1901 and named for the famous Sauk chief, *Ma-ka-ta-mi-ci-kiak-kiak,* "Black Sparrow Hawk."

Blaine [blān], village in Jay County (F-10).

Platted in 1883 and named for James G. Blaine, presidential candidate in 1884.

Blairsville ['blerz‚vil], village in Posey County (O-2).

Laid out in 1837 by Ebenezer Phillips and Stephen Blair, and named for Blair.

Blanford ['blæn‚fərd], village in Vermillion County (H-3).

Platted in 1912 and named for L. S. Blanford, large landowner here.

Blocher ['blachər], village in Scott County (M-8).

Laid out in 1860 and named for

Daniel Blocher, founder. Formerly called Holman Station and Holman.

Bloomfield ['blūm‚fēld], county seat, town in Greene County (L-5).
Laid out in 1824 and named by Dr. Hallet B. Dean for his birthplace, Bloomfield, New Jersey. A common local legend says early settlers saw blooming fields here.

Bloomfield ['blūm‚fēld], village in Spencer County (O-4).
Laid out in 1853. Perhaps a transfer name.

Bloomingdale ['blūmiŋ‚dāl], town in Parke County (H-4).
Settled in 1826 by Quakers who named it Elevatis for the elevation where the meeting house was built. In 1827 the name was changed to Bloomfield, allegedly because a Quaker leader wanted a name with more "bloom" in it. In 1860 the name was changed to Bloomingdale to avoid confusion with another Bloomfield in Indiana. Apparently a commendatory name.

Blooming Grove [‚blūmiŋ 'grōv], village in Franklin County (J-10).
Platted in 1816 and originally called Greensboro. Renamed for Blooming Grove Township.

Bloomingport ['blūmiŋ‚pōrt], village in Randolph County (G-10).
Laid out in 1829 and formerly called Bloomingsport.

Bloomington ['blūmiŋ‚tən], county seat, second class city in Monroe County (K-6).
Settled in 1815 and platted in 1818. According to local legend, the name was "suggested when a group of pioneers, picnicking on a nearby hillside, were impressed by the blooming flowers and foliage below them." Probably named for an early settler, William Bloom.

Blountsville ['blənts‚vil], town in Henry County (G-9).
Platted in 1832 and named for Andrew D. Blount, the original proprietor.

Bluecast ['blū‚kæst], village in Allen County (C-10).
Apparently this is a descriptive name.

Blue Creek ['blū‚krēk], village in Franklin County (J-10).
Also called Klemmes Corner, for Albert Klemme, who operated a general store here. Blue Creek, originally Blue Creek Post Office, established in 1849, is for a nearby stream.

Bluegrass ['blū‚græs], village in Fulton County (D-6).
Established as a post office in 1851. Apparently a descriptive name.

Blue Lake [‚blū 'lāk], lake in Whitley County.
This 239-acre lake is located 2 miles northwest of Churubusco. The name is descriptive of its deep bluish cast.

Blue Lick Creek ['blū 'lik ‚krēk], stream in Clark County.
This small stream in northwestern

Clark County was so named for the blue slate that forms its bed.

Blue Ridge ['blū ˌrij], village in Shelby County (J-8).

Platted in 1835 and named Cynthiana, for the town in Kentucky; the name was changed to Blue Ridge because there was another Cynthiana in Indiana. The present name is commendatory.

Blue River ['blū ˌrivər], stream.

Blue is a descriptive name applied to several streams and lakes in Indiana. Streams in northern, south-central, and southern Indiana are called Blue River. Probably the best known of these streams is the principal tributary of East Fork White River, as it is the subject of Charles Major's book, *The Bears of Blue River*. Sometimes called Big Blue River, it heads in northern Henry County and flows southwest for about 80 miles through Rush, Hancock, Shelby, and Johnson counties.

Blue River ['blū ˌrivər], village in Washington County (M-7).

A post office was located here in 1876 and named for the nearby stream of the same name.

Bluff Creek [ˌbləf 'krēk], village in Johnson County (J-7).

Established around 1850 and named for a nearby stream of the same name.

Bluff Point [ˌbləf 'point], village in Jay County (F-10).

Platted in 1854 and apparently so named because of its location on a small hill.

Bluffton ['bləfˌtən], county seat, fifth class city in Wells County (E-10).

Laid out in 1838 and so named because it is situated on the bluffs of the south bank of the Wabash River.

Bobo ['bōˌbō] (Rivare), village in Adams County (D-11).

See Rivare.

Boggstown ['bogzˌtaun], village in Shelby County (J-7).

Platted in 1867 and named for Joseph Boggs, early settler of the county.

Bono ['bōnō], village in Lawrence County (M-6).

Laid out in 1816 and, according to local legend, named for a French settler who was driven out of town a few years following settlement. Probably named for the Bono brothers, early settlers. In other states the name is an adaptation of the Latin word for "good."

Bono ['bōnō], village in Vermillion County (H-3).

Settled in 1848. Perhaps a commendatory name meaning "good."

Boone [būn] County (G-6).

Organized in 1830 and named for the famous frontiersman, Daniel Boone.

Boone Grove [ˌbūn 'grōv], village in Porter County (C-4).

Founded in 1857 and named for the Boones, a pioneer family.

Boonville ['būnˌvil], county seat, fifth class city in Warrick County (O-3).

15

Platted in 1818 and named for Ratliff Boon, early settler and prominent politician, who was instrumental in locating the county seat here.

Boston ['bostən], town in Wayne County (H-11).

Platted in 1832 and apparently named for Boston, Massachusetts.

Boswell ['baz‚wel], town in Benton County (F-3).

Platted in 1872 and named for a local family, probably for Charles P. Boswell, a pioneer settler. Among the early landowners were Parnham Boswell and John F. Boswell.

Boundary City [‚baund(ə)rē 'sitē], village in Jay County (F-10).

Platted in 1853 and named for its location on an Indian treaty line.

Bourbon ['bərbən], town in Marshall County (C-7).

Laid out in 1853 and named for Bourbon Township, which was named for Bourbon County, Kentucky, home of founders.

Bowers ['bauərz], village in Montgomery County (G-5).

A post office was established in 1861 as Clouser's Mills, for Daniel Clouser, first postmaster. In 1876 the name was changed to Bowers, for the Bowers family, who were numerous here.

Bowling Green ['bōliŋ ‚grēn], village in Clay County (J-4).

Founded in 1825 and named for Bowling Green, Kentucky.

Boxley ['baks‚lē], village in Hamilton County (G-7).

Laid out in 1836 and named Boxleytown for George Boxley, father of the founders, Addison and Thomas P. Boxley.

Boyleston ['boilz‚tən], village in Clinton County (F-6).

Named for Louis N. Boyle of Indianapolis who platted the town in 1875.

Bracken ['brækən], village in Huntington County (D-8).

Platted in 1853 as Claysville, but since there already was a Claysville in Indiana, the name was changed to Bracken, for the county in Kentucky from which the founders came.

Bradford ['bræd‚fərd], village in Harrison County (N-7).

Laid out in 1838. Probably for the personal name.

Bramble ['bræmbəl], village in Martin County (L-5).

Founded about 1875 and named for local landowners.

Branchville ['brænch‚vil], village in Perry County (0-6).

Established in 1866 and originally called Oil Creek, for the nearby stream. The present name comes from its location near the branches of Oil Creek.

Brazil ['brā‚zil; brə'zil], county seat, fifth class city in Clay County (J-4).

Settled before 1834, founded in 1844, and named for Brazil, South America, which was in the news at the time.

Bremen ['brēmən], town in Marshall County (B-7).

Platted in 1851 and named for the city in Germany by German settlers. First called New Bremen.

Brems [brimz], village in Starke County (C-5).

Platted in 1881 and named for Louis Brems, a large landowner here.

Bretzville ['brets‚vil] (Newton), village in Dubois County (N-5).

Laid out in 1866 by William Bretz and named for him. A post office, called Bretz, was established the same year. Apparently the alternate name, Newton, is for a personal name.

Brewersville ['brūərz‚vil], village in Jennings County (K-8).

Laid out in 1837 by Jacob Brewer and named for him.

Brice [brais], village in Jay County (F-10).

Platted in 1886. A post office called Brice, probably from the personal name, was established here in 1883.

Brick Chapel [‚brik 'chæpəl], village in Putnam County (H-5).

The village was established around and named for a church built here in the early 1830's. A post office was established in 1873.

Bridgeport ['brij‚pōrt] (Locust Point), village in Harrison County (N-7).

Laid out in 1849 as Bridgeport, probably a transfer from an eastern state. Locust Point, apparently descriptive, was the post office name applied in 1875.

Bridgeport ['brij‚pōrt], village in Marion County (H-6).

Platted in 1830 and probably named for Bridgeport, Connecticut.

Bridgeton ['brij‚tən], village in Parke County (H-4).

Originally called Lockwood Mills, for a mill owner, the town was platted in 1857. The present name comes from the bridge here over Big Raccoon Creek.

Brighton ['braitn], village in Lagrange County (A-9).

Laid out in 1836 and originally called Lexington. Brighton was the post office name.

Brimfield ['brim‚fēld], village in Noble County (B-9).

Laid out in 1861. Probably for the English village via New England.

Brinckley ['briŋklē], village in Randolph County (F-10).

Established as a post office in 1881 and named for a local family, probably Alonzo Brinckley, first postmaster.

Bringhurst ['briŋ‚hərst], village in Carroll County (F-6).

Founded in 1872. Known earlier as U Know and Plank, it received its present name for Colonel Bringhurst of Logansport.

Bristol ['bristəl], town in Elkhart County (A-8).

Founded in 1830 and named for Bristol, England.

Bristow ['bristō], village in Perry County (O-5).

Laid out in 1875 and named for a prominent family here.

Broad Park [ˌbrŏd 'park], village in Putnam County (J-5).

Surveyed in 1893 and named for J. C. Broadstreet and Hugh Parker, large landowners in the area.

Bromer ['brŏmər], village in Orange County (M-6).

A post office called Bromer was established here in 1884. Allegedly the name is an acronym formed from the names of six early settlers: Boyd, Roll, Oldham, McCoy, Ellis, and Reid.

Bronson ['bransən] (Losantville), town in Randolph County (G-10).

See Losantville.

Brook [bruk], town in Newton County (D-3).

Setted in 1832, and a post office was established here in 1837. Allegedly so named because a small stream runs through the town.

Brookfield ['bruk,fēld], village in Shelby County (J-7).

Laid out in 1853 by Robert Means, who called it Brookville.

Brooklyn ['bruk,lun; -lən], town in Morgan County (J-6).

Settled as early as 1819, though not laid out until 1854. Probably influenced by Brooklyn, New York.

Brooksburg ['bruks,bərg], town in Jefferson County (M-9).

Named around 1839 for Noah Brooks, co-founder. Laid out in 1843.

Brooks Creek ['bruks ˌkrēk], stream in Jay County.

This tributary of the Salamonie River in western Jay County was named for the Brooks family, early settlers along its banks.

Brookston ['bruks,tən], town in White County (E-5).

Platted in 1853 and named for James Brooks, president of the Louisville, New Albany, and Chicago Railroad.

Brookville ['bruk,vil], county seat, town in Franklin County (J-10).

Platted in 1808 by Amos Butler and Jesse Brooks Thomas and named Brooksville for Thomas' mother, whose maiden name was Brooks. In 1811 the name was shortened to Brookville.

Brouilletts Creek [ˌbrū'lets ˌkrēk], stream.

About 45 miles long, it heads in Edgar County, Illinois, and flows southeast through Vermillion County to the Wabash River about 2 miles east of Shepardsville in Vigo County. On a map of 1778 the name is *Rivière à la Brouette,* "River of the Wheelbarrow." The stream probably gets the present form of its name from Michael Brouillette, an Indian interpreter from Knox County. Perhaps *Rivière à la Brouette* was first, though misunderstood, and Brouillette's name substituted.

Brown [braun] County (K-7).

Organized in 1836 and named for General Jacob Brown, hero of the War of 1812.

Brownsburg ['braunz̩bərg], town in Hendricks County (H-6).

Laid out in 1835 by William Harris and called Harrisburg. The name was changed to Brownsburg when the post office was established.

Brownstown ['braunz̩taun], county seat, town in Jackson County (L-7).

Platted in 1816 and named for General Jacob Brown of the War of 1812.

Browns Valley ['braunz 'vælē], village in Montgomery County (G-4).

Laid out in 1836 as Brownsville, and probably named for its location in Brown Township.

Brownsville ['braunz̩vil], village in Union County (H-10).

Established in 1815 in Wayne County and named for the Brown family, early settlers.

Bruce Lake ['brūs ̩lāk], lake in Fulton County.

This 245-acre lake is located 6 miles northeast of Kewanna and was named for the Bruce family, local landowners. Originally called Bruce's Lake.

Bruce Lake [̩brūs 'lāk], village in Fulton County (D-6).

A post office called Bruce's Lake, for the nearby lake, was established in 1855. In 1895 the name was changed to Bruce Lake.

Bruceville ['brūs̩vil], town in Knox County (L-3).

For the first settler, Major William Bruce, who came here in 1805. A fort was built on the Bruce farm, and the town was founded in 1811. Bruce had the town laid out in 1829.

Brummetts Creek [̩brəməts 'krēk], stream in Monroe County.

This tributary of North Fork Salt Creek was named for the Brummett families who settled near it.

Brunerstown ['brūnərz̩taun], village in Putnam County (H-4).

Named for Joseph Bruner, who laid out the town in 1837.

Brunswick ['brənz̩wik], village in Lake County (B-3).

Established about 1858 and named for the state and city in Germany.

Brushy Prairie [̩brəshē 'prerē], village in Lagrange County (B-9).

Established as a post office in 1834. Apparently this is a descriptive name.

Bryant ['brai̩ənt], town in Jay County (F-10).

Platted in 1872 and originally named Bryan, for a railroad construction boss who helped establish a railroad station here, but the railroad called it Briant and the Post Office Department called it Bryant.

Bryantsburg ['brai̩ənts̩bərg], village in Jefferson County (L-9).

Named for Jacob Bryant, who laid out the town in 1834.

Bryantsville ['brai̩ənts̩vil], village in Lawrence County (L-6).

Platted in 1835 and named for Robert Bryant, pioneer farmer here.

19

Buck Creek ['bək ˌkrēk], stream.

This stream name, for the male deer, is fairly popular in Indiana, with at least 6 streams bearing the name. In western Greene County allegedly the best place to kill deer was along Buck Creek, hence the name.

Buck Creek ['bək ˌkrēk], village in Tippecanoe County (F-5).

Platted in 1856 and originally called Transitville. The present name comes from the nearby stream of the same name.

Buckskin ['bəkˌskin], village in Gibson County (N-3).

A post office was established here in 1847. Several legends attempt to explain this name. One goes: "The town of Buckskin got its name from the deerskins that hung on the trading post walls. In the early 1800's there was a small trading post at what now is Buckskin. The owners of the post used to hang deerskins on the side of the building to dry. When people had skins or furs to sell they would go to the Buckskin trading post. When it became a town the name of Buckskin was used as the name."

Bud [bəd], village in Johnson County (J-7).

The first store was built here around 1832. The settlement was named for Bud Vandivier, son of the first merchant.

Buddha ['būdē; -ə], village in Lawrence County (L-6).

In 1895 a post office was located here. Allegedly the name was sug-gested by a traveling salesman who stopped at a store here. A former name was Flynn's Cross Roads. One legend says the traveler's name was Buddha: "Buddha was named for a tramp. Back in [the] 1800's, according to legend, a tramp named Budha [sic] used to pass through the town, and it was later named after him. He's now buried in an old cemetery west of here." Buda, for one of the two cities now Budapest, Hungary, was applied to post offices in Illinois and Iowa in the nineteenth century and likely is the source of this name too.

Buena Vista [ˌbyūnə 'vistə] (Stips Hill), village in Franklin County (J-9).

Platted in 1848 and named for the Battle of Buena Vista in the Mexican War. The post office name is Stips Hill, for Isaac Stips, who came here in 1814.

Buena Vista [ˌbyūnə 'vistə] (Giro), village in Gibson County (M-3).

Laid out in 1848 and named for the battle during the Mexican War. In 1887 a post office was established and called Giro.

Buena Vista [ˌbyūnə 'vistə], village in Harrison County (O-7).

Laid out in 1850. This popular name commemorates the Battle of Buena Vista.

Buena Vista [ˌbyūnə 'vistə], village in Randolph County (G-10).

Platted in 1851. The post office here was called Cerro Gordo, probably for the American victory in Mexico in 1847. Apparently the present name commemorates another battle in the Mexican War.

Buffalo ['bəfəlō], village in White County (D-5).

Platted in 1886 and named for Buffalo, New York, hometown of the first postmaster.

Buffaloville ['bəfəlō,vil], village in Spencer County (O-4).

Laid out in 1860 and, according to tradition, the name comes from Buffalo Grounds, as Clay and Jackson townships were called by early settlers.

Bullocktown ['bulik,taun] (Bullock), village in Warrick County (O-4).

Named for the Bullock family, pioneer settlers here. John A. Bullock was the first postmaster of Bullock, established in 1892.

Bunker Hill [,bəŋkər 'hil], town in Miami County (E-7).

Laid out in 1851 and named for the Battle of Bunker Hill.

Bunker Hill [,bəŋkər 'hil], village in Washington County (M-7).

Apparently named for the famous battle.

Burdick ['bərdik], village in Porter County (B-4).

Founded in 1870 and named for A. C. Burdick, lumber dealer from Coldwater, Michigan, who owned a sawmill here.

Burket ['bərkət; -'ket], town in Kosciusko County (C-7).

Established in the early 1880's and named for its founder.

Burkhart Creek [,bərk,hart 'krēk], stream in Johnson County.

This tributary of Youngs Creek was named for Harry and George Burkhart, early settlers.

Burlington ['bərliŋ,tən], town in Carroll County (F-6).

Laid out in 1828 and named for a Wyandotte Indian, Chief Burlington.

Burnett [,bər'net], village in Vigo County (J-3).

A post office called Burnett was established in 1870. Named for a prominent family who owned a tanyard here.

Burnettsville ['bərnətz,vil], town in White County (E-5).

Formerly called Farmington. A post office was established here in 1836 and called Burnetts Creek, for a nearby stream. Platted in 1854 and named for the stream.

Burney ['bərnē], village in Decatur County (K-8).

Laid out in 1882 and named for the Burney family, early settlers and prominent citizens.

Burns City ['bərn(z) 'sid̲ē], village in Martin County (L-5).

Originally called Kecksville, which was laid out in 1852 and named for the Keck family, early settlers. The present name was applied by a railroad engineer whose wife's maiden name was Burns.

Burnsville ['bərnz,vil], village in Bartholomew County (K-8).

Platted in 1845 by Brice Burns, for whom it was named.

21

Burr Oak ['bər 'ōk], village in Marshall County (C-6).

Platted in 1882. The post office formerly was called Oakington. Both names apparently are for the presence of oak trees here.

Burr Oak ['bər 'ōk], village in Noble County (C-9).

A post office was established here in 1848. Apparently the name is descriptive.

Burrows ['bərəz; -ōz], village in Carroll County (E-6).

Laid out in 1856 and earlier called Cornucopia, the name was changed to Burrows in 1864 in honor of a local family.

Bushrod ['bush,rad], village in Greene County (L-4).

Laid out in 1889 and named for Bushrod Taylor, who laid out switches here for the Penn Central Railroad.

Busseron ['bəsərən], village in Knox County (L-3).

Laid out in 1854 and named for Busseron Township, in which it is located.

Busseron Creek ['bəsərən 'krēk], stream.

About 50 miles long, it heads in Vigo County and flows southwest through Sullivan County and Knox County to the Wabash River. It was named for Francis Busseron, a judge of the Northwest Territory.

Butler ['bətlər], fifth class city in Dekalb County (B-10).

Called Norristown in 1853 for Charles Norris, real estate promoter. In 1859 the name was changed to Jarvis, and in 1868 the name was changed again to Butler, for pioneer David Butler. The Butler family was prominent in county history.

Butler Center [,bətlər 'sentər], village in Dekalb County (C-10).

A post office, called Butler, was established in 1840. Named for its location near the center of Butler Township.

Butlerville ['bətlər,vil], village in Jennings County (L-9).

Platted in 1853. The name was first applied to a post office near here which was named for Butlerville, Ohio.

Butternut Creek ['bətərnət ,krēk], stream in Jay County.

Flows north to the Little Salamonie River. The present name is for the tree, but it was formerly known as *Atchepongquawe*, "Snapping Turtle Eggs."

Byrneville ['bərn,vil], village in Harrison County (N-7).

For Temple C. Byrne, who platted the town in 1838.

Byron ['bai,rən; 'ba(i)ərn], village in LaPorte County (A-5).

Laid out in 1837. Apparently the name comes from the personal name. A post office was established in 1832 as Kankakee, but the name was changed to Byron in 1841.

Byron ['bai,rən; 'ba(i)ərn], village in Parke County (H-4).

A post office was established here in 1884. Allegedly this name honors the British poet, Lord Byron.

22

C

Caborn ['kā͵bōrn; -born], village in Posey County (O-2).

Named for Cornelius Caborn, who laid it out in 1871. Formerly called Caborn Summit and Caborn Station.

Cadiz ['kæ͵dis; -z; kə'diz], town in Henry County (G-9).

Laid out in 1836 and named for Cadiz, Ohio. Ultimately the name comes from the Spanish city.

Cagle's Mill Reservoir [͵kāgəlz ͵mil 'rezə͵voi], lake.

See Cataract Lake.

Cairo ['kairō], village in Tippecanoe County (F-5).

Apparently named for the city in Egypt.

Cale ['kā(i)l], village in Martin County (L-5).

Founded in 1889 and named for a school near the village, Kale School, apparently named for a resident here.

Calvertville ['kælvərt͵vil], village in Greene County (K-5).

Founded in 1885 and named for a prominent resident, John Calvert.

Cambria ['kæmbr(ē)ə], village in Clinton County (F-6).

A post office was established here in 1883. The name comes from the Latin name of Wales, perhaps via New York or Pennsylvania.

Cambridge City [͵kāmbrij 'sitē], town in Wayne County (H-10).

Founded in 1836 as a depot on the Whitewater Canal. Named for the English county or town, perhaps via New England.

Camby ['kæmbē], village in Marion County (F-6).

Platted in 1890 and formerly called West Union Station. The first postmaster, Don Carlos Morgan, gave the town its present name "because it was short and different from any post office in the state and was the name of a river in South America."

Camden ['kæm͵dən], town in Carroll County (E-6).

Platted in 1833. The name is probably a transfer from an eastern state.

Cammack [kə'mæk], village in Delaware County (G-9).

Laid out in 1882 by David Cammack, for whom it was named.

Campbellsburg ['kæm(b)əlz͵bərg], town in Washington County (M-6).

Named for Robert Campbell, who laid out the town in 1851.

Canaan ['kānən], village in Jefferson County (L-9).

Platted in 1836 and named for the promised land in the Bible, although the name of the founder, John Cane, probably suggested the name.

Canal [kə'næl] (Millersburg), village in Warrick County (O-3).

See Millersburg, Warrick County.

Caney Fork [ˌkānē 'fork], stream in Clark County.

This small stream in northwestern Clark County received its name from the thickets of cane that once grew along it.

Cannelburg ['kænəlˌbərg], town in Daviess County (M-4).

Originally called Clark's Station, for A. Clark, the first settler, the town was laid out in 1872 and named for the cannel coal here, mined by the Buckeye Cannel Coal Company.

Cannelton ['kænəlˌtən], county seat, fifth class city in Perry County (O-5).

Laid out in 1844 as Cannelsburg, for the cannel coal mined here, but the present name was more popular and was adopted in 1844.

Canton ['kæntn], village in Washington County (M-7).

Formerly called Greensburg, for the Green family here, and Egg Harbor, for the large quantity of eggs sold here, it was laid out in 1838. The present name, probably borrowed from an eastern state, was suggested when the post office was established.

Carbon ['karbən], town in Clay County (J-4).

Founded in 1870 by the Carbon Coal Co. and so named for the coal here.

Carbondale ['karbənˌdāl], village in Warren County (F-3).

A post office was established here about 1846 and named Clark's Cross Roads for Dr. Wesley Clark, the first postmaster. About 1873 the name was changed to Carbondale, for the coal deposits here.

Cardonia [ˌkar'dōnēə; -yə], village in Clay County (J-4).

Founded in 1871 by the Clay County Coal Co. and named for John F. Card, then president of the company.

Carlisle [ˌkar'lail], town in Sullivan County (L-3).

Settled in 1803 and platted in 1815. Named for Carlisle, Pennsylvania, home of some settlers.

Carlos ['karləs], village in Randolph County (G-10).

The post office here, established in 1882, formerly was called Carlos City. It became Carlos in 1895.

Carmel ['karməl], town in Hamilton County (G-7).

Founded in 1837. The name was suggested by Levi Haines, Sr., probably for the biblical mountain.

Carpentersville ['karpəntərzˌvil], village in Putnam County (H-5).

Laid out in 1840 and named for Philip Carpenter, who came here about 1831 and established a tannery and harness factory.

Carroll ['kerəl] County (E-6).

Organized in 1828 and named for Charles Carroll, a signer of the Declaration of Independence.

Carroll ['kerəl] (Wheeling), village in Carroll County (E-6).

See Wheeling, Carroll County.

Carrollton ['kerəl‚tən], village in Carroll County (F-6).

Platted in 1835 and named for Carroll County. Ultimately the name comes from Charles Carroll, a signer of the Declaration of Independence.

Carrollton ['kerəl‚tən] (Finley), village in Hancock County (H-8).

This community has had several names. A post office called Kinder was established here in 1847. In 1869 the post office name was changed to Carrollton, probably for Charles Carroll, and this remained the name until 1905, when the post office was taken away. The railroad called its station here Reedville. In 1913 the post office was reestablished as Finly, for Congressman Finly Gray. A local name, Tailholt, was immortalized by James Whitcomb Riley. The original plat of Carrollton was surveyed in 1854.

Cartersburg ['kartərz‚bərg], village in Hendricks County (H-6).

Laid out in 1850 by John Carter, for whom it was named.

Carthage ['karthij; -ēj], town in Rush County (H-8).

Laid out in 1834 and named for Carthage, North Carolina, home of Quaker settlers.

Carwood ['kar‚wud], village in Clark County (N-8).

A post office was established in 1858 as Muddy Fork. In 1902 the name was changed to Carwood, a coined name honoring General John Carr, an early settler and prominent citizen, and General Wood.

Cass [kæs] County (E-6).

Organized in 1829 and named for General Lewis Cass, who served in the War of 1812, was Governor of Michigan Territory, 1813–31, and was the Democratic candidate for President in 1848.

Cass [kæs], village in Sullivan County (K-4).

Laid out in 1880 and named for Cass Township, in which it is located. Formerly called Buell and Lyontown.

Cassville ['kæs‚vil], village in Howard County (F-7).

Laid out in 1848 and named for Lewis Cass, general, senator, and presidential candidate.

Castleton ['kæsəl‚tən], town in Marion County (H-7).

Platted in 1852 by Thomas P. Gentry, who named it for his home, Castleton, North Carolina.

Cataract ['kætəræk], village in Owen County (J-5).

Laid out in 1851 and named for the cataract (waterfall) here on Mill Creek.

Cataract Lake [‚kætəræk 'lāk] (Cagle's Mill Reservoir), lake.

This artificial lake, located 6 miles southwest of Cloverdale, covers 1400 acres in Owen and Putnam counties. It was named Cataract for the falls at the head of the lake. The alternate name, Cagle's Mill Reservoir, is for an early mill near the present lake.

25

Cates [kāts], village in Fountain County (G-3).

Platted in 1903 and named for David Cates who settled here in 1844.

Catlin ['kæt₁lən], village in Parke County (H-4).

Named for Thomas Catlin, who built a warehouse here in 1861 and became the first postmaster.

Cato ['kātō], village in Pike County (N-4).

A post office called Cato was established here in 1894. A classical name, it probably is a transfer from New York.

Cayuga [₁kai'yūgə; kā-; kə-], town in Vermillion County (G-3).

Platted in 1827 and formerly called Eugene Station. The present name is for the New York lake and city. The name is a corruption of the Iroquois *Gwa-u-geh,* "the place of taking out," referring to the beginning of a portage. Naturally, local legends have been created to explain this name. One goes: "When the Model T Ford first was made, the people would drive through Cayuga and blow their horns. The sound of the horn seemed to say CAYUGA. And that is how Cayuga, Indiana, received its name."

Cedar ['sēdər], village in Dekalb County (C-10).

Settled in 1868, laid out in 1872, it was formerly called Cedar Creek Station, for Cedar Creek.

Cedar Creek ['sēdər ₁krēk], stream

About 40 miles long, it heads in Dekalb County and flows south to its confluence with the St. Joseph River in Allen County. The name is a literal translation of the Potawatomi name, *Mes-kwah-wah-se-pe.*

Cedar Creek ['sēdər ₁krēk], stream in Lake County.

About 12 miles long, it heads at the outlet of Cedar Lake, for which it was named, and flows south through Lake Dalecarlia to Singleton Ditch.

Cedar Grove [₁sēdər 'grōv], town in Franklin County (J-10).

Platted in 1837 and originally called Rochester. Apparently the present name is descriptive.

Cedar Lake [₁sēdər 'lāk], lake in Lake County.

Formerly called The Lake of the Red Cedars, this 281-acre lake was named for the red cedars along its shores.

Cedar Lake [₁sēdər 'lāk], town in Lake County (C-3).

A Cedar Lake Post Office was established in the county as early as 1839. Named for the nearby lake of the same name.

Cedarville ['sēdər₁vil], village in Allen County (C-10).

Platted in 1838 and named for Cedar Creek.

Celestine ['seləs₁tēn], village in Dubois County (N-5).

26

Platted in 1843 by Father Joseph Kundek and named in honor of the Right Reverend Celestine René Lawrence de la Hailandière, Bishop of Vincennes.

Celina [ˌsēˈlainə], village in Perry County (N-5).
A post office named Celina was located here in 1870. Probably named for Celina, Ohio.

Cementville [ˌsēˈmentˌvil], village in Clark County (N-8).
Founded in 1870 and named for the cement industry.

Centenary [ˈsentnˌerē], village in Vermillion County (H-3).
Platted in 1910. Perhaps named for a local church.

Center [ˈsen(t)ər], village in Howard County (F-7).
Laid out in 1852. A Pennsylvania Railroad survey showed this point as midway between Cincinnati and Chicago, hence the name.

Center [ˈsen(t)ər], village in Jay County (F-10).
So named because of its location near the center of Greene Township.

Center Point [ˈsen(t)ər ˌpoint], town in Clay County (J-4).
Founded in 1856 and named for the post office established here in 1854, which was so named because it was located near the center of the county.

Center Square [ˌsentər ˈskwer], village in Switzerland County (L-10).

The name is locational and descriptive, as the town was laid out in 1835 in the form of a square near the center of the county.

Centerton [ˈsen(t)ərˌtən], village in Morgan County (J-6).
Laid out in 1854 and so named for its location near the center of the county.

Centerville [ˈsentərˌvil], town in Wayne County (H-10).
Laid out in 1814 and named for its location near the center of the county.

Central [ˈsentrəl], village in Harrison County (O-7).
Laid out in 1890 and so named because of its location as a central point of mail delivery.

Ceylon [ˈsēˌlən], village in Adams County (E-10).
Platted in 1873 by B. B. Snow and named Florence for Snow's daughter. The name was changed to Ceylon when it was discovered there was another town named Florence. Apparently named for the island in the Indian Ocean.

Chalmers [ˈchælmərz], town in White County (E-5).
Originally called Mudge's Station, for a local storekeeper, it was platted in 1873. Apparently the present name is for a personal name, too.

Chambersburg [ˈchāmbərzˌbərg], village in Orange County (M-6).
Laid out in 1840 by Samuel

27

Chambers, who named it for himself.

Chandler ['chæn(d)ˌlər], town in Warrick County (O-3).
Settled in 1879. Apparently a personal name.

Chapel Hill [ˌchæpəl 'hil], village in Monroe County (L-6).
Platted in 1856 and named for the Chapel Hill Methodist Church, already here when the town was laid out.

Charlestown ['char(ə)lzˌtaun], fifth class city in Clark County (N-8).
Laid out in 1808 and named for Charles Biggs, who surveyed the town.

Charley Creek ['charlē ˌkrēk], stream in Wabash County.
Named for a Miami Indian whose reservation was near the city of Wabash. His Indian name was *Ke-ton-gah,* or sometimes written *Ke-tun-ga,* meaning "Sleepy."

Charlottesville ['sharlətsˌvil], village in Hancock County (H-8).
Laid out in 1830 and named for Charlottesville, Virginia.

Chase [chās], village in Benton County (F-3).
A post office was established in 1873. Named for a local landowner, Simon P. Chase.

Chatterton ['chætərˌtən], village in Warren County (F-4).
Founded in 1896 and a post office was established in 1900. The Post Office Department selected the name from several suggested names.

Chelsea ['chelsē], village in Jefferson County (M-9).
A post office was located here in 1883. Named for the district in London, perhaps via Maine.

Cherry Grove [ˌcherē 'grōv], village in Montgomery County (G-5).
A railroad switching station was established here around 1851. Apparently this is a descriptive name for wild cherry trees here.

Chester ['chestər], village in Wayne County (H-11).
Settled about 1820 and platted in 1866.

Chesterfield ['chestərˌfēld], town in Madison County (G-8).
Platted in 1830 and first called West Union for its location in Union Township. The name was changed to Chesterfield in 1834, apparently for an early settler and Indian trader named McChester.

Chesterton ['chestərˌtən], town in Porter County (B-4).
A post office was established here in 1833 and named Coffee Creek, for the nearby stream. Around 1853 the name was changed to Calumet, for another stream. The present name comes from Westchester Township, in which it is located.

Chili ['chaiˌlai], village in Miami County (D-7).
Laid out in 1839 as New Market. Chili is an older spelling of Chile. The presence of a Mexico and Peru in this county probably influenced the renaming of this town for the country in South America. The spel-

ling and pronunciation are found in the name of a New York settlement, so there is a possibility of borrowing from that state.

China ['chainə], village in Jefferson County (L-9).
First called Indiana Kentucky but changed by the Post Office Department to China in 1833, apparently for the country.

Chippewanuck Creek [ˌchipə'wanək ˌkrēk], stream.
About 14.8 miles long, it heads in Kosciusko County at the outlet of Rock Lake and flows northwest to its confluence with the Tippecanoe River in Fulton County. The name comes from Potawatomi *Che-pyuk,* "spirits" or "ghosts," and *Wah-nuk,* "hole"—thus, "Ghost Hole."

Chrisney ['krisˌnē], town in Spencer County (O-4).
Originally called Spring's Station, as there was a spring here beside the railroad. Named Chrisney in 1882 for John B. Chrisney, who first owned the site and arranged for the post office and railroad station here.

Christiansburg ['krisˌchənzˌbərg], village in Brown County (K-7).
Founded about 1850 by Thomas Carmichael. The name is found in other states, where it honors Col. William Christian, who was killed by Indians in Kentucky in 1786. Thus, the name probably is a transfer.

Churubusco [ˌcherə'bəskō; ˌcheryu-], town in Whitley County (C-9).

Formerly two towns were platted here—Franklin in 1845 and Union in 1855. In 1870 they merged and were renamed Churubusco, for the Mexican town where American troops won a battle in the Mexican War.

Cicero ['sisərō], town in Hamilton County (G-7).
Laid out in 1835 and named for nearby Cicero Creek.

Cicero Creek ['sisərō 'krēk], stream in Hamilton County.
This stream heads in Tipton County and flows south through Morse Reservoir to West Fork White River near Noblesville in Hamilton County. Allegedly it was named for an early settler's son named Cicero who fell into the stream while fishing.

Cincinnati [ˌsintsə'næd̲ē], village in Greene County (L-5).
Founded about 1840 and named for Cincinnati, Ohio.

Clanricarde [ˌklænri'kard], village in Porter County (C-4).
Established in 1865. Named for Clanricarde, Wales, hometown of the wife of Jim Burk, co-owner of a ranch here.

Clare [kler], village in Hamilton County (G-7).
Settled around 1830 and named by William W. Conner, one of the founders, for a son of an early settler.

Clark [klark] County (M-8).
Organized in 1801 and named for

General George Rogers Clark, hero of the Revolution.

Clarksburg ['klarks͵bərg], village in Decatur County (J-9).
Laid out by Woodson Clark in 1832 and named for him.

Clarks Hill [͵klarks 'hil], town in Tippecanoe County (F-5).
Named for Daniel D. Clark, who platted the town in 1850.

Clarksville ['klarks͵vil], town in Clark County (N-8).
Founded in 1784 by George Rogers Clark, for whom it was named.

Clarksville ['klarks͵vil], village in Hamilton County (G-7).
Named for General George Rogers Clark.

Clay [klā] County (J-4).
Organized in 1825 and named for Henry Clay, Kentucky orator and statesman.

Clay City ['klā 'sidē], town in Clay County (K-4).
Founded in 1873 and called Markland, for Colonel Markland, Hoosier soldier and statesman. When it was found that another Indiana town had the same name, a local committee changed the name to Clay City, for the county.

Claypool ['klā͵pūl], town in Kosciusko County (C-8).
A post office named Claypool, apparently for the personal name, was established here in 1841.

Claysville ['klāz͵vil], village in Washington County (M-6).
Laid out in 1828 and formerly called Middletown. The present name was adopted in 1839 when a post office was established.

Clayton ['klātn], town in Hendricks County (H-6).
Laid out in 1851 and originally called Claysville, for Henry Clay, Kentucky statesman.

Clear Creek ['klir ͵krēk], village in Monroe County (K-6).
Founded in 1854 and named for a nearby stream of the same name.

Clear Lake ['klir ͵lāk], town in Steuben County (A-11).
Named for the nearby lake of the same name. Incorporated in 1933.

Clear Spring ['klir ͵spriŋ], village in Jackson County (L-7).
Founded in 1839 and named for a spring that runs through the village.

Clermont ['kler͵mant], town in Marion County (H-6).
Platted in 1849 as Mechanicsburg, but it was renamed six years later because there were other Indiana towns of the same name. The name is fairly common in the U. S. and was probably selected for its commendatory quality.

Cleveland ['klēv͵lənd], village in Hancock County (H-8).
Laid out in 1834 and called Portland until about 1855. The origin of

the present name is unknown but probably is for the city in Ohio.

Clifford ['klifərd], town in Bartholomew County (K-8).

Laid out in 1853, and a post office was established here in 1855. Apparently for the personal name.

Clifty Creek ['kliftē ˌkrēk], stream.

About 50 miles long, it heads in Rush County and flows southwest through Decatur and Bartholomew counties to the East Fork White River, about 3 miles south of Columbus. The present name comes from the Indian name *Es-the-nou-o-ne-ho-neque,* "Cliff of Rocks River."

Clinton ['klintn] County (F-6).

Organized in 1830 and named for DeWitt Clinton, governor of New York.

Clinton ['klintn], fifth class city in Vermillion County (J-3).

Platted in 1829 and named for DeWitt Clinton, governor of New York.

Clinton Falls [ˌklintn 'folz], village in Putnam County (H-4).

Formerly called Quincy until the post office was established in 1874 when the name was changed to Clinton Falls for the township it is located in and the nearby falls.

Cloverdale ['klōvərˌdāl], town in Putnam County (J-5).

A post office was established here in 1836 and named Clover Dale,

"for the many large fields of clover, and the lovely shady dales."

Cloverland ['klōvərˌlænd], village in Clay County (J-4).

Founded in 1834 and named for the growth of native clover on the site.

Clymers ['klaimərz], village in Cass County (E-6).

Founded by George Clymer about 1856 and presumably named for him. Laid out in 1869 by David Clymer.

Coal Bluff ['kōl ˌbləf], village in Vigo County (J-4).

A post office was established here in 1876. Named for the Coal Bluff Mining Co., which owned a local mine.

Coal City [ˌkōl 'sidē], village in Owen County (K-4).

Laid out in 1875 and named for the coal mining here.

Coal Creek ['kōl ˌkrēk; ˌkrik], stream.

About 45 miles long, it heads in Fountain County and flows southwest to the Wabash River at the northwest corner of Parke County. It received its name from a rich coal bank discovered near its mouth.

Coal Creek ['kōl ˌkrēk], village in Fountain County (G-3).

A post office was established in 1840 as Headley's Mills. In 1864 the name was changed to Snoddy's Mills, and in 1888 it was changed again to Coal Creek, for the stream of the same name.

Coalmont ['kōl‚mant], village in Clay County (K-4).

Founded in 1900 and named for the coal here and allegedly the elevation of the site.

Coatesville ['kōts‚vil], town in Hendricks County (H-5).

The original plat and records have been lost. A church was established here in the 1830's.

Coburg ['kō‚bərg], village in Porter County (B-5).

Named by Jacob T. Forbes, who settled here in 1854, for his home, Cobourg, Ontario. Forbes owned the land on which the town was laid out.

Coesse [‚kō'esē], village in Whitley County (C-9).

Laid out in 1854–55. The name is a corruption of a Potawatomi nickname of a Miami chief, *Ku-wa-zi,* "Old Man." The Miami pronunciation was *Ko-wa-zi.*

Colburn ['kōl‚bərn], village in Tippecanoe County (E-5).

Laid out in 1858 by Jacob Chapman and called Chapmanville for him.

Cold Springs ['kōld ‚spriŋz], village in Dearborn County (K-10).

Originally called Jones' Station in 1857. The name was changed to Cold Springs in 1874.

Colfax ['kōl‚fæks], town in Clinton County (G-5).

Platted in 1854 and originally called Midway. In 1857 the name was changed to Colfax, for Schuyler Colfax, prominent Hoosier who became Vice President of the U. S.

Collamer ['kal(ə)mar], village in Whitley County (D-8).

Platted in 1846 and formerly called Millersburg, for Elias Miller, who had a gristmill here. The present name was the post office name, which honors Jacob Collamer, Postmaster-General, 1849–50.

College Corner ['kalij 'kornər], village in Jay County (F-10).

Platted in 1857 and named for a former college here.

Collegeville ['kalij‚vil], village in Jasper County (D-4).

Founded in 1889 and so named because of the establishment of St. Joseph's College nearby.

Collett ['kalət], village in Jay County (F-10).

Platted in 1872 by John Collett, for whom it was named.

Collins ['kalənz], village in Whitley County (C-9).

Platted in 1872 and named for James Collins, president of the Detroit, Eel River, and Illinois Railroad.

Coloma [kə'lōmə; kō-], village in Parke County (H-3).

Settled in 1830 and called Rocky Run, for a nearby stream. Renamed Coloma in 1868, probably for Coloma, California, famous in the Gold Rush of 1849.

Columbia [kə'ləmbēə], village in Fayette County (J-10).

Platted in 1832 and named for the township in which it is located.

Columbia City [kə͵ləmbēə 'sidē], county seat, fifth class city in Whitley County (C-9).

Laid out in 1839 and formerly called Columbia. Later, City was added to the name to distinguish it from another Columbia, Indiana. The name, a Latinized form of Columbus, is a very popular place name in the U. S. and was chosen here for its inspirational quality.

Columbus [kə'ləmbəs; -bus], county seat, third class city in Bartholomew County (K-7).

Settled by General John Tipton, John Lindsay, and Luke Bonesteel in 1820 and called Tiptonia for General Tipton, who in 1821 offered 30 acres for the county seat if it were named for him. The county commissioners readily accepted the land but named the seat Columbus when the town was platted in 1821.

Commiskey [kə'mis͵kē], village in Jennings County (L-8).

Platted in 1870 and a post office was established the same year. Apparently the name is for the personal name.

Como ['kōmō], village in Jay County (F-10).

Founded in 1879. Probably named for the Italian city and lake.

Concord ['kan͵kord], village in Dekalb County (C-10).

Apparently named for Concord Township, in which it is located. Platted in 1832.

Concord ['kan͵kord], village in Tippecanoe County (F-5).

A post office was established here in 1837. Probably a transfer name from an eastern state.

Connersville ['kanərz͵vil], county seat, fourth class city in Fayette County (J-10).

Named for John Conner, who established a fur-trading post here in 1808 and founded the town in 1813.

Conrad ['kan͵rəd; -͵ræd], village in Newton County (C-3).

Named for Jennie M. Conrad, who laid out the town in 1908.

Contreras [kən'trerəs], village in Union County (J-11).

Apparently named for the Mexican village of the same name, site of the American victory over the Mexicans in August 1847.

Converse ['kan͵vərs], village in Blackford County (F-9).

A flag station was established here around 1860 and named for Dr. Converse, president of the Pan Handle Railroad.

Converse ['kan͵vərs], town in Miami County (E-8).

A post office was established in 1854 and called Xenia. The town was platted in 1849 and named Converse for a large landowner in the area. In 1892 the post office name was changed to Converse, too.

Cornelius [ˌkorˈnēlˌyəs], village in Brown County (K-6).

Once known locally as Cottonwood, for a tree near a present cemetery. The official name, Cornelius, honoring an early settler, was applied to a post office here in 1893.

Cornettsville [ˈkornətsˌvil], village in Daviess County (M-4).

Platted in 1875 and named for Samuel Cornet, who, with others, laid out the town.

Corning [ˈkorniŋ], village in Daviess County (M-4).

First settled in 1828 and allegedly named by a priest for the corn growing here. The name is both a personal and place name in the U. S., though, so the name probably comes from a person or another place.

Cornstalk Creek [ˈkornˌstok ˌkrēk], stream in Montgomery County.

This tributary of Big Raccoon Creek was named for a nearby Indian village.

Correct [kəˈrekt], village in Ripley County (L-9).

Allegedly William Will, postmaster at Versailles, was asked to suggest a name when a post office was established here in 1881. Since it was at the time of Halley's Comet, he wrote "Comet" on the form and sent it to the Post Office Department. The Department found his handwriting difficult to read so returned a card with "Comet" on it and asked Will to verify the name. He wrote "correct," and that became the name of the town.

Cortland [ˈkortˌlənd], village in Jackson County (L-7).

Founded in 1847 by Cyrus L. Dunham, who named the town for his birthplace, Cortland, New York.

Corunna [kəˈrōnə], town in Dekalb County (B-10).

Settled around 1855 and perhaps named for Corunna, Michigan, although ultimately the name comes from a Spanish city.

Corwin [ˈkorˌwən], village in Tippecanoe County (F-5).

Platted in 1832 and first called Columbia. The name probably is from a personal name.

Cory [ˈkōrē], village in Clay County (J-4).

Founded in 1872 and named for Simeon Cory, pioneer hardware merchant of Terre Haute.

Corydon [ˈkorədən], county seat, town in Harrison County (N-7).

Founded in 1808. General William Henry Harrison, who originally owned the site of the town, named it Corydon when he was governor of the Territory for the shepherd in his favorite song, "Pastoral Elegy," which was in the popular songbook *Missouri Harmony*. It was the first state capital.

Cosperville [ˈkaspərˌvil], village in Noble County (B-9).

Formerly called Springfield, it was laid out in 1844. The name is probably from a personal name.

Cottage Grove [ˌkadij ˈgrōv], village in Union County (J-11).

This is most likely a commendatory name applied to a post office in 1848.

Courter ['kōrtər], village in Miami County (D-7).
Laid out in 1869, and a post office was established the same year.

Coveyville ['kōvē,vil; 'kəvē-], village in Lawrence County (L-6).
Formerly called Goat Run.

Covington ['kəviŋ,tən], county seat, fifth class city in Fountain County (G-3).
Platted in 1828 by Isaac Coleman, a Virginian who settled here in 1826, so possibly it was named for Covington, Virginia.

Cowan ['kau,(w)ən], village in Delaware County (G-9).
Laid out in 1869 by several men, including Charles McCowen, for whom it was named. A variant spelling was Cowen.

Coxville ['kaks,vil], village in Parke County (H-3).
A post office was established here in 1823 and named Roseville, for Chauncey Rose, early settler and prominent citizen. The name was changed to Coxville in 1890 for William Cox, local miller.

Craig [kreg], village in Switzerland County (M-10).
Established as a post office in 1849 and named for Craig Township, in which it is located. The township was named for George Craig, early settler.

Craigville ['kreg,vil], village in Wells County (E-10).
Laid out in 1879 and named for William J. Craig, county clerk when the town was platted.

Crandall ['krændəl], town in Harrison County (N-7).
Laid out in 1872 by Cornelius F. Crandall, for whom it was named.

Crawford ['krofərd] County (N-6).
Organized in 1818 and named for Colonel William Crawford, Indian fighter and land agent for George Washington.

Crawfordsville ['krofərdz,vil], county seat, fourth class city in Montgomery County (G-5).
Laid out in 1823 and named for Colonel William H. Crawford, a famous Indian fighter from Virginia, who was Secretary of War, 1815–16, Secretary of the Treasury, 1816–25, and candidate for the presidency, 1824.

Crawleyville ['krolē,vil], village in Gibson County (N-2).
Settled in 1811 and named for a prominent local family whose name was spelled Crowley.

Creston ['kres,tən], village in Lake County (C-3).
Cedar Lake Post Office, named for a nearby lake, was established about ½ mile from Creston around 1842 and moved to the present site of Creston in 1875. In 1882 the name was changed to Creston.

Crete [krēt], village in Randolph County (G-11).

A post office was established here in 1882. Allegedly named for a local resident's sweetheart, whose name was Lucretia or Cretia. Perhaps the present spelling was influenced by the Mediterranean Island, although not necessarily since Crete, North Dakota, also was named from the nickname of a girl named Lucretia.

Crocker ['krakər], village in Porter County (B-4).

Laid out in 1875 by Fred La-Hayn, and called LaHayn for him. The present name, originally spelled Croker, allegedly was for the engineer of the first train to pass through town.

Cromwell ['kram̩wel], town in Noble County (B-8).

Laid out in 1853 by Harrison Wood, who allegedly said, "[Oliver] Cromwell was a good Republican and I'll name the town in his honor."

Crooked Creek ['krukud ̩krēk], stream in Cass County.

About 24 miles long, the stream flows southwest to the Wabash River about 8 miles below Logansport. The name is descriptive of its course.

Crooked Creek ['krukud ̩krēk], stream in Marion County.

Heads in northern Marion County and flows southeast, then southwest, and then east to West Fork White River 5 miles above Indianapolis. The name is descriptive of its circuitous course.

Crooked Creek ['krukud ̩krēk], stream in Steuben County.

About 14 miles long, it heads at the outlet of Lake George and flows southwest through Mud Lake, Snow Lake, and Lake James and then northwest through Jimmerson Lake to a small lake near Orland. The name is descriptive.

Cross Plains [̩kros 'plānz], village in Ripley County (L-10).

Laid out in 1826 and so named for its location on a cross roads on level ground.

Cross Roads ['kros̩ rōdz], village in Delaware County (G-9).

A post office called Cross Roads was established here in 1879. Apparently the name is descriptive of its location.

Crothersville ['krəth̲ərz̩vil], town in Jackson County (L-8).

Founded in 1835 and originally called Haysville. Shortly after this the name was changed to Crothersville, for Dr. Crothers, a railroad superintendent.

Crown Center [̩kraun 'sen(t)ər], village in Morgan County (J-6).

Originally called Mount Tabor, but presumably because there was another Hoosier town of that name, the Post Office Department applied the present name in 1891.

Crown Point [̩kraun 'point], county seat, fourth class city in Lake County (B-3).

Founded about 1834 and first known as Robinson's Prairie, for

36

Solon and Milo Robinson. Allegedly, when Solon Robinson saved his neighbors' lands from speculators, he was nicknamed "King of the Squatters," and the settlement was renamed Crown Point: "Crown" for the "king" and "Point" for the elevation on which the courthouse and Robinson's cabin stood. The town was laid out in 1840 as a new county seat, and according to one source, "The name Crown Point was applied under the following circumstances: 'I have a name to propose,' said George Earle, County Agent. 'So have I,' replied Solon Robinson. 'What is your name?' 'Crown Point.' 'And that is also mine.' " Probably the name was suggested by that of a nearby settlement, West Point, and borrowed from New York for its commendatory value.

Crumstown ['krəmz‚taun], village in St. Joseph County (B-6).

Formerly called Crum's Point, for Nathaniel H. Crum, early settler and prominent citizen, it was laid out in 1875.

Crystal ['kristəl], village in Dubois County (M-5).

Never platted, but a post office was established here in 1889.

Cuba ['kyūbə], village in Allen County (C-10).

Laid out in 1855 and apparently named for the island.

Cuba ['kyūbə], village in Owen County (J-5).

Laid out in 1851 and called Santa Fe. The post office name was Cuba, apparently for the island.

Culver ['kəlvər], town in Marshall County (C-6).

Laid out in 1844 and named for the founder of Culver Military Academy, Henry Harrison Culver. Former names were Union Town, 1844–51, and Marmount, 1851–95.

Cumback ['kəm‚bæk], village in Daviess County (M-4).

Settled in 1883 and named for Hoosier politician William Cumback.

Cumberland ['kəmbər‚lənd], town in Marion County (H-7).

Platted in 1831 and named for the Cumberland Road, on which it was located.

Curryville ['kərē‚vil], village in Adams County (E-10).

Located on the Adams-Wells county line, it was founded in 1859 and called Coryville, for Peter Corey, on whose land it was located. Platted in 1880.

Curtisville ['kərtəs‚vil], village in Tipton County (F-7).

Laid out in 1873. Apparently named for the personal name.

Cutler ['kət‚lər], village in Carroll County (F-6).

Settled in 1828 and named for a railroad official of the same name.

Cuzco ['kuz‚kō], village in Dubois County (M-5).

Platted in 1905 and originally called Union Valley because the residents were opposed to slavery. The present name comes from the city in Peru.

Cyclone [‚sai'klōn], village in Clinton County (G-6).

Named for the cyclone of June 14, 1880.

Cynthiana [‚sinthē'ænə], town in Posey County (N-2).

Laid out in 1817 and named by William Davis for Cynthiana, Kentucky, home of its settlers.

D

Dabney ['dæbnē], village in Ripley County (K-9).

Laid out in 1855 and named Poston, "but because it sounded so much like Holton, people often got off the train at the wrong station. According to a story, a train dispatcher got the towns mixed up and almost caused a wreck, so the railroad company called the town Dabney," for the postmaster whose name was Dabney.

Daggett ['dægit; -ət], village in Owen County (K-4).

Laid out in 1880 and named for Charles Daggett, who owned a mill here.

Dale [dāl], town in Spencer County (N-4).

Laid out in 1843 and named Elizabeth, but since there were already two other towns named Elizabeth in the state, it was renamed Dale, for Robert Dale Owen of New Harmony, who was a congressman when the name was changed.

Daleville ['dāl‚vil], village in Delaware County (G-9).

Platted in 1838 by Campbell Dale and originally called Dalesville for him.

Dalton ['doltn], village in Wayne County (G-10).

Platted in 1828. The post office formerly was Palmyra. Probably the name comes from a personal name.

Dana ['dānə], town in Vermillion County (H-3).

Platted in 1874. The name honors Charles Dana, a stockholder in the railroad through here.

Danville ['dæn‚vil], county seat, town in Hendricks County (H-6).

Laid out in 1824 and named by William Watson Wick, judge of the fifth circuit, for his brother Dan.

Darlington ['darliŋ‚tən], town in Montgomery County (G-5).

First settled in 1823 and platted in 1836. Named for the English town by Quaker settlers.

Darmstadt ['darm‚stæt], village in Vanderburgh County (O-3).

Established about 1860 by Ger-

38

mans who named it for Darmstadt, Germany.

Daviess ['dāvəs] County (M-4).

Organized in 1817 and named for Colonel Joseph Hamilton Daviess, who was killed in the Battle of Tippecanoe. Dunn says the "Colonel's name was Daveiss and he always wrote it that way."

Daylight ['dā͵lait], village in Vanderburgh County (O-3).

A post office was located here in 1900. Allegedly this community was named for the remark of a railroad engineer. Each evening when he dropped off a construction crew here, he said, "I'll pick you men up at daylight." Eventually Daylight became the name of the place.

Dayton ['dātn], village in Tippecanoe County (F-5).

Laid out in 1827 and named Fairfield; however, since there was another town of that name in Indiana, the name was changed in 1830 to Dayton, for the city in Ohio.

Dayville ['dā͵vil], village in Warrick County (O-3).

Named for the Day family, descendants of Thomas Day, who settled in the county in 1850. A post office was established here in 1900, with George O. Day as the postmaster.

Deacon ['dēkən], village in Cass County (E-6).

Never platted, the town was named for William C. Deacon, merchant and first postmaster when a post office was established in 1884.

Dearborn ['dir͵bərn] County (K-10).

Organized in 1803 and named for General Henry Dearborn, who served in the Revolution and was Secretary of War, 1801–09.

Decatur [di'kātər] County (K-9).

Organized in 1822 and named for Commodore Stephen Decatur, naval hero of the War of 1812.

Decatur [͵dē'kātər; di-], county seat, fifth class city in Adams County (D-10).

Platted in 1836 and named for the naval hero, Stephen Decatur.

Decker ['dekər], town in Knox County (M-3).

Laid out in 1869 by Isaac Decker, and named for him. Formerly called Deckertown and Deckers.

Deedsville ['dēdz͵vil], village in Miami County (D-7).

Platted in 1870 and named for William Deeds, who owned the land.

Deep River [͵dēp 'rivər], village in Lake County (B-4).

First settled in 1836 and named for the nearby stream of the same name.

Deer Creek ['dir ͵krēk], stream.

About 40 miles long, it heads in Howard County and flows west to the Wabash River near Delphi. The name comes from the Miami name,

Passeanong, "The Place of the Fawn."

Deer Creek ['dir ˌkrik], village in Carroll County (E-6).

A post office called Deer Creek was established here in 1832. Named for nearby Deer Creek.

Deerfield ['dirˌfēld], village in Randolph County (F-10).

Laid out in 1833. The post office formerly was named Mississinewa, then Randolph.

Dekalb [di'kælb; ˌdē-] County (B-10).

Organized in 1837 and named for Baron Johann de Kalb, Revolutionary War general. Baron De Kalb, a Bavarian who entered the French service in 1743 and the American service in 1777, was killed at Camden in 1780.

Delaware ['delaˌwer] County (F-9).

Organized in 1827 and named for the Delaware Indians, who had villages in the area from 1770 to 1818.

Delaware ['delaˌwer], village in Ripley County (K-10).

Platted in 1870. The post office name first was Delaware Station, then Rei, then Delaware. The present name is for Delaware Township, in which it is located.

Delong [dē'loŋ], village in Fulton County (C-6).

Established in 1871 and named for early settlers. An earlier spelling was DeLong.

Delphi ['delˌfai], county seat, fifth class city in Carroll County (E-5).

Laid out as the county seat in 1828 and first called Carrollton, for the county, but later the same year the name was changed to Delphi, for the Greek shrine, at the suggestion of General Samuel Milroy, a leader in the organization of the county.

Deming ['demiŋ; -ēŋ], village in Hamilton County (G-7).

Laid out in 1837 and named for an abolition candidate for president.

Demotte [dē'mat], town in Jasper County (C-4).

Laid out in 1884. The name probably is from the personal name.

Denham ['denəm], village in Pulaski County (C-5).

Originally called Gundrum, for the first merchant, Paul Gundrum. The name was changed by railroad officials. A store was established here in 1868 and a post office about the same time. The name probably is a personal name.

Denmark ['denˌmark], village in Owen County (K-4).

A post office was established at this unplatted community in 1874. Apparently named for the country.

Denver ['denˌvər], town in Miami County (D-7).

Originally called Urbana, the town was platted in 1872. The present name was applied to a post office here in 1869.

Depauw [ˌdē'po], village in Harrison County (N-7).

Platted in 1884. The name probably is from the personal name, perhaps for industrialist Washington C. DePauw of nearby New Albany, for whom DePauw University was named the same year.

Deputy ['depyudē], village in Jefferson County (L-8).

Laid out in 1871 and named for James Deputy, prominent citizen.

Derby ['dərbē], village in Perry County (0-6).

Laid out in 1835 and named for Derby, Ireland.

Desoto [dē'sōtō; di-; də-], village in Delaware County (F-9).

Platted in 1881 and originally called Woodlawn. Because of confusion with a town of the same name in Allen County, the name was changed to Desoto, for the Spanish explorer.

Devore [di'vōr; dē-], village in Owen County (J-5).

Established in 1835 and named for the Devore family, early settlers. Originally it was called Mill Grove, for a mill here.

Diamond ['dai(ə)mən(d)], village in Parke County (J-4).

Originally called Caseyville, for a local storekeeper. The name was changed to Diamond in 1891 for the coal, "black diamond," here when a post office was established.

Dillman ['dilmən], village in Wells County (E-9).

Named for Andrew Dillman who came here in 1854 from Ohio.

Dillsboro ['dilz‚bərō], town in Dearborn County (L-10).

Laid out in 1830 and originally called Dillsborough. The present spelling was adopted in 1893. Probably named for General James Dill, prominent in the history of the county.

Dillsboro Station [‚dilz‚bəro 'stāshən], village in Dearborn County (L-10).

Named for Dillsboro.

Disko ['diskō], village in Fulton County (D-7).

Laid out in 1856 and originally called New Harrisburg. The present name is for the railroad station here. The name may come from Disco, a bay and island west of Greenland. The name is found in Michigan, too, where it comes from a nineteenth century school named for the Latin "I learn."

Dixon Lake [‚diksən 'lāk], lake in Marshall County.

Located 1½ miles southwest of Plymouth, this 27-acre lake was named for George Dixon, who lived near the lake.

Doans [dōnz], village in Greene County (L-5).

Originally called Snake Hollow, for a rattlesnake found here, the town was renamed Doans, for nearby Doans Creek, when a post office was established in 1899.

Doans Creek [‚dōnz 'krēk], stream in Greene County.

About 10 miles long, this stream

flows west and then southwest to West Fork White River about 2½ miles above Newberry. It was named for an early settler, Isaac Doan.

Dodd [dad], village in Perry County (0-5).

A post office, established here in 1898, was named for George Dodd, early settler.

Dogwood ['dog͵wud], village in Harrison County (O-7).

Established about 1895. Apparently named for the tree.

Dolan ['dōlən], village in Monroe County (K-6).

Laid out in 1851 and named for a pioneer miller, John Dolan.

Domestic [də'mestik], village in Wells County (E-10).

Formerly called Ringville. A post office called Domestic, apparently a commendatory name, was established in 1884.

Donaldson ['danəl(d)sən], village in Marshall County (C-6).

Platted in 1871. A varied spelling was Donelson. Apparently the name is from the personal name.

Doolittle Mills ['dū͵lutl 'milz], village in Perry County (N-5).

A post office was established in 1870 and named for the Doolittle family, who operated a mill here.

Door Village [͵dōr 'vilij] village in LaPorte County (B-5).

Settled about 1830 and surveyed in 1836 on Door Prairie. The name

of the town and prairie are translations of the name of the county, LaPorte, "the Door."

Dover ['dōvər], village in Boone County (G-5).

First known as Crackaway, it was platted in 1850. In 1860 a post office was established here and called Dover, perhaps a transfer from an eastern state.

Dover ['dōvər] (Kelso), village in Dearborn County (K-10).

John Kelso, a native of Ireland, settled in the county in 1813, and a township and this town were named for him. McKenzie Cross Roads, for early settler Henry McKenzie, was another former name.

Dover Hill [͵dōvər 'hil], village in Martin County (M-5).

Laid out in 1844 and called Hillsborough. A few years later the name was changed to Dover Hill, apparently because the high cliffs here suggested the cliffs of Dover, England.

Downeyville ['daunē͵vil], village in Decatur County (J-8).

Never platted, the town was named for the first settler, J. F. Downey. Downey and his sons had a general store here. When a post office was established in 1876, Amos F. Downey became the first postmaster.

Drewersburg ['drūərz͵bərg], village in Franklin County (K-11).

Platted in 1833 and named for a resident, William S. Drewer.

Driftwood River ['driftwud 'rivər], stream.

This is the name of the East Fork of White River, especially that part of it after Blue River unites with Sugar Creek near the Johnson-Bartholomew county line until it is joined by Flat Rock River near Columbus, but all of the East Fork has been called Driftwood Fork. Driftwood is said to be a literal translation of the Miami name, *Ongwah-sah-kah*.

Dublin ['dəblən], town in Wayne County (H-9).

Settled in 1821 and platted in 1830. Probably named for the Irish city, but according to local anecdote: "Dublin, in the early days, was a famous mud hole just west of Cambridge City. Wagons and stagecoaches when passing this spot had to double team to get through. This condition continued until the National Road was built. When the town was platted, it was decided to call it Dublin, because of always having to double team at that place. There is a marker to designate the place." According to another legend, "Dublin, Indiana, got its name from the old home place, [the] Huddleston House. The home place used to be called Double Inn because it had double doors."

Dubois ['dū͵boiz] County (N-5).

Organized in 1818 and named for Toussaint Dubois, a French soldier who fought with General William Henry Harrison at Tippecanoe.

Dubois ['dū͵boiz], village in Dubois County (N-5).

Platted in 1885 and named for the county.

Dudleytown ['dədlē͵taun], village in Jackson County (L-7).

Laid out in 1837 by James Dudley, for whom it was named.

Duff [dəf], village in Dubois County (N-4).

Founded in 1833 and named for Colonel B. B. "Duff" Edmonstan.

Dugger ['dəgər], town in Sullivan County (K-4).

Founded in 1879 by F. M. Dugger and named for him.

Dundee [͵dən'dē], village in Madison County (F-8).

Originally called Mudsock, for the marshy quality of the soil, the town was platted in 1883. Probably named for the city in Scotland.

Dune Acres [͵dūn 'ākərz], town in Porter County (B-4).

Incorporated in 1925 and named for the Indiana Dunes.

Dunfee ['dən͵fē; dəm-], village in Whitley County (D-9).

A post office called Dunfee was established here in 1883. Probably named for an official with the New York, Chicago, and St. Louis Railroad.

Dunkirk ['dən͵kərk], fifth class city in Blackford and Jay counties (F-9).

Platted in 1853 and originally called Quincy. The name was changed because there was another town named Quincy in the state. The present name might be for Dunkirk, New York.

Dunlap ['dənˌlæp], village in Elkhart County (A-7).

Unplatted, the town was named for a railroad official. When a post office was established in 1886, the name was spelled Dunlaps.

Dunlapsville ['dənˌlæpsˌvil], village in Union County (J-10).

Laid out in 1817 and named for John Dunlap, early settler and proprietor.

Dunn [dən], village in Benton County (E-3).

A post office was located here in 1907 and named for Captain James Dunn, who founded nearby Dunnington.

Dunnington ['dəniŋˌtən], village in Benton County (E-3).

Named for the founder, Captain James Dunn. Mannella Dunn was the first postmaster when a post office was established in 1888.

Dunreith ['dənˌrēth], town in Henry County (H-9).

Platted in 1865, the settlement first was known as Coffin's Station, for Emery Dunreith Coffin. The present name comes from Coffin's middle name.

Dupont ['dūˌpant], town in Jefferson County (L-9).

Laid out in 1849 by James Tilton of Wilmington, Delaware, who named the town for the Du Pont family, manufacturers of gunpowder.

Durham ['durəm], village in La-Porte County (B-5).

Laid out in 1847, although the village grew up around 1837, and named for New Durham Township, which was named for Durham, Greene County, New York.

Dyer ['daiˌər], town in Lake County (B-3).

A post office named Dyer, probably for the personal name, was established here in 1857.

E

Eagletown ['ēgəlˌtaun], village in Hamilton County (G-7).

Laid out in 1848. It was established as a railroad station and named after Little Eagle Creek.

Eagle Village [ˌēgəl 'vilij; -ēj], village in Boone County (G-6).

Laid out in 1831 in Eagle Township, for which it was named.

Earle [ərl], village in Vanderburgh County (O-3).

Named for John Earle, an English settler who came here in 1828.

Earl Park [ˌərl 'park], town in Benton County (E-3).

Laid out in 1872 and named for Adams Earl of Lafayette, a large landowner and co-founder of the town.

East Chicago [ˌēs(t) shiˈkagō], second class city in Lake County (A-3).

Incorporated in 1889. A locational name, as the city is located east of Chicago, which means "place of wild onions."

East Enterprise [ˌēs ˈtenərˌpraiz], village in Switzerland County (L-10).

Formerly called Clapboard Corner, for a clapboard mill here. A post office was established in 1823 as Allensville, and the name was changed to East Enterprise in 1864. The present name is commendatory.

East Fork Tanners Creek [ˌēst ˌfork ˈtænərz ˌkrēk], stream in Dearborn County.

A tributary of Tanners Creek, q.v., for which it was named.

East Fork White River [ˌēst ˌfork ˈhwait ˌrivər], stream.

See White River and Driftwood River.

East Gary [ˌēst ˈgerē], fifth class city in Lake County (B-4).

Laid out in 1852. The name is locational, as the town is east of Gary, q.v.

East Germantown [ˌēst ˈjərmənˌtaun] (Pershing), town in Wayne County (H-10).

See Pershing, Wayne County.

East Glenn [ˌēs(t) ˈglen], village in Vigo County (J-3).

Named for nearby Glen Ayr, q.v., although East Glenn actually is north of Glen Ayr. Glenn Post Office was established in 1887 and discontinued in 1902.

East Liberty [ˌēs(t) ˈlibərdē], village in Allen County (D-11).

Laid out in 1848. The name is commendatory.

East Mount Carmel [ˌēs(t) ˌmaunt ˈkarməl], village in Gibson County (N-2).

Established about 1885. The name is locational, for Mt. Carmel, Illinois, located just across the Wabash.

East Oolitic [ˌēst ōˈlitik], village in Lawrence County (L-6).

Platted in 1900. The name is locational, as the town is east of Oolitic, q.v. Formerly called Spien Kopj, for the battle in the Boer War.

East Union [ˌēst ˈyūnyən], village in Tipton County (G-7).

Apparently this name is commendatory.

Eaton [ˈētn], town in Delaware County (F-9).

Laid out in 1854 and probably named for the personal name.

Eckerty [ˈekərdē], village in Crawford County (N-5).

Named for Christopher Eckerty, a leading citizen who laid out the town in 1873.

Economy [ēˈkanəmē], town in Wayne County (G-10).

Named by Charles Osborn in 1825 when, according to tradition, he was short of funds and laid out his land in lots and sold them, as this was "the most economical way of proceeding." Economy is a common commendatory name meaning "thrift."

Eddy ['edē], village in Lagrange County (B-9).

A post office was established here in 1893 and called Eddy, probably from the personal name.

Eden ['ēdn], village in Hancock County (H-8).

Laid out in 1835 and formerly called Lewisburg. The origin of the present name is unknown, but probably is a commendatory name influenced by the biblical garden.

Edgewood ['ejˌwud], town in Madison County (G-8).

Laid out in 1916 and so named because a forest bordered it on the east.

Edgewood ['ejˌwud], village in Marion County (H-7).

Platted in 1907 and so named because it was located at the edge of a large forest.

Edinburg ['ednˌbərg], town in Johnson and Bartholomew counties (J-7).

Laid out in 1826 and named for Edinburgh, Scotland.

Edna Mills [ˌednə 'milz], village in Clinton County (F-5).

Never formally laid out. A post office was located here in 1861. Named for Edna Kellenbarger, wife of a local mill owner.

Edwardsport ['edwərdzˌpōrt], town in Knox County (L-4).

Platted in 1839 and named for Edward Wilkins, who was instrumental in laying out the town. It was once a prominent flatboat landing place, hence the generic *port*.

Edwardsville ['edwərdzˌvil], village in Floyd County (N-7).

Laid out in 1853 by Henry Edwards, for whom it was named.

Eel River [ˌēl 'rivər], stream.

About 100 miles long, it heads in Allen County and flows southwest to the Wabash River near Logansport. Both the French name, *L'Anguille,* and the English name are literal translations of the Miami name, *Ken-na-pe-kwo-ma-kwa.*

Eel River [ˌēl 'rivər], stream.

About 120 miles long, including the Big Walnut Fork, which heads in Boone County and flows southwest through Hendricks and Putnam counties, where it meets Mill Creek. At this point the stream, Eel River proper, flows southwest, then southeast, through Clay and Owen counties to the West Fork White River near Worthington in Greene County. The name is a translation of the Delaware name, *Schack-a-mak,* "slippery fish," i.e., "eel."

Effner ['efˌnər], village in Newton County (E-3).

Established about 1860, but a post office was not located here until 1899. Probably named for a personal name.

Ehrmandale ['ərmənˌdāl], village in Vigo County (J-4).

A post office was established as Elsie in 1896, but the name was changed to Ehrmandale in 1898, for local landowners, the Ehrman family.

Ekin ['ēkin], village in Tipton County (G-7).

A post office was established here in 1875. Named for General Ekin, supervisor of a government depot in Jeffersonville.

Elberfeld ['elbər͵feld], town in Warrick County (O-3).

Platted in 1885 and named for Elberfeld, Germany, as many settlers were Germans.

Elizabeth [ə'liz(ə)bəth], town in Harrison County (O-7).

Platted in 1812 and named for Elizabeth Veach, wife of the man who donated land to the town.

Elizabethtown [(ə)'liz(ə)bəth͵taun], town in Bartholomew County (K-8).

Laid out in 1845 by George W. Branham, who named the town for his wife, Elizabeth.

Elizaville [ə'laizə͵vil], village in Boone County (G-6).

Laid out in 1851 or 1852 on the farm of Hiram Brinton. The name probably is for the christian name.

Elkhart ['elkart] County (B-8).

Organized in 1830 and named for the Elkhart River.

Elkhart ['elkart], second class city in Elkhart County (A-7).

Platted in 1832 and named for the Elkhart River.

Elkhart River [͵elkart 'rivər], stream.

About 100 miles long, it heads in Noble County and flows northwest through Elkhart County to the St. Joseph River. On early maps the name was written Elkheart or Elksheart in English and *Coeur de Cerf* in French, which are literal translations of the Potawatomi name of the stream, *Me-sheh-weh-ou-deh-ik*. It derives its name from an island at its mouth which the Indians thought resembled an elk's heart.

Elkinsville ['elkinz͵vil], village in Brown County (K-6).

Founded in the 1850's and named for William Elkins, first settler and founder of the town.

Ellettsville ['eləts͵vil], town in Monroe County (K-5).

Named for Edward Elletts, who kept a tavern here before the settlement was platted in 1837.

Ellis ['eləs], village in Greene County (K-4).

Founded about 1873 and named for William Ellis, who donated land for a school here.

Elliston ['eləstən], village in Greene County (L-4).

Platted in 1885 and named for an early settler named Ellis.

Ellsworth ['elz͵wərth], village in Dubois County (N-5).

A post office was located here in 1878. Named for early settlers, the Ellsworth family. James Ellis was the first postmaster.

Elmdale ['elm‚dāl], village in Montgomery County (G-4).

Originally called Boston Store in 1866. The name was changed to Elmdale in 1882. The present name probably is descriptive, for the tree, although presently Elm has commendatory quality.

Elmira [‚el'mairə], village in Lagrange County (B-9).

Apparently named for Elmira, New York.

Elnora [‚el'nōrə], town in Daviess County (L-4).

Laid out in 1885 and named for Elnora Griffith, wife of a merchant here.

Elon [ē'lan], village in Orange County (N-5).

A post office named Elon was established in 1892. Probably the name is biblical.

Elrod ['el‚rad], village in Ripley County (K-10).

Established as a post office in 1849. Named for early settler and first postmaster George W. Elrod.

Elwood ['el‚wud], fourth class city in Madison County (F-8).

Laid out in 1853 and called Quincy, but since there was another town of that name in Indiana, the name was changed to Elwood in 1869. The post office formerly was Duck Creek. The origin of Elwood is uncertain. One account says the name was arbitrarily selected from a directory, and another more likely explanation says the name honors Elwood Frazier, a seven-year-old boy here when the town was renamed.

Elwren ['el‚rən], village in Monroe County (K-5).

Settled in 1906. Supposedly the name is an acronym coined to satisfy four local families who wanted the railroad station here named for them: E̲ller, W̲haley, Baker̲, and Breede̲n̲.

Eminence ['emənənts], village in Morgan County (J-5).

Laid out in 1855. The name probably is commendatory.

Emison ['eməsən; 'im-], village in Knox County (L-3).

Laid out in 1867 and named for the proprietor, Samuel A. Emison.

Emma ['emə], village in Lagrange County (B-9).

Formerly called Eden Mills. A post office was established here in 1880 and called Emma, apparently for a personal name.

Emporia [im'pōrēə; em-], village in Madison County (G-8).

Laid out around 1891 and probably a commendatory name; however, the name was applied to two ancient cities and several American settlements, so the name may have been borrowed.

English [ãŋglish; 'iŋ-], county seat, town in Crawford County (N-6).

Platted in 1839 and named for William Hayden English, Hoosier statesman.

English Lake [‚iŋglish 'lāk], village in Starke County (C-5).

Established in 1865 and named for an adjoining lake, now drained.

Enochsburg ['ēniks,bərg], village in Franklin County (J-9).

Laid out in 1836 by Woodson Clark and Enoch Abrahams, for whom it was named.

Enos ['ēnəs], village in Newton County (D-3).

Laid out in 1907. Probably the name comes from the personal name.

Enterprise ['entər,praiz], village in Spencer County (P-4).

Laid out in 1862. The name is commendatory.

Epsom ['eps(ə)m], village in Daviess County (L-4).

Settled in 1815 or 1816 and allegedly named for a well dug here that tasted like Epsom salts. The name is also found in England and New Hampshire.

Erie ['irē], village in Lawrence County (L-6).

Laid out in 1867. The name comes from the Indian tribe, perhaps via Lake Erie.

Erie ['irē], village in Miami County (E-7).

Named for Erie Township, in which it is located.

Etna ['et,nə] (Hecla), village in Whitley County (C-8).

Laid out in 1849 and formerly called Hecla, apparently for the Ohio town. Etna is for the township in which it is located.

Etna Green [,et,nə 'grēn], town in Kosciusko County (C-7).

The post office here first was called Camp Creek in 1849, but the name was changed to Etna Green in 1954. The town is located in Etna Township, and the first part of the name comes from that. The complete name probably is a parody of Gretna Green, a Scottish town.

Eugene ['yūjēn], village in Vermillion County (G-3).

Laid out in 1827. According to local legend, an habitual drunk frequently searched for his wife, calling, "Oh, Jane!" "But his condition rendered his speech ineffective, and his call would sound more like, 'Eu, Jene!' Finally his popular call became the name of the town." The actual origin of the name is unknown.

Eureka [yu'rēkə], village in Spencer County (P-4).

Laid out in 1858 and named French Island City, for the nearby island on the Ohio River. In 1860 the post office name, French Island, was changed to Eureka, as the settlement informally was known. According to local legend, early settlers were looking for a tract of land opposite French Island. A watchman sighted the island at dawn and shouted "Eureka," which became the name of the settlement.

Evansville ['evənz,vil], county seat, second class city in Vanderburgh County (O-3).

Colonel Hugh McGary built a

cabin here in 1812. In 1817 he sold a section of land to General Robert Evans, and the town was replatted, becoming the county seat of newly created Vanderburgh County, and named for General Evans.

Everton ['evərˌtən], village in Fayette County (J-10).

Founded around 1840. Originally called Lawstown or Lawsburg, then West Union, it was renamed for the post office.

F

Fairbanks ['ferˌbæŋks], village in Sullivan County (K-3).

Platted in 1840 and named for Lt. Fairbanks, who, along with most of his command, was killed here by Indians in 1812.

Fairfield ['ferˌfēld], village in Franklin County (J-10).

Platted in 1815. Apparently the name is commendatory, "suggested by the general beauty of the country" here.

Fairfield ['ferˌfēld] (Oakford), village in Howard County (F-7).

See Oakford.

Fairland ['ferˌlænd], village in Shelby County (J-8).

Laid out in 1852. The name is commendatory, meaning "beautiful land."

Fairmount ['ferˌmaunt], town in Grant County (F-8).

Laid out in 1850 and named by James Baldwin for the Fairmount waterworks of Philadelphia "because of its resemblance in cleanliness and beauty."

Fairview ['ferˌvyū], village in Fayette County (H-9).

A post office was established here in 1835 and apparently named for Fairview Township, in which it is located.

Fairview ['ferˌvyū], village in Randolph County (L-10).

Laid out in 1838. The name is subjectively descriptive.

Fairview ['ferˌvyū], village in Switzerland County (L-10).

Unplatted. The post office, established in 1835, was called Sugar Branch. The name was changed to Fairview in 1911. The present name, fairly popular in Indiana, is subjectively descriptive.

Fairview Park [ˌferˌvyū 'park], town in Vermillion County (H-3).

Platted in 1902. Fairview, generally a subjectively descriptive name, is the name of three other communities in Indiana. Fairview Park is especially commendatory.

Fall Creek ['fol ˌkrēk], stream.

About 75 miles long, it heads in

Henry County and flows southwest through Madison, Hamilton, and Marion counties to the West Fork White River near Indianapolis. The name is a translation of the Delaware word for a waterfall, *sokpehellak* or *sookpehelluk,* which refers to the falls near Pendleton. The Miami name of the stream was *Chank-tun-oon-gi,* "Makes a Noise Place," which also refers to the falls.

Falmouth ['fælməth], village in Fayette County (H-9).

Originally called Old Baker Settlement for the Baker family who settled here, the village was laid out in 1832 and renamed for the English town, Falmouth, home of the Bakers.

Fancher Lake [ˌfænchər 'lāk], lake in Lake County.

This ten-acre lake located at the fairgrounds in Crown Point was named for early settler Richard Fancher or his family.

Farabee ['ferəbē], village in Washington County (M-7).

Formerly a railroad stop that was named for the first station agent.

Farlen ['farlən], village in Daviess County (L-5).

Originally called McFarlen, for early settler W. N. McFarlen, who had a general store here. A post office was established as Farlen in 1884, with Wyatt M. McFarlen as postmaster.

Farmers ['farmərz], village in Owen County (K-5).

A post office named Farmer's Station was established in 1882. In 1882 the name was changed to Farmer. Named for a storeowner here named Farmer.

Farmersburg ['farmərzˌbərg], town in Sullivan County (K-3).

Settled in 1853 by Seventh-Day Adventists, who named it Ascension. Renamed Farmersburg about 1875 because the town served farmers in the area.

Farmers Retreat [ˌfarmərz ri'trēt], village in Dearborn County (L-10).

A post office was established here in 1852. Apparently this name is commendatory.

Farmersville ['farmərzˌvil], village in Posey County (O-2).

Settled about 1812. Formerly it was called Yankee Settlement and Yankeetown, as the settlers were from New England. It also has been called The Corners, for its location at the corner of four farms. Apparently the present name is for these surrounding farms.

Farmland ['farmˌlænd], town in Randolph County (G-10).

Platted in 1852 and named for the rich farmland surrounding it.

Farrville ['farˌvil], village in Grant County (E-9).

A post office was located here in 1887. So named because Farr is a common local personal name. Alfred C. Farr was the first postmaster.

Fawcetts ['fosuts], village in Greene County (L-5).

51

Founded before 1897 and named for the Fawcett family, local landowners.

Fayette [fā'et] County (H-10).

Organized in 1819 and named for the Marquis de la Fayette, the French general who fought in the American Revolution.

Fayette [fā'et], village in Boone County (G-6).

Apparently named for the Marquis de la Fayette.

Fayetteville ['fā͵ət͵vil], village in Lawrence County (L-6).

Platted in 1838 and supposedly named for John Fayette, early settler. Originally called Danville.

Ferdinand ['fərd(ə)nænd; -nænt], town in Dubois County (N-5).

Platted in 1840 and named for the Austrian emperor, Ferdinand.

Ferguson Hill [͵fərgəsən 'hil], village in Vigo County (J-3).

Named for a farmer who owned most of the land here.

Ferndale ['fərn͵dāl], village in Parke County (H-4).

Settled in 1839 and named for the abundance of ferns growing here. A post office was established here in 1884.

Fickle ['fikəl], village in Clinton County (F-5).

Named for an early settler, Isaac Fickle or William Fickle, who bought land here in 1832.

Fillmore ['fil͵mōr], village in Putnam County (H-5).

Laid out in 1837 and named Nicholsville or Nicholsonville, for one of the founders, Carter F. Nicholson. In 1851 the name was changed to Fillmore, for President Millard Fillmore.

Fincastle ['fin͵kæsəl], village in Putnam County (H-5).

Laid out in 1838 and probably named for Fincastle, Virginia, especially the old county of which Kentucky was a part until it was made a separate county in 1776.

Finley ['fin͵lē] (Carrollton), village in Hancock County (H-8).

See Carrollton, Hancock County.

Fishers ['fishərz], town in Hamilton County (G-7).

Named for Salathel Fisher, who laid out the town in 1872. Earlier called Fishers Switch and Fishers Station.

Fishersburg ['fishərz͵bərg], village in Madison County (G-8).

Laid out in 1830 and named by Charles Fisher, postmaster, for his father, John Fisher, an early settler.

Five Points ['faiv ͵points], village in Marion County (H-7).

So named because five roads converge at this point.

Five Points ['faiv ͵points], village in Morgan County (J-6).

Named for five converging roads here.

Flat Rock ['flæt ͵rak], village in Shelby County (J-8).

Platted in 1855 and named for nearby Flat Rock River.

Flat Rock River [ˌflæt ˌrak 'rivər], stream.

About 100 miles long, it heads in Henry County and flows south through Rush, Decatur, Shelby, and Bartholomew counties to the East Fork White River, at Columbus. The name comes from the Delaware name, *Puck-op-ka*. *Puck* means "rock," though *op-ka* does not mean "flat," as the translation implies. It may mean "bed of a stream."

Fletcher ['flechər], village in Fulton County (D-6).

A post office was established here in 1888. Apparently named for the personal name.

Flint Creek [ˌflint 'krēk], stream.

Heads in Tippecanoe County and flows west to the Wabash River at the extreme northeast tip of Fountain County. The name is descriptive of an abundance of flint found near the mouth of the stream.

Flora ['flōrə], town in Carroll County (E-6).

Named for John Flora, who laid out the town in 1872.

Florence ['florənts], village in Switzerland County (L-10).

Laid out in 1817 and called New York. Apparently for the christian name.

Florida ['florədə], village in Madison County (G-8).

Laid out in 1856 and named Clark's Station, for T. G. Clark, resident. The present name comes from the railroad station here, Florida Station, apparently named for the state.

Floyd [floid] County (N-8).

Organized in 1819 and named, according to most sources, for Colonel John Floyd, who was killed by Indians on the Kentucky side of the Ohio River. Colonel Davis Floyd, an associate of Aaron Burr and member of the Indiana General Assembly, was an important figure in the history of the county, and it is likely that the county was named for him. At least, a village in the county, Floyds Knobs, honors Davis Floyd.

Floyds Knobs [ˌfloid 'nabz], village in Floyd County (N-8).

A gristmill was built here in 1815, and the present name was adopted in 1843 in honor of Colonel Davis Floyd of Jeffersonville. The town is located in a valley surrounded by hills, called "knobs."

Folsomville ['fōlsəmˌvil], village in Warrick County (O-4).

Formerly called Lickskillet. The present name is for Benjamin Folsom, proprietor, who laid out the town in 1859.

Foltz [fōlts], village in Jefferson County (L-9).

A post office was established here in 1883. Named for a local family. Nicholas Foltz was the first postmaster.

Fontanet [ˌfauntn'et; ˌfantn-], village in Vigo County (J-4).

Formerly called Fountain Station, allegedly because "the village sprang up overnight." In 1877 a post office was established as Hunter. In 1881 the name was changed to Fontanet, apparently formed from Fountain Station.

Foraker ['fōrˌākər; 'forə-], village in Elkhart County (B-7).

Platted in 1892 and named for Senator Joseph B. Foraker of Ohio.

Foresman ['fōrzmən], village in Newton County (D-3).

Named for J. B. Foresman, who laid out the town in 1882.

Forest ['forəst], village in Clinton County (F-6).

Platted in 1874 and named for the extensive timber here. A variant spelling has been Forrest.

Forest ['forəst] (Laud), village in Whitley County (D-9).

Named for the dense forests here. The post office name is Laud.

Forest City [ˌforəst 'sitē], village in Jasper County (C-4).

So named because of the surrounding forest.

Forest Hill [ˌforəst 'hil], village in Decatur County (K-8).

Laid out in 1852 by Newberry Wheeldon as Newburg. Apparently the present name is descriptive, so named because "it was heavily wooded and stood on a hill."

Fort Branch [ˌfōrt 'brænch], town in Gibson County (N-3).

Laid out in 1852 and named for the pioneer outpost, Fort Branch, built in 1811, which was near the present town.

Fort Ritner [ˌfōrt 'ritˌnər], village in Lawrence County (L-6).

Named for Michael Ritner, foreman of a construction crew building the railroad tunnel near here, who platted the town in 1857.

Fortville ['fōrtˌvil], town in Hancock County (G-8).

Laid out in 1849 by Cephas Fort, who owned the land, and named for the Fort family. Years before the town was platted a local name was Phoebe Fort's Corner. A post office established here was called Walpole, for Thomas D. Walpole, a prominent attorney. When the town was incorporated in 1865, the official name became Fortville.

Fort Wayne [ˌfōrt 'wān], county seat, second class city in Allen County (C-10).

Platted in 1824 and named for General Anthony Wayne, who built a stockade here after defeating Little Turtle in 1794.

Foster ['fostər], village in Warren County (G-3).

Platted in 1893 and named for Joseph Foster, an early settler.

Fountain ['fauntn] County (G-4).

Organized in 1826 and named for Major James Fountain of Kentucky who was killed near Ft. Wayne in the Battle of Maumee in 1790.

Fountain ['fauntn], village in Fountain County (F-3).

Platted in 1828 as Portland, since it was an important port at one time. The present name comes from the county.

Fountain City [‚faunt(ə)n 'sitē], town in Wayne County (G-10).

A Quaker settlement, it was laid out in 1818 as New Garden. When it was incorporated in 1834, it was renamed Newport. In 1878 it became Fountain City, for fountain wells here.

Fountaintown ['fauntn‚taun], village in Shelby County (H-8).

Platted in 1854 by Matthew Fountain, and named for him.

Fourteen Mile Creek [‚fōr(t)tēn ‚mail 'krēk], stream.

Heads in Jefferson County and flows south through Scott and Clark counties to the Ohio River, 14 miles above the Falls at Louisville, from which it gets its name.

Fowler ['faulər], county seat, town in Benton County (E-3).

Named for Moses Fowler of Lafayette, who laid out the town in 1872.

Fowlerton ['faulərtən], town in Grant County (F-8).

Originally called Leach, for a local family. The present name apparently comes from Elbert and Jeff Fowler, who built a mill here in 1895.

Fox [faks], village in Grant County (E-8).

Formerly called Fox Station for Edward Fox, prominent citizen. A post office established in 1884 was called Fox.

Frances ['frænsəs], village in Johnson County (J-7).

Named for the wife of a man who helped establish a railroad station here and assisted in laying out the town.

Francesville ['frænsəs‚vil], town in Pulaski County (D-5).

Laid out in 1852 by James Brooks and named for his daughter.

Francisco [‚fræn'siskō], town in Gibson County (N-3).

Platted in 1851. According to legend, it was named for a Spanish laborer working on the Wabash and Erie Canal. He was fired, built a shack here, and became the first settler.

Frankfort ['fræŋk‚fərt], county seat, fourth class city in Clinton County (F-6).

Laid out in 1830 and named for Frankfurt am Main, Germany, home of the grandfather of the Pence Brothers, who owned the land on which the city is located.

Franklin ['fræŋklən] County (J-10).

Organized in 1811 and named for the famous statesman, Benjamin Franklin.

Franklin ['fræŋk‚lən; -lun], county seat, fourth class city in Johnson County (J-7).

Founded in 1823 and named for Benjamin Franklin.

Franklin ['fræŋkˌlən], village in Wayne County (G-10).

Platted in 1830. A post office was established here in 1876 and called Nettle Creek, for the nearby stream.

Frankton ['fræŋkˌtn], town in Madison County (G-8).

Laid out in 1853 by Alfred Makepeace and Francis Sigler and probably named for Sigler's nickname, Frank.

Fredericksburg ['fredriksˌbərg], town in Washington County (N-7).

First settled in 1805 and called Bridgeport, apparently for a bridge here. It was laid out in 1815 by Frederick Royse and named for him.

Fredonia [ˌfrē'dōnēə], village in Crawford County (N-6).

Platted in 1818. The name was coined around 1800 by giving a Latin ending to freedom and by 1876 it had been applied to at least 12 post offices in the U. S. Since the name means "place of freedom," the name is commendatory.

Freedom ['frēdəm] (Bear Branch), village in Ohio County (L-10).

Laid out in 1845 by Jonathan Cole, who named it Cole's Corner. Bear Branch was the post office here, named for Bear Creek. Apparently Freedom is commendatory.

Freedom ['frēdəm], village in Owen County (K-5).

Laid out in 1834. The name was formed from the name of the proprietor, Joseph Freeland.

Freeland Park [ˌfrēlən(d) 'park], village in Benton County (E-3).

Platted in 1898 and named for Antone Freeland, who owned the land.

Freelandville ['frēləndˌvil], village in Knox County (L-3).

Laid out in 1866 and named for Dr. John T. Freeland, prominent local physician.

Freeman ['frēmən], village in Owen County (K-5).

A post office was established here in 1886. Named for the Freeman family, early settlers.

Freeport ['frēˌpōrt], village in Shelby County (J-8).

Platted in 1836 on the site of a trading post, allegedly "a free place to load cargo." Probably the name is commendatory.

Freetown ['frēˌtaun], village in Jackson County (L-7).

Laid out in 1850 and called Freeport, apparently a commendatory name changed to Freetown because of another town in Shelby County of the same name.

Fremont ['frēˌmant], town in Steuben County (A-10).

Platted in 1837. Originally called Willow Prairie, for willow trees growing here, then Brockville, for local residents. At the time there was another town in Indiana named Brockville, so the town was renamed Fremont, for the famous explorer, J. C. Fremont.

French Lick [ˌfrench 'lik], town in Orange County (M-5).

Laid out in 1857 in French Lick Township, which in 1847 was named for the famous springs. A French settlement here near an animal lick gave the salt spring its name.

Frenchtown ['french‚taun], village in Harrison County (N-7).

Settled in 1840 by about 50 families from France and first called St. Bernard, for a local church. When a post office was established, the name was changed to Frenchtown, for the settlers.

Friendship ['fren(d)‚ship], village in Ripley County (L-10).

Laid out in 1849 by William Hart and originally called Hart's Mills. In 1870 the postmaster changed the name to Friendship "because most of the people were friendly."

Friendswood ['frenz‚wud], village in Hendricks County (H-6).

Settled in 1820. A post office called Friendswood, a commendatory name perhaps suggesting a Quaker influence, was established in 1868.

Fritchton ['frich‚tən], village in Knox County (M-3).

Laid out in 1839 as Richland, for the character of the soil here. In 1893 a post office named Fritchton, for the Fritch family, was established. Emil H. Fritch was the first postmaster.

Fruitdale ['frūt‚dāl], village in Brown County (K-6).

A post office was located here in 1909. The name is of unknown origin, although it is generally believed that it comes from the location in the fruit belt. Probably the name is commendatory.

Fulda ['fuldə], village in Spencer County (O-5).

Established around 1840 and apparently named for the German river or city.

Fulton ['fultn] County (D-6).

Organized in 1836 and named for the inventor of the steamboat, Robert Fulton.

Fulton ['fultn], town in Fulton County (D-6).

Named for Fulton County. A post office was established here in 1850.

Furnessville ['fərnəs‚vil], village in Porter County (A-4).

Founded in 1861 and named for Edwin Furness, who settled here in 1856 and became the first postmaster.

G

Galena [gə'lēnə], village in Floyd County (N-7).

Platted in 1837, it first was called Germantown because many Germans lived here. When a post office was established in 1860, it was named Galena. Galena often is a name descriptive of the principal ore of lead, but in this case may be a transfer.

Galveston [ˌɡælˈvesˌtən], town in Cass County (E-7).

Laid out by James Carter in 1852. The name is explained by an amusing anecdote. "Mr. Carter was puzzled as to what name to give it and on looking out the window noticed a girl passing by with a vest on. The name of Galveston sprang up in his mind." More likely the name was borrowed from Texas.

Gar Creek [ˌɡar ˈkrēk; krik], village in Allen County (C-10).

A post office was established here in 1873 and named for Gar Creek, a nearby stream, now dredged.

Garden City [ˌɡardn ˈsitē], village in Bartholomew County (K-7).

Established in 1886 and allegedly so named because "most everyone living there has a large vegetable garden." Probably the name is commendatory.

Garfield [ˈɡarˌfēld], village in Montgomery County (G-5).

A post office was established here in 1880. Probably named for James A. Garfield, who was elected President of the U. S. that year.

Garrett [ˈɡerət], fifth class city in Dekalb County (C-10).

Laid out in 1875 and named for John W. Garrett, president of the B. & O. Railroad.

Garrison Creek [ˈɡerəsən ˌkrēk], stream in Fayette County.

About 6 miles long, this tributary of Whitewater River flows southeast. Named for Samuel Garrison, who first settled near its mouth around 1812.

Gary [ˈɡerē], second class city in Lake County (B-3).

Founded in 1906 and named for Judge Elbert H. Gary, chairman of the board of directors of U. S. Steel.

Gasburg [ˈɡæsˌbərɡ], village in Morgan County (J-6).

A post office named Gasburgh was located here in 1874. In 1892 the name was changed to Gasburg. According to local legend, "Gideon Johnson, an early settler of Monroe Township, Morgan County, was regarded in his day as the 'windiest' man in that part of Morgan County. In fact, a little village in Monroe Township, which he is accredited as having founded, soon became named or nicknamed Gas Burg on account of his 'gas' and 'tall' stories."

Gas City [ˌɡæ(s) ˈsitē], fifth class city in Grant County (F-8).

Named for the natural gas discovered here in 1887. The town was laid out in 1867 and formerly called Harrisburg, for John S. Harris, a local lawyer.

Gaston [ˈɡæstən], town in Delaware County (F-9).

Platted in 1855 as New Corner, but the name was changed to Gaston in the 1880's for the gas boom here.

Gates Corner ['gāts 'kornər], village in Delaware County (G-9).
Probably named for Albert L. Gates, who settled here in 1838 and divided his 250 acres among his children.

Gaynorsville ['gānərz,vil], village in Decatur County (K-9).
A post office was established here in 1871. Probably the name comes from the personal name.

Geetingsville ['gēdēŋz,vil], village in Clinton County (F-6).
Founded about 1830 and named for the first postmaster, Henry W. Geeting.

Gem [jem], village in Hancock County (H-7).
A post office named Gem, for Gem Station, a nearby railroad station, was established in 1877.

Geneva [jə'nēvə; ji-], town in Adams County (E-10).
Platted in 1853 and first called Buffalo. Perhaps named for the Swiss city or lake.

Geneva [ji'nēvə; jə-], village in Shelby County (J-8).
Platted in 1853. Perhaps named for the Swiss city. Sulphur Hill was the post office name.

Gentryville ['jentrē,vil], town in Spencer County (O-4).
Platted in 1854 and named for James Gentry, one of the town's first merchants.

Georgetown ['jorj,taun], village in Cass County (E-6).
Platted in 1835 and named for George Cicott, an Indian whose reservation was partly in the town's plat.

Georgetown ['jorj,taun], town in Floyd County (N-7).
Laid out around 1833 by George Waltz, for whom it was named.

Georgetown ['jorj,taun], village in Randolph County (G-10).
Platted in 1850, although established as early as 1830.

Georgia ['jorjə], village in Lawrence County (M-6).
Platted in 1853 by John and Alexander Case. A post office was established in 1857.

Gerald [jə'rald], village in Perry County (O-6).
A post office called Gerald, probably for the personal name, was established here in 1905.

Germantown ['jərmən,taun], village in Decatur County (J-8).
This fairly common name usually indicates a German settlement and here honors the large number of Germans who settled in the county.

Gessie ['gesē], village in Vermillion County (G-3).
Platted in 1872 and named for Robert J. Gessie, owner of the townsite.

Gibson ['gib,sən] County (N-3).
Organized in 1813 and named for General John Gibson, secretary of

Indiana Territory, 1801–16, and acting governor for about a year after Harrison's resignation.

Gifford ['gifərd], village in Jasper County (D-4).

Named for Benjamin J. Gifford, who founded the town in 1899.

Gilead ['gilēud; -əd; -id], village in Miami County (D-7).

Platted in 1844 and apparently named for the biblical district and mountain.

Gilman ['gilmən], village in Madison County (G-8).

Laid out in 1893 and named for an early resident.

Gilmour ['gilmōr], village in Sullivan County (K-4).

Established in 1900 and named for Jackson Gilmour, who operated a coal mine here.

Gimco City [ˌgimkō 'sitē], town in Madison County (F-8).

Located near a factory of the General Insulating and Manufacturing Co. (G. I. M. Co.), and named for the company's initials.

Gings [giŋz; gēŋz], village in Rush County (H-9).

Platted in 1870 and named for local storeowner and postmaster Michael Ging.

Giro ['ga(i)ˌrō] (Buena Vista), village in Gibson County (M-3).

See Buena Vista, Gibson County.

Glen Ayr [ˌglen 'er], village in Vigo County (J-3).

Originally a mining town owned by the Glen Ayr Coal Company, and presumably named for the coal company. Glenn Post Office was established in 1887.

Glendale ['glinˌdāl], village in Daviess County (M-4).

Laid out in 1866 and named for Glendale, Ohio.

Glenhall ['glenˌhol], village in Tippecanoe County (F-4).

Platted in 1831 by Joseph Hall, who named it Glen Hall for himself.

Glenns Valley [ˌglenz 'vælē], village in Marion County (J-7).

Founded in 1831 and named for the Glenn family, early settlers.

Glenwood ['glenˌwud], village in Elkhart County (A-7).

This is a fairly commonplace name in the U. S., so possibly it is a transfer from an eastern state, most likely applied because of its commendatory quality.

Glenwood ['glenˌwud], town in Rush and Fayette counties (J-9).

Originally called Steel's for the first postmaster, David Steel, and later named Vienna, the town was laid out in 1882. The present name probably is commendatory.

Glezon ['glēsən] (Hosmer), village in Pike County (N-3).

Laid out in 1854 by Stephen R. Hosmer and named for him. Glezon is the name of a prominent family in the county, as Joseph C. Glezon was a member of the first board of trustees of Petersburg.

Gnaw Bone ['no ˌbōn], village in Brown County (K-7).

Several legends try to explain this colorful name. One story says the Hawkins family built a store and sawmill here, and when one man asked another if he had seen Hawkins, the latter replied, "I seed him settin' on a log above the sawmill gnawin' a bone." Another legend tells of a drunk who got lost on the way home, and one of his friends who found him said, "Thar he sets on that er' log gnawin' his bones." Other stories tell about early settlers who were snowed in, and when help arrived the settlers were found gnawing on old bones. A more plausible theory is that French settlers named the town *Narbonne,* for the French city, and through folk etymology the town became Gnaw Bone.

Gnaw Bone Creek [ˌno ˌbōn 'krēk], stream in Brown County.

About 6 miles long, it flows south and then west to North Fork Salt Creek about 2.2 miles west of the village of Gnaw Bone, for which it was named. Formerly called Henderson Creek, for an early settler.

Goblesville ['gōbəlzˌvil], village in Huntington County (D-9).

Named for the Goble family, prominent in the development of the community. The village is unplatted, but Peter R. Goble settled here as early as 1855.

Goldsmith ['gōldˌsmith], village in Tipton County (F-7).

Laid out in 1876 and named for a railroad official.

Goodland ['gudˌlən(d)], town in Newton County (E-3).

Platted in 1861 and so named because of its surroundings and fertile soil.

Goodwins Corner [ˌgudwənz 'kornər], village in Union County (H-11).

Named for B. L. Goodwin, who had a store and post office here. The post office was established in 1871.

Goshen ['gōshən], county seat, fourth class city in Elkhart County (B-8).

Platted in 1831 and named for the biblical land because of the fertile prairie here.

Gosport ['gasˌpōrt], town in Owen County (J-5).

Laid out in 1829 by Ephraim and Abner Goss, for whom it was named.

Gowdy ['gaudē], village in Rush County (J-8).

Established in 1830 and apparently named for the personal name. A post office was located here in 1890.

Grabill ['grābəl; -ˌbil], town in Allen County (C-10).

Platted in 1902 and named for Joseph A. Grabill.

Grafton ['græfˌtən], village in Posey County (O-1).

Laid out in 1852 and named for Grafton, Illinois.

Graham ['græm; 'grā͵əm], village in Daviess County (M-4).

Founded about 1900 and named for nearby Graham Farms.

Graham Creek ['græm 'krēk], stream in Fountain County.

About 11 miles long, it flows south to Coal Creek and was named for the Graham family who settled here about 1823.

Grammer ['græmər], village in Bartholomew County (K-8).

Platted in 1896. A railroad was built through here in 1891, and allegedly the name comes from the surname of a railroad conductor.

Grand Calumet River [͵græn(d) ͵kæl͵yū'met 'rivər], stream in Lake County.

Flows west across northern Lake County into the State of Illinois. Generally the name is thought to be a corruption of the French *Chalemel,* literally "little reed," but in the corrupted form "pipe of peace." Actually the name is a corruption of the Indian name, appearing in various forms on old maps—*Cal-la-mick, Kil-la-mick,* and *Ken-no-mick,* among others. All these forms are Algonquian dialectical variations, meaning "a long body of deep, still water."

Grandview ['græn(d)͵vyū], town in Spencer County (O-4).

Laid out in 1851 and so named because of its location on a bluff that offers a view of the Ohio River in each direction.

Grange Corner [͵grānj 'kornər], village in Parke County (G-4).

Named Grangeburg about 1871 for John Lundgren's Grange Store and the local Jefferson Grange lodge. It received its present name about 1879.

Granger ['grānjər], village in St. Joseph County (A-7).

Founded in 1883 and named in commemoration of the Grange, a nineteenth century farmer's organization.

Grant [grænt] County (F-8).

Organized in 1831 and named for Samuel and Moses Grant, both killed by Indians in 1789 in Switzerland County.

Grant City [͵grænt 'sitē], village in Henry County (H-9).

Laid out in 1868 and named for President U. S. Grant.

Grantsburg ['grænts͵bərg], village in Crawford County (N-6).

A post office was established here in 1848 and called Sterling. In 1854 the name was changed to Grantsburg, supposedly for General U. S. Grant, but more likely for a local personal name since Grant was not nationally known until the Civil War.

Grants Creek [͵grænts 'krēk], stream in Switzerland County.

A tributary of the Ohio River, it was named for Captain Samuel Grant and Moses Grant, who in 1789 were killed by Indians near the stream.

Granville ['græn‚vil; -vəl], village in Delaware County (F-9).

Founded in 1836 and named for Granville Hastings, who established two mills and a store here.

Grass Creek ['græs ‚krēk], village in Fulton County (D-6).

Established in 1882 and named for a stream of the same name.

Gravel Hill [‚grævəl 'hil], village in Benton County (E-3).

Formerly called The Summit, for a hill here composed largely of gravel; thus, the present name is descriptive.

Graysville ['grāz‚vil], village in Sullivan County (K-3).

Established around 1850 and named for Joseph Gray, early miller and storekeeper here.

Greencastle ['grēn‚kæsəl], county seat, fifth class city in Putnam County (H-5).

Named for Greencastle, Pennyslvania, the hometown of the earliest settler, Ephraim Dukes, who came here in 1821. One local legend that attempts to explain the name goes: "The first man that settled in this area built a home and built it on— I don't know whether it was on posts or he had it laying down for a footing—but they started, after the house was built, they started to sprout, you know, and grow, so he called it his green castle."

Green Center [‚grēn 'sentər], village in Noble County (C-9).

Settled about 1836 and so named because it is near the center of Green Township.

Greendale ['grēn‚dāl], town in Dearborn County (K-11).

Laid out in 1883. Apparently the name is commendatory.

Greene [grēn] County (L-4).

Organized in 1821 and named for Nathaniel Greene, Revolutionary War general.

Greene [grēn], village in Jay County (F-10).

A post office was established here in 1862 and was named for the township in which it is located. The township was named for Greene County, Ohio, home of settlers.

Greenfield ['grēn‚fēld], county seat, fifth class city in Hancock County (H-8).

On April 11, 1828, a committee chose this city as the seat of Hancock County and ordered that it "shall be known and designated by the name and title of Greenfield," for reasons unknown. An early settler in the county was John Green, for whom Green Township was named, so the name may have come from a local family name.

Green Hill [‚grēn 'hil], village in Warren County (F-4).

Platted in 1832 and named Milford, for the Delaware town. In 1869 the name was changed to Green Hill when the Green Hill Seminary was established here.

Green Oak [ˌgrēn 'ōk], village in Fulton County (D-7).

A post office was established here in 1853. Named for a large oak tree on the land where a general store was built. The name has commendatory value.

Greensboro ['grēnzˌbərə; -ō], town in Henry County (H-9).

Platted in 1830 and named for Greensboro, North Carolina, by settlers from there.

Greensburg ['grēnzˌbərg], county seat, fifth class city in Decatur County (K-9).

Laid out in 1822 on ground donated by Thomas Hendricks and John Walker and named for Mrs. Hendricks' home in Pennsylvania.

Greensfork ['grēnzˌfork], town in Wayne County (H-10).

Platted in 1818 and originally called Washington, but since there already was a town of that name in the state, it was renamed for the nearby stream, Greens Fork.

Greentown ['grēnˌtaun], town in Howard County (F-7).

Platted in 1848 on the site of an Indian town, Green's Village, named for Chief Green, a Miami Indian here.

Greenville ['grēnˌvil], town in Floyd County (N-7).

First settled in 1807 and platted in 1818 near the center of Greenville Township, for which it was named.

Greenwood ['grēnˌwud], fourth class city in Johnson County (J-7).

First called Greenfield, apparently for a church here, it was platted in 1864.

· **Greenwood** ['grēnˌwud], village in Wells County (D-10).

Platted in 1872 by Samuel Greenwood and named for him.

Griffin [ˌgrifən], town in Posey County (N-2).

Laid out in 1881 and named for Samuel Griffin, first postmaster.

Griffith ['grifith; -əth], town in Lake County (B-3).

Dates from 1891 and named for Benjamin Griffith, civil engineer for a railroad.

Groomsville ['grūmzˌvil], village in Tipton County (F-7).

Established in 1860 and named for Dr. Groom of Tipton.

Groveland ['grōvˌlənd], village in Putnam County (H-5).

Laid out in 1854. Probably so named for the forest here. It is a popular name applied to nine U. S. post offices by 1875.

Grovertown ['grōvərˌtaun], village in Starke County (B-6).

Laid out in 1858 and formerly called Grovestown. Named for Stephen Grover, engineer on the Pennsylvania Railroad.

Guernsey ['gərnzē], village in White County (E-5).

In 1883 a railroad station was established here. The name of the community was derived from the post office name.

Guilford ['gilfərd], village in Dearborn County (K-10).

Laid out in 1850. Probably named for the English town, perhaps via an eastern state.

Guion ['gai‚ən], village in Parke County (H-4).

Settled in 1821 and called Bruin's Crossroads, for a local family. The present name honors William H. Guion, a New York stockholder in the railroad that came through here in 1872. Platted in 1882.

Guionsville ['gai‚ənz‚vil] (Milton), village in Ohio County (L-10).

Laid out in 1825 by Pinkney James and called by him Jamestown. James built a mill here the same year, and the place also was known as James Mills. In 1837 a post office was established and named Guionsville, for Thomas Guion, early settler and first postmaster. The name was changed to Milton Mills in 1847, hence the alternate name, and back to Guionsville in 1850.

Guthrie ['gəthrē], village in Lawrence County (L-6).

Platted in 1865 and probably named for Daniel Guthrie, one of the first settlers in the county, or his family.

Gwynneville ['gwin‚vil], village in Shelby County (H-8).

Platted in 1881 and named for O'Brien Gwynne, merchant from Carthage, Indiana, who owned land here.

H

Hackleman ['hækəl‚mən], village in Grant County (F-8).

A post office was established here in 1871 and named for General Hackleman, apparently a resident.

Hadley ['hædlē], village in Hendricks County (H-6).

Laid out in 1872 and named for the Hadley family here.

Hagerstown [hāgərz‚taun; 'hæg-], town in Wayne County (H-10).

Laid out in 1830 and called Elizabethtown. In 1836 the name was changed to the present one for Hagerstown, Maryland.

Halfmoon Lake [‚hæf‚mūn 'lāk], lake in Posey County.

This 45-acre lake is located 10 miles southwest of Mt. Vernon. Its name is descriptive, as its shape resembles a half-moon.

Half Way Creek [hæf ‚wā ‚krēk], stream.

This tributary of the Mississinewa River is located in southwestern Jay County and northeastern Delaware County. It was so named for its location about half way between Portland and Muncie.

Hall [hol], village in Morgan County (J-6).

Laid out in 1861. Apparently the name comes from the personal name.

Hamburg ['hæm‚bərg], village in Clark County (N-8).

Laid out in 1837 and named for the German city.

Hamburg ['hæm‚bərg], village in Franklin County (J-9).

Platted in 1864 and named for the city in Germany.

Hamilton ['hæməl‚tən] County (G-7).

Organized in 1823 and named for Alexander Hamilton, the American statesman.

Hamilton ['hæməl‚tən], village in Clinton County (F-5).

Platted in 1839 and named for Alexander Hamilton.

Hamilton ['hæməl‚tən], village in St. Joseph County (A-6).

Established in 1837 and formerly called Terre Coupee. The present name is for Hamilton's Tavern once here.

Hamilton ['hæməl‚tən], town in Steuben County (B-10).

Established about 1836 and named for Alexander Hamilton.

Hamlet ['hæm‚lət], town in Starke County (B-5).

For John Hamlet, who platted the town in 1863.

Hammond ['hæmənd], second class city in Lake County (B-3).

First settled in 1851 and platted in 1875. Formerly called Hohman, for an early settler, then State Line because of its location on the Indiana-Illinois line. It was named Hammond for George H. Hammond, a Detroit butcher who founded the local slaughterhouse and adapted the refrigeration boxcar for shipping dressed beef.

Hancock ['hæn‚kak] County (H-8).

Organized in 1828 and named for John Hancock, a signer of the Declaration of Independence.

Handy ['hændē], village in Benton County (F-3).

Named for a man who operated a grain business in the area.

Handy ['hændē], village in Monroe County (K-6).

The name probably comes from the personal name.

Hanfield ['hæn‚fēld], village in Grant County (E-8).

Founded about 1880. Supposedly the name was coined as a compromise between advocates for the names Garfield and Hancock.

Hanna ['hænə], village in LaPorte County (B-5).

Laid out in 1858 and named for Judge Hanna of Ft. Wayne, who was involved with building a railroad here.

Hanover ['hæn͵ōvər], town in Jefferson County (M-9).

Platted in 1832 and named for Hanover Church, which was named as a compliment to the wife of the Rev. Searle, who before her marriage lived in Hanover, New Hampshire.

Hardinsburg ['hardnz͵bərg] (Hardintown), town in Dearborn County (K-11).

Settled in 1796 by Henry Hardin and named for him. Laid out on his land in 1815.

Hardinsburg ['hardn(z)͵bərg], town in Washington County (M-6).

Named for Aaron Hardin, who laid it out in 1838.

Hardintown ['hardn͵taun] (Hardinsburg), town in Dearborn County (K-11).

See Hardinsburg, Dearborn County.

Harlan ['harlən], village in Allen County (C-10).

Laid out in 1853 by Mr. and Mrs. Lewis Reichelderfer, who named it Harlan. In 1859 an adjoining town, Maysville, was laid out by and named for Ezra May. Harlan was retained as the post office name, but both towns were called Maysville by residents.

Harmony ['harmənē], village in Clay County (J-4).

Originally laid out in 1839 and replatted in 1854. The name is inspirational. "There is no reason to be assigned for the naming of this town and the postoffice, also, other than that of euphony and suggestiveness."

Harper ['harpər], village in Decatur County (K-8).

A post office was established here in 1881 and called Bigrest. In 1882 the name was changed to Harper, probably for the personal name.

Harris ['herəs], village in Marshall County (B-6).

A post office established here in 1884 was called Linkville. In 1888 the name was changed to Harris Station, apparently for the personal name. The post office was called Linkville again from 1889 to 1903.

Harrisburg ['herəs͵bərg], village in Fayette County (H-10).

A post office was formed here in 1828 and called Harrisburg, probably for the personal name.

Harris City [͵herəs 'sidē], village in Decatur County (K-9).

Formerly called Harris, for B. B. Harris who rode through here with General John Hunt Morgan in 1863 and returned in 1869 to open a quarry.

Harrison ['herəsən] County (N-7).

Organized in 1808 and named for William Henry Harrison, first Governor of Indiana Territory, commander at the Battle of Tippecanoe, and ninth President of the United States.

Harristown ['herəs͵taun] (Norris), village in Washington County (M-7).

Founded in 1850 by Thomas M. Harris and named for him. The railroad station here was named Norris, for the first station agent, Thomas B. Norris, to avoid confusion with Harrisburg.

Harrisville ['herəs̩vil], village in Randolph County (G-10).
Platted in 1854 and named for its founder, Job Harris.

Harrodsburg ['herədz̩bərg], village in Monroe County (L-6).
Formerly called Newgene, it was platted in 1836. In 1837 the name was changed to Harrodsburg "for some reason unknown," possibly for the Kentucky town.

Hartford ['hart̩fərd] (Laugherty), village in Ohio County (L-10).
Laid out in 1817. Laugherty is for nearby Laughery Creek, q.v. Apparently Hartford is for the English town, probably via an eastern state.

Hartford City [ˌhart̩fərd ˈsitē], county seat, fifth class city in Blackford County (F-9).
Platted in 1845 as Blackford, the name was changed in 1854 to Hartford, then Hartford City to distinguish it from another Indiana town of the same name. Probably named for Hartford, Connecticut, home of early settlers, although some say for the Hart family who forded Licking Creek here.

Hartleyville ['hart̩lē̩vil], village in Lawrence County (L-6).
Charles Hartley named the town for himself.

Hartsville ['harts̩vil], town in Bartholomew County (K-8).
Laid out in 1832 and probably named for local pioneer leader Gideon B. Hart or his family.

Harveysburg ['harvēz̩bərg], village in Fountain County (G-3).
Laid out in 1856 by L. B. Lindley and named for his wife's father, Harlan Harvey.

Haskell ['hæskəl], village in LaPorte County (B-5).
Formerly called Haskell Station. A store was established here in 1855 and a post office in 1857. The name probably is from the personal name.

Hatfield ['hæt̩fēld], village in Spencer County (O-4).
Originally called Fair Fight, it was founded in 1883 by James Hatfield, the first postmaster, and named for him.

Haubstadt ['habz̩stat], town in Gibson County (N-3).
Laid out in 1855 and originally called Haub's Station, for Henry Haub, who had a general store and stage station here. The generic -stadt, German for "town," is rare in Indiana place names.

Hayden ['hādn], village in Jennings County (L-8).
Platted in 1854. The name probably comes from the personal name.

Haymond ['hāmənd] (St. Marys), village in Franklin County (K-10).
See St. Marys, Franklin County.

Haysville ['hāz͵vil], village in Dubois County (M-5).

Platted in 1835 and named for Judge Willis Hays, who donated some land for the town.

Hazel [hāzəl] (Mt. Pleasant), village in Delaware County (G-9).

See Mt. Pleasant, Delaware County.

Hazelrigg ['hāzəl͵rig], village in Boone County (G-6).

Laid out on land owned by H. G. Hazelrigg and named for him. A post office was established here in 1873.

Hazelton ['hāzəltən], town in Gibson County (M-3).

Named for Gervas Hazelton, who laid out the town in 1856.

Hazelwood ['hāzəl͵wud], village in Hendricks County (J-6).

Named for Daniel Hazelwood who settled here in 1832.

Headlee ['hed͵lē; 'hæd-], village in White County (D-5).

Named for Harry Headlee, who, with several others, platted the village in 1888.

Hebron ['hēbrən], town in Porter County (C-4).

Originally called The Corners, it was first laid out in 1844 and named for the biblical city by Rev. Hannan.

Hecla ['heklə] (Etna), village in Whitley County (C-8).

See Etna.

Hedrick ['hedrik], village in Warren County (F-3).

Platted in 1881 and named for an early resident whose surname was Hedrick.

Heilman ['hailmən], village in Warrick County (O-4).

A post office was established here in 1881. Named for the Heilman family, early settlers.

Helmer ['helmər], village in Steuben County (B-10).

Platted in 1892 by Cyrus Helmer, for whom it was named.

Helmsburg ['helmz͵bərg], village in Brown County (K-6).

Named for John Helms, an early settler. The post office name was changed from Helms to Helmsburg in 1905.

Heltonville ['heltn͵vil], village in Lawrence County (L-6).

Platted in 1845 by Andrew Helton and named for him.

Hemlock ['him͵lak; 'hem-] (Terre Hall), village in Howard County (F-7).

Originally called Terre Hall. When a post office was established in 1881, it was named Hemlock, apparently for the tree.

Henderson ['hendərsən], village in Rush County (H-9).

Named for Ida M. Henderson, who laid out the town in 1890.

Hendricks ['hendriks] County (H-6).

Organized in 1824 and named for William Hendricks, governor of Indiana (1822–25) when the county was established.

Hendricksville ['hendriks,vil], village in Greene County (K-5).

Settled in 1888 and named for an early settler, Philip Hendricks, or his family.

Henry ['henrē] County (G-9).

Organized in 1822 and named for Patrick Henry, famous orator of the Revolution.

Henryville ['henrē,vil], village in Clark County (M-8).

Laid out in 1850 and first called Morristown. In 1853 the name was changed to Henryville for Colonel Henry Ferguson.

Herbst [hərbzd; hərpst], village in Grant County (F-8).

Named for August H. Herbst, the first storekeeper here. When a post office was established in 1880, he became postmaster.

Hessen Cassel [,hæsən 'kæsəl], village in Allen County (D-10).

Platted in 1863 and named for Hesse, Germany, home of early settlers. Hessen-Kassel was a former landgraviate.

Hesston ['hestən], village in LaPorte County (A-5).

In 1877 a post office was established here. It was named for Peter M. Hess, storekeeper and first postmaster.

Heusler ['hūslər], village in Posey County (O-2).

Probably named for Ernst H. C. Heusler, first postmaster. The post office was established here in 1893.

Hibbard ['hibərd], village in Marshall County (C-6).

Platted in 1883. Formerly known popularly as Helltown and officially as Dante, apparently for the poet. Hibbard, probably for a personal name, was applied to the railroad station and post office here.

Highland ['hailənd], town in Lake County (B-3).

A post office established in 1883 was named Clough, apparently for the personal name. In 1888 the name was changed to Highland because of its location on land higher than the surrounding area. The name, popular in the U. S., usually is commendatory.

Hillham ['hil,hæm; -əm], village in Dubois County (M-5).

Never platted, but a post office was established here in 1860.

Hillisburg ['hiləs,bərg], village in Clinton County (F-6).

Named for John E. Hillis, who platted the town in 1874.

Hillsboro ['hilz,bərō], town in Fountain County (G-4).

Platted in 1826 and presumably named for its location.

Hillsboro ['hilz,bərə; -ō], village in Henry County (G-9).

Platted in 1831 and named for its elevation.

Hillsdale ['hilz‚dāl], village in Vermillion County (H-3).

Laid out in 1873 and named for its location on high ground.

Hindustan [hin'dəstən; -tæn], village in Monroe County (K-6).

Platted in 1853. A variant spelling has been Hindostan. Apparently named for India, or a region of it.

Hitchcock ['hich‚kak] (Oxonia), village in Washington County (M-7).

A post office established here in 1861 was called Heffren. In 1865 the name was changed to Hitchcock's Station, and in 1882 it became Hitchcock for a local family. William Hitchcock had the first store here. In 1900 the post office was named Oxonia by O. K. Hobbs, apparently honoring residents of Oxford, England, or graduates of Oxford University.

Hoagland ['hōglənd; -‚lænd], village in Allen County (D-10).

Platted in 1872 and named for the Hon. Pliny Hoagland.

Hobart ['hō‚bart], third class city in Lake County (B-4).

Platted in 1849 and named for Hobart Earle, a brother of George Earle, the founder. A local legend explaining the name is: "The people of the town were standing in front of the old country store when a man came through with his horse and buggy and said, 'Ho, Bart!' to his horse. So the name just stuck."

Hobbieville ['habē‚vil], village in Greene County (L-5).

Settled in 1816 and laid out in 1837. It first was called Jonesboro. Apparently both names are from personal names. A post office was established here in 1840.

Hobbs [habz], village in Tipton County (F-7).

Established about 1878 by Henderson Hobbs on his farm and named for him.

Holland ['halənd], town in Dubois County (N-4).

Laid out in 1859 by Henry Kunz, who named it for his native country.

Hollandsburg ['halənz‚bərg], village in Parke County (H-4).

Settled in 1853 and named by John and Abraham Collings for a Kentucky Baptist minister.

Holton ['hōltn], village in Ripley County (K-9).

Laid out in 1854 on land owned by Jesse Holman, and although some people wanted to name the town Holman, Mr. Holman suggested naming it Holton.

Home Place ['hōm 'plās], village in Hamilton County (H-7).

Laid out in 1814. The name was selected from several by vote of the residents, probably for its commendatory quality.

Homer ['hōmər], village in Rush County (J-8).

Originally called Slabtown, the village was laid out in 1876. The name was changed to Homer because it was felt that the original name might hurt business. The post office formerly was called Goddard, for Joseph Goddard, first postmaster.

Honduras [ˌhanˈdurəs; -əs], village in Adams County (E-10).

A post office was established here in 1890. Apparently named for the Central American republic.

Honey Creek [ˈhənē ˌkrēk], village in Henry County (G-9).

Founded in 1858 and originally called Warnock Station, for a pioneer landowner. The present name comes from a nearby stream of the same name.

Hoosier [ˈhūˌzhər], state nickname.

The origin of Hoosier has been much disputed, and a number of legends, anecdotes, and theories have arisen to explain the nickname. According to the most widely held account, pioneers in Indiana greeted visitors at the doors of their log cabins by calling out, "Who's 'ere?" Another anecdote holds that a Louisville contractor named Samuel Hoosier preferred hiring Indiana men, and his employees were known as "Hoosier men" or "Hoosiers." Other sources maintain that there was a lot of fighting in early Indiana taverns, and the frontiersmen scratched, gouged, and bit—often biting off noses and ears. Frequently following a fight a settler found an ear on the sawdust floor of a tavern and asked, "Whose ear?"

Two other accounts agree that early settlers or Ohio River boatmen were vicious fighters and were called "hussars" because they fought like those European soldiers or "hushers" because they could hush any opponent. Other theories hold the term comes from the French *houssières,* "the bushy places," or from an English dialectical word, "hoose," for roundworms. Apparently this disease of cattle caused the animals' hair to turn back and gave their eyes a wild look, as Indiana frontiersmen in their coonskin caps appeared to others. Still other explanations are that the nickname comes from *hoosa,* an alleged Indian word for maize, from "huzza," an exclamation of early settlers, or from "hoozer," a southern dialectical word meaning something especially large.

Field records for the Linguistic Atlas of the Middle and South Atlantic States, however, reveal that in the southern states Hoosier is a derogatory epithet connoting uncouthness and is synonymous with hick, hayseed, and hillbilly. Probably the term first was applied to early settlers in southern Indiana, themselves from southern states, who were considered uncouth rustics by their cousins back home in more established states. Hoosier, as a derogatory name, is still current in West Virginia, the Upper Piedmont of Virginia, the Carolinas, and Georgia; however, it is extremely rare as a derogatory term west of the Appalachians, where it simply means a native of Indiana.

Hoosier Highlands [ˌhūzhər ˈhai-ˌlənz], village in Putnam County (J-5).

Platted in 1924. The name was suggested by the Hoosier poet William Herschel, from the state nickname and the hills here. It was established as a recreational area.

Hoosierville [ˈhūzhərˌvil], village in Clay County (J-4).

Laid out in 1871 and so named for its location in the Hoosier state.

Hoovers [ˈhūvərz], village in Cass County (D-7).

Named for Riley Hoover, who platted the town in 1874.

Hope [hōp], town in Bartholomew County (K-8).

Settled in 1830 by a Moravian congregation from North Carolina. Called Goshen until a post office was established in 1833, when the name was changed to Hope, for an earlier Moravian settlement in North Carolina. Platted in 1836.

Hopewell [ˈhōpˌwel], village in Johnson County (J-7).

Nearly 20 post offices in the U. S. bore this name by 1876, so possibly it is a transfer for its commendatory quality.

Horace [ˈhorəs], village in Decatur County (K-8).

Laid out in 1881 and called Wyncoop, for the founder, James Wyncoop. Horace was the post office name.

Horney Creek [ˈhornē ˌkrik], stream in Cass County.

This small tributary of Eel River near Logansport was named for John Horney, who settled here in 1831.

Hortonville [ˈhortnˌvil], village in Hamilton County (G-7).

A post office was established here in 1883 and named Hortonville, for the first postmaster, John B. Horton. An alternate name of the community is Horton.

Hosmer [ˈhazˌmər] (Glezon), village in Pike County (N-3).

See Glezon.

Houston [ˈhaustən], village in Jackson County (L-7).

Laid out in 1853 and named for an early settler, Leonard Houston.

Hovey [ˈhəvē], village in Posey County (O-1).

Apparently named for Hoosier Governor Alvin P. Hovey.

Hovey Lake [ˌhəvē ˈlāk], lake in Posey County.

Located 9 miles southwest of Mt. Vernon, this 242-acre lake was named for Alvin P. Hovey, Union officer and Indiana governor, 1888–92, who is buried nearby in Bellefontaine Cemetery.

Howard [ˈhauərd] County (F-7).

Organized in 1844 as Richardsville, honoring the famous Miami chief, but in 1846 the name was changed to Howard, for Tilghman

A. Howard, Hoosier lawyer and statesman.

Howard ['hauərd], village in Parke County (H-3).

Platted in 1848 and named for Tilghman A. Howard, famous statesman who lived here.

Howe [hau], village in Lagrange County (A-9).

Platted in 1834 on the site of a Potawatomi village called *Mongoquinong,* "Big Squaw," and originally called Lima. In 1884 it was renamed for John B. Howe, a leading citizen who founded Howe School here.

Howesville ['hauz‚vil], village in Clay County (K-4).

Named for Robert Howe, who founded it in 1856.

Hubbells Corner [‚həbəlz 'kornər], village in Dearborn County (K-10).

Formerly called Hubbell's Cross Roads, it was named for Merritt Hubbell who settled here and operated a store around 1832.

Hudson ['həd‚sən], town in Steuben County (B-10).

Established as a post office in 1868 and platted in 1869 as North Benton. Formerly called Benton, for the personal name. Hudson, apparently for the personal name, became the post office name in 1875.

Hudson Lake [‚həd‚sən 'lāk], village in LaPorte County (A-6).

Settled around 1829 and named for nearby Hudson Lake.

Hudsonville ['həd‚sən‚vil], village in Daviess County (M-4).

Laid out in 1856 and named for the Hudson family, who were among the early settlers.

Huff [həf] (New Boston), village in Spencer County (O-5).

See New Boston, Spencer County.

Huffman ['həf‚mən], village in Spencer County (O-5).

A post office was established here in 1883. Originally called Huffman's Mills, as the Huffman family had a mill here, which was built around 1815 by John R. Huffman.

Huntersville ['hən(t)ərz‚vil], village in Franklin County (K-9).

Platted in 1841 and supposedly named for a man named Hunter, who was instrumental in founding the town.

Huntertown ['həntər‚taun], town in Allen County (C-10).

Platted in 1870, although settled in the 1830's, and named for William T. Hunter, who established the town.

Huntingburg ['hən(t)iŋ‚bərg], fifth class city in Dubois County (N-4).

Founded in 1839 by Joseph Geiger who named it Huntingdon, allegedly because he came here from Kentucky to hunt even before he purchased the land. Since the name was confused with Huntington, it was changed to Huntingburg.

Huntington ['hən(t)iŋ‚tən] County (D-9).

Organized in 1834 and named for Samuel Huntington of Connecticut, member of the first Continental Congress and signer of the Declaration of Independence.

Huntington [ˈhən(t)iŋˌtən], county seat, fourth class city in Huntington County (D-9).

Named in 1831 for Samuel Huntington, member of the first Continental Congress.

Huntsville [ˈhəntsˌvil], village in Madison County (G-8).

Laid out in 1830 by Enos Adamson and Eleazer Hunt and named for the Hunt family, who were among the earliest settlers.

Huntsville [ˈhəntsˌvil], village in Randolph County (G-10).

Named for the proprietors, William and Miles Hunt, who platted it in 1834.

Hurlburt [ˈhərlˌbət], village in Porter County (C-4).

Founded in 1833 and named for an early settler.

Huron [ˈhyurən], village in Lawrence County (M-5).

Platted in 1859. Originally called Hoard's Station, for William Hoard, pioneer landowner, but renamed for

Huron County, Ohio, by settlers who came from there about 1855.

Hurricane Creek [ˈhərəkān ˌkrēk], stream in Johnson County.

About 10 miles long, this stream flows south to Youngs Creek at Franklin. It was so named for the evidence left by a hurricane in the area.

Hutton [ˈhətn], village in Vigo County (K-3).

Settled in 1833 and named for a prominent family here. Charles N. Hutton was the first postmaster.

Hymera [ˌhaiˈmerə], town in Sullivan County (K-3).

Platted in 1870 and called Pittsburg, for William Pitt, who owned land here. According to one legend, the town was named by John Badders, the postmaster, for his unusually tall adopted daughter, "High Mary." Another legend says a woman named "Mary" worked in the post office, and everyone who passed would wave and call, "Hi, Mary!" It seems more likely, however, that the name is classical, for the ancient city, Himera, founded 648 B.C. on the northern coast of Sicily. The town's name was changed to Hymera, already the post office name, in 1890.

I

Idaville [ˈaidəˌvil], village in White County (E-5).

Platted in 1860 by Andrew

Hanna and called Hanna for him. Since there was another town named Hanna in the state, the name was changed to Ida, for Ida M. Baxter, a local woman.

Ijamsville ['aijəmz‚vil], village in Wabash County (D-8).

Platted in 1872 and originally called South Laketon, for its location south of Laketon. The present name honors the Ijam family who ran a general store and post office here.

Ilene [‚ai'lēn], village in Greene County (L-4).

Named for the daughter of John Morgan, local landowner.

Independence [‚indi'pendənts], village in Warren County (F-4).

Founded in 1832 by Zachariah Cicott—a French-Indian trader and scout for General William Henry Harrison—on ground given him by the government for his services. The name is commendatory.

Indiana [‚indē'ænə; indi-], state.

Admitted to the Union December 11, 1816, and named for Indiana Territory, established in 1800. The first use of the name Indiana was for a tract of land in Pennsylvania ceded by Indians in 1768.

Indianapolis [‚indē(ə)'næp(ə)ləs], state capital, county seat, first class city in Marion County (H-7).

Settled in February 1820, it was called the Fall Creek Settlement by fur traders. On June 7, 1820, the site was selected for a new state capital because of its central location. It was laid out in 1821 and

named Indianapolis, coined by adding the Greek -polis, "city," to the state name.

Indian Creek ['indin ‚krēk; ‚krik], stream.

This is one of the most popular stream names in Indiana, with at least nine streams bearing this name and several others being called Little Indian Creek. As with the stream named Indian Creek heading in Johnson County, in most cases these streams were so named because Indians either lived or camped near them.

Indian Springs [‚indin 'sprinz], village in Martin County (L-5).

Laid out in 1889 and named for mineral springs here of the same name.

Ingalls ['inɡəlz], town in Madison County (G-8).

Laid out in 1883 and named for M. E. Ingalls, then president of The Big Four Railroad.

Inglefield ['inɡəl‚fēld], village in Vanderburgh County (O-3).

Named for John Ingle, who laid out the town in 1819 and first called it Sandersville. Ingle, still an alternate name of the community, was the name of a railroad station here.

Inwood ['in‚wud], village in Marshall County (C-7).

Platted in 1854 by Ezra G. Pearson and named Pearsonville for him. The railroad changed the name to

Inwood, descriptive of the thick woods once here.

Ireland ['air‚lənd], village in Dubois County (N-4).

Platted in 1865 and so named because early settlers were mainly Irish.

Ironton ['ai‚ərn‚tən], village in Martin County (M-5).

Laid out in 1873 by the Southern Indiana Coal and Iron Company and formerly called Irondon for the iron industry here.

Iroquois River ['irə‚kwoi ‚rivər], stream.

About 50 miles long in Indiana. Heads in Jasper County, where it is called Pickamink River until it is met by Slough Creek, and flows southwest to the state of Illinois, where it turns north to the Kankakee River. The Potawatomis called this stream *Pick-amik,* or *Pick-a-mink,* which means "full-grown beavers." The name Iroquois appears before 1700 and comes from the Iroquois Indians, supposedly defeated on the stream by a party of Illinois.

J

Jacks Defeat Creek [‚jæks di'fēt ‚krēk], stream in Monroe County.

A variety of legends, usually about Jack Storm falling into the creek, explain the name of this stream in western Monroe County. One version runs: "In the early days of Monroe County, before it was organized, probably as early as 1812 or 1813, some men were on a trip to the West Fork of White River. Several miles northwest of what is now Bloomington, they had to cross a little stream which flows into Beanblossom Creek. A man named Jack Storm attempted to cross this little stream. He got his horse mired down in the mud and had a hard time getting out. From that time, the stream was called Jack's Defeat and is still so called."

Jackson ['jæks(ə)n] County (L-7).

Organized in 1816 and named for Andrew Jackson, general in the Battle of New Orleans in 1815 and later President of the U. S.

Jacksonburg ['jæksən‚bərg], village in Wayne County (H-10).

Platted in 1814 and named for Jackson Township, as it was then the voting precinct of that township.

Jacksons ['jæksənz] (Parrottsville), village in Tipton County (F-7).

In 1863 a post office named Jackson Station was established about two miles south of a sawmill operated by George Kane and Newton Jackson. In 1882 the post office name was changed to Jackson. Newton Jackson already had founded a settlement called Jackson, for him, in 1846. Parrottsville, apparently for a personal name, was established as a railroad station in 1853.

Jacksonville ['jæks(ə)n͵vil], village in Switzerland County (L-10).
Laid out in 1815 and named for a local Jackson family.

Jalapa [jə'læpə], village in Grant County (E-8).
Laid out in 1849 and named for the Mexican city occupied by Americans during the Mexican War.

Jamestown ['jāmz͵taun], town in Boone County (H-5).
Platted in 1832 and named for James Mattlock, one of the founders.

Jamestown ['jāmz͵taun], village in Elkhart County (B-7).
Founded in 1835 and named for James Davis, who laid out the town. Formerly called Jimtown.

Jamestown ['jāmz͵taun], village in Steuben County (A-10).
Settled in 1835 and platted soon after.

Jasonville ['jāsən͵vil], fifth class city in Greene County (K-4).
Named around 1855 for Jason Rogers, who purchased the original plat in 1853.

Jasper ['jæspər] County (D-4).
Organized in 1838 and named for Sgt. William Jasper of Fort Moultrie, South Carolina, who was killed in the Revolution.

Jasper ['jæspər], county seat, fifth class city in Dubois County (N-5).
Founded about 1818 and platted in 1830. Only legend explains this name: "Jasper was named when some ol' lady opened the Bible and put her finger on the word Jasper. She was the oldest in the community, so she got the honor of naming the town."

Jay [jā] County (F-10).
Organized in 1836 and named for John Jay, famous American statesman and jurist.

Jay City [͵jā 'sitē], village in Jay County (E-11).
Platted in 1839 and named for Jay County.

Jeff [jef], village in Wells County (E-9).
A post office was established here in 1891. Allegedly named for Jeff Jones, son of the owner of the land on which the town was located.

Jefferson ['jefərsən] County (L-9).
Organized in 1811 and named for President Thomas Jefferson.

Jefferson ['jefərsən], village in Clinton County (F-6).
Laid out in 1829 and named for President Thomas Jefferson.

Jeffersonville ['jefərsən͵vil], county seat, third class city in Clark County (N-8).
A settlement was made here at Ft. Steuben in 1786. In 1802 the city was laid out according to a plan suggested by Thomas Jefferson and

named in honor of him by William Henry Harrison.

Jennings ['jeniŋz] County (L-8).
Organized in 1817 and named for Jonathan Jennings, first governor of the State of Indiana.

Jerome [jə'rōm], village in Howard County (F-7).
Laid out in 1847 by Hampton Brown, who named the town for his son, Jerome.

Jessup ['jesəp], village in Parke County (H-4).
A post office was established here in 1867 and called Jessup's Station, for a local landowner, C. Jessup.

Jockey ['jakē], village in Warrick County (N-4).
This name is of uncertain origin. One explanation is that residents had a reputation for dealing shrewdly, so the community was named Jockey for that meaning of the word.

Johnson ['jan,sən] County (J-7).
Organized in 1823 and named for John Johnson, judge of the Indiana Supreme Court.

Johnson ['jan,sən], village in Gibson County (N-2).
Settled in 1911 and named for a railroad construction superintendent.

Johnsonville ['jan,sən,vil], village in Warren County (F-3).
Laid out in 1874 by G. W. Johnson and named for him.

Jolietville [,jalē'et,vil], village in Hamilton County (G-7).
A post office named Jollietville was established here in 1875. In 1883 the spelling was changed to Jolietville. Perhaps named for the explorer, Louis Joliet.

Jonesboro ['jōnz,bərō], town in Grant County (F-8).
Platted in 1837 by Obediah Jones, for whom it was named. Formerly spelled Jonesborough.

Jonestown ['jōnz,taun], village in Vermillion County (H-3).
Platted in 1862 by Phillip Jones and named for him.

Jonesville ['jōnz,vil], town in Bartholomew County (K-8).
Platted in 1851 by Benjamin Jones, for whom it was named.

Jordan ['jordn; 'jərdn], village in Owen County (J-5).
A post office, originally called Jordan Village, was established here in 1854. Apparently named for a resident of that name.

Judson ['jəd,sən], town in Parke County (H-4).
Originally called Buchanan's Springs, for an early settler. Platted in 1872 by Alexander Buchanan, who named it for Adoniram Judson, a Kentucky Baptist minister and missionary who died in 1850.

Judyville ['jūdē,vil], village in Warren County (F-3).
Named for John Judy, who platted the town in 1903.

Julian ['jūlē͵in; -ən], village in Newton County (D-4).

Platted in 1882 by Martha and J. B. Julian, for whom it was named.

K

Kankakee River [͵kæŋkə'kē 'rivər], stream.

Heads in St. Joseph County near South Bend and flows southwest into the State of Illinois. Apparently the name is a corruption of the Potawatomi, *Tian-kakeek,* pronounced "Teh-yak-ke-ki" by the Indians and meaning "low land" or "swampy country." A further corruption is *Kiakiki,* which appeared in French as *Qui-que-que* and *Quin-qui-qui,* the latter pronounced nearly the same as Kankakee.

Kappa ['kæpə], village in Howard County (F-6).

A post office was located here in 1886. Although the name appears to be the tenth letter of the Greek alphabet, it perhaps comes from the Indian tribal name, *Kappa,* sometimes spelled *Quapaw.*

Keller ['kelər], village in Vigo County (J-3).

A post office was established here as Ferrell on January 9, 1903. On February 24, 1903, the name was changed to Keller, probably from the personal name, by the Southern Indiana Railroad.

Kellerville ['kelərz͵vil], village in Dubois County (M-5).

Settled in 1867 and named for John C. Keller, prominent local merchant.

Kelso ['kelsō] (Dover), village in Dearborn County (K-10).

See Dover, Dearborn County.

Kelso ['kelsō] (Majenica), village in Huntington County (E-9).

See Majenica.

Kempton ['kem(p)tən], town in Tipton County (F-7).

Established in 1874 on land owned by David Kemp and named for him.

Kendallville ['kendəl͵vil], fifth class city in Noble County (B-9).

Settled in 1833, and a post office was established in 1836. Named for Postmaster General Amos Kendall, under President Jackson, when a post office was reestablished in 1848.

Kennard ['kenərd], town in Henry County (H-9).

Platted in 1882 and named for Jenkins Kennard, prominent early citizen.

Kenneth ['kenəth], village in Cass County (E-6).

A post office was located here in 1892. Named by railroad officials, apparently for the personal name.

Kent [kent], village in Jefferson County (M-9).

Platted in 1853 and named for James Kent, chief justice of New York. Formerly called Ramsey's Mills Post Office.

Kentland ['kent͵lənd], county seat, town in Newton County (E-3).

Platted in 1860 by A. J. Kent and named Kent for him. The name was changed to Kentland to avoid confusion with another Indiana town called Kent.

Kent Station [͵kent 'stāshən], village in Newton County (D-3).

A post office established in 1860 was called Kent Station. The name comes from the personal name.

Kersey ['kərzē], village in Jasper County (C-4).

A post office was located here in 1900. Named for a local landowner.

Kewanna [kē'wanə; kə-], town in Fulton County (D-6).

Laid out in 1845 as Pleasant Grove. The present name is for a Potawatomi chief, *Ki-wa-na,* "Prairie Chicken."

Keystone ['kē͵stōn], village in Wells County (E-9).

Platted in 1872 by Luther Twibell and named by his wife for Pennsylvania, "The Keystone State."

Kickapoo Creek ['kikəpū 'krik], stream in Warren County.

Named for the Indian tribe.

Killbuck Creek ['kil͵bək 'krik; 'krēk], stream.

Heads in Delaware County and flows southwest through Madison County to the West Fork White River near Anderson. Named for Charles Killbuck who lived nearby in the Delaware village Killbuck, or Buck's Town. Killbuck became a common Delaware family name.

Kilmore ['kil͵mōr], village in Clinton. County (F-6).

Originally called Penceville, for Abner Pence, who laid out the town in 1854. The present name, formerly spelled Killmore, was applied in 1872 and is for a nearby stream, Killmore Creek, itself named for early resident John Killmore.

Kimmell ['kiməl], village in Noble County (B-8).

Settled in 1831 and named for the Kimmell family, prominent in county history, perhaps for Orlando Kimmell, wealthy farmer and member of the state legislature.

Kinder ['kindər], village in Johnson County (J-7).

A post office was established here in 1886. Probably named for William Kinder, who lived here.

Kingman ['kiŋ͵mən], town in Fountain County (G-3).

Platted in 1886 and presumably named for a local man of the same name.

Kings [kiŋz], village in Gibson County (N-3).

Formerly called King's Station, the town was named for John King, who settled here around 1818.

Kingsbury [ˈkiŋzˌberē], town in La-Porte County (B-5).

Laid out in 1835 and named for an early settler whose surname was Kingsbury.

Kingsland [ˈkiŋzˌlənd], village in Wells County (D-10).

Laid out in 1883 and originally called Parkinson, for Ebenezer Parkinson, prominent citizen and first postmaster. The town was re-named by Isaac Hatfield.

Kingston [ˈkiŋzˌtən], village in Decatur County (J-9).

Laid out in 1851 by John King and others and presumably named for King.

Kintner Creek [ˈkintˌnər ˌkrēk; ˈkent-], stream in Wabash County.

About 10 miles long, it flows southwest to the Wabash River about 5 miles west of Wabash. It was named for Frederick and James Kintner who built a harness and saddle shop near the stream's mouth in 1827. Formerly called Kintner's Creek and sometimes spelled Kentner Creek.

Kirby [ˈkərbē], village in Monroe County (K-5).

Named for a local man named Kirby.

Kirklin [ˈkərklən], town in Clinton County (G-6).

Named for Nathan Kirk, who bought land here in 1828, built a tavern, and founded the town in 1837.

Kirkpatrick [ˌkərkˈpætrik], village in Montgomery County (G-5).

Platted in 1882 and named for Wesley Kirkpatrick, who owned the land where the town is located.

Kirksville [ˈkərksˌvil], village in Monroe County (L-5).

A post office was established here in 1879. Named for the Kirk family, early settlers who owned a store here.

Kirksville [ˈkərksˌvil] (Wheeling), village in Gibson County (N-3).

See Wheeling, Gibson County.

Kitchel [ˈkichəl], village in Union County (H-11).

A post office was located here in 1901. Named for the Kitchel family, owner of the site.

Klaasville [ˈklasˌvil], village in Lake County (C-3).

Named around 1850 for an early settler, H. Klaas, but founded by August Klaas, local storekeeper.

Klondike [ˈklanˌdaik], village in Tippecanoe County (F-4).

A post office was established here in 1897. Apparently named for the region or river in Canada, famous for gold discoveries.

Klondyke [ˈklanˌdaik], village in Parke County (H-3).

Platted in 1907 and probably named for the Klondike River, noted for the Gold Rush of 1898.

Klondyke [ˈklanˌdaik], village in Vermillion County (H-3).

Named for the Klondyke Mines, active near here in the first part of this century.

Knightstown ['naits‚taun], town in Henry County (H-9).

Laid out in 1827 and named for John Knight, an engineer in the construction of the National Road through here.

Knightsville ['naits‚vil], town in Clay County (J-4).

Laid out in 1867 by A. W. Knight, for whom it was named.

Kniman ['naimən], village in Jasper County (C-4).

Laid out in 1887 by H. Kniman, for whom the town was named.

Knox [naks] County (M-3).

Organized in 1790 and named for General Henry Knox, artillery officer of the Revolution and Secretary of War, 1785–95.

Knox [naks], county seat, fifth class city in Starke County (C-5).

Laid out in 1851 and named for General Henry Knox, officer in the Revolution and member of Washington's cabinet.

Kokomo ['kōkə‚mō], county seat, second class city in Howard County (F-7).

Laid out in 1844 and named for a Thorntown Miami Indian, *Ko-ka-ma,* "The Diver."

Koleen [kō'lēn], village in Greene County (L-5).

Platted in 1853 and named by

railroad officials because kaolin clay, used in making pottery, was mined here.

Koontz Lake [‚kūnts 'lāk], lake.

This lake, located 6 miles northeast of Hamlet, covers 346 acres in Starke and Porter counties. It was named for Samuel Koontz, who operated a nearby mill.

Koontz Lake [‚kūnts 'lāk], village in Starke County (B-6).

Named for nearby Koontz Lake.

Kosciusko [‚kaskē'əs‚kō; ‚kasē'os-] County (C-8).

Organized in 1837 and named for General Tadeusz Kosciuszko, a famous Polish soldier who served with Washington in the Revolution.

Kossuth [ka'sūth; kə-], village in Washington County (M-7).

Probably named for the Hungarian orator and patriot, Lajos Kossuth (1802–94). A post office was established here beween 1850 and 1853.

Kouts [kauts], town in Porter County (C-4).

The name dates from about 1865 when surveyors for a railroad boarded at the house of early settler Barnardt Kouts, originally spelled Kautz, and named the place Kouts Station. The name became Kouts in 1882.

Kramer ['krāmər], village in Warren County (F-3).

A post office called Cameron Springs, for William Cameron, first postmaster, was established here in 1885. In 1889 the name was changed to Indiana Mineral Springs and in 1901 to Kramer for H. L. Kramer, who built a resort hotel here to take advantage of the springs, which were thought to have therapeutic properties.

Kurtz [kərts], village in Jackson County (L-7).

Founded in 1890 and named in honor of an engineer named Kurtz who built the railroad through here.

Kyana [ˌkaiˈænə; ˈkai-], village in Dubois County (N-5).

Platted in 1882 by John L. Wheat, President of the Louisville Mining and Manufacturing Company. The name, coined by the company, consists of the abbreviation for Kentucky and the last three letters of Indiana.

L

Laconia [ləˈkōnˌy(ē)ə], town in Harrison County (O-7).

Platted in 1816 and said to be named for Laconia, New Hampshire. It was the name of a district in ancient Greece.

LaCrosse [ləˈkros], town in LaPorte County (C-5).

A post office was established here in 1868. Said to mean "The Crossing," thus descriptive of the location at the junction of four railroads. But a crossing in French is *croisement* and a railroad crossing is *passage à niveau. Crosse* means "crosier" or "stick," and *lacrosse* is the Indian game played with a crosier-like stick. Thus, either Indians played lacrosse here, the name was borrowed from one of the other American settlements called LaCrosse, or the name was misapplied.

Lacy [ˈlāsē], village in Martin County (M-5).

A post office was located here in 1901. According to local anecdote, the town was so named for "the small lace caps which the women of a peculiar religious sect near the village always wear to church." Probably the name honors a local family.

Ladoga [ləˈdōgə], town in Montgomery County (H-5).

Laid out in 1836 and named for the largest lake in Europe, Lake Ladoga in Russia.

Lafayette [ˌlæfēˈet; la-; lā-], county seat, second class city in Tippecanoe County (F-5).

Named in 1824 by its founder, William Digby, for the Marquis de la Fayette.

LaFontaine [ləˈfauntn], town in Wabash County (E-8).

Settled in 1834 by William Grant and called Grant's Land. In 1845

Grant changed the name to Ashland, for Henry Clay's home. In 1862 the town was incorporated as LaFontaine, for Chief LaFontaine, leader of the Miami nation.

Lagrange [lə'grānj] County (B-9).
Organized in 1832 and named for the Marquis de la Fayette's country home near Paris.

Lagrange [lə'grānj], county seat, town in Lagrange County (B-9).
Platted in 1836 and named for Lagrange County.

Lagro ['lāgrō], town in Wabash County (D-8).
Settled around 1829 and named for LeGros, the French nickname of a Miami chief who lived here.

Lake [lāk] County (B-3).
Organized in 1837 and named for Lake Michigan, which borders the county on the north.

Lake Cicott [ˌlāk 'saiˌkat; 'sēkət], lake in Cass County.
This 65-acre lake is located 9 miles west of Logansport and was named for George Cicott, who owned a reservation here.

Lake Cicott [ˌlāk 'saiˌkat; 'sēkət], village in Cass County (E-6).
Laid out in 1868 and named for the lake.

Lake Freeman [ˌlāk 'frēmən], lake.
This lake, located 3 miles south of Monticello, covers 1547 acres in Carroll and White counties. It was named for Roger M. Freeman, chief

engineer of the Oakdale Dam, which backs up the Tippecanoe River to form the lake.

Lake James [ˌlāk 'jāmz], village in Steuben County (A-10).
A post office was established here in 1851. Named for the nearby lake of the same name.

Lake Lemon [ˌlāk 'lemən], lake in Monroe County.
This 17-acre artificial lake is located south of the Morgan-Monroe State Forest and was first called Beanblossom Lake for Beanblossom Creek, q.v. The present name honors Thomas Lemon, a former mayor of Bloomington.

Lake Lenape [ˌlāk lə'napē; lə'næp], lake.
This 36-acre lake in Shakamak State Park was named for the Delaware Indians, who called themselves *Lenni Lenape,* "virile men," "true men," or "men of men."

Lake Lincoln [ˌlāk 'liŋkən], lake in Spencer County.
This 58-acre lake is located in Lincoln State Park. Both the lake and the park are named for Abraham Lincoln, who spent his boyhood years nearby.

Lake Manitou [ˌlāk 'mænətō], lake in Fulton County.
This 713-acre lake is located one mile east of Rochester. The name is from the Potawatomi *ma-ne-to,* referring to a supernatural spirit, said to be a monster, believed to live in the lake.

Lake Maxinkuckee [ˌlāk ˈmæksən-ˌkəkē], lake in Marshall County.

The name of this 1854-acre lake at Culver is a corruption of the Potawatomi name, *Mog-sin-kee-ki,* "Big Stone Country," apparently so named for the extensive rock bars in the lake.

Lake Michigan [ˌlāk ˈmishigən], lake in northern Indiana.

About 220 square miles of this lake are located in Indiana. The name probably is a compound of the Ojibwa, *mi-shi,* "great," and *sa-gie-gan,* "lake."

Lake of the Woods [lākə thə ˈwudz], lake in Marshall County.

This 416-acre lake is located 5 miles south of Bremen and was named for its setting in a forest of virgin hardwood.

Lakeside [ˈlākˌsaid], village in Pulaski County (D-5).

A post office was established here in 1885. Apparently the name is commendatory.

Laketon [ˈlākˌtən], village in Wabash County (D-8).

Platted in 1836 and named for the numerous lakes in the area.

Lake Village [ˈlāk ˈvilij; -ēj], village in Newton County (C-3).

Laid out in 1876. So named because the site was a swamp before it was reclaimed by artificial drainage.

Lakeville [ˈlākˌvil], town in St. Joseph County (B-6).

Platted in 1857 and named for a chain of small lakes nearby.

Lamar [ləˈmar], village in Spencer County (O-5).

A post office was located here in 1888. Apparently named for the personal name.

Lamb [læm], village in Switzerland County (M-10).

Laid out in 1815 and called Erin. The present name is for the Lamb family here who established the post office. William Lamb was the first postmaster.

Lancaster [ˈlæŋkəstər] (River), village in Huntington County (E-9).

Originally the post office was called River, for its location on the Salamonie River. The town was platted in 1836, and it is believed the name Lancaster comes from the English town and county, perhaps via several eastern states.

Lancaster [ˈlæŋkəstər], village in Jefferson County (L-9).

Established as a post office in 1830 and probably named for Lancaster Township, in which it is located.

Landersdale [ˈlændərzˌdāl], village in Morgan County (J-6).

Apparently the name comes from the personal name.

Landess [ˈlændəs], village in Grant County (E-8).

Formerly called Landesville, the town was laid out in 1882 by William Landess, for whom it was named.

Lanesville [ˈlānzˌvil], town in Harrison County (N-7).

Settled in 1792 and platted in 1817, the town was named for General Lane, a government surveyor who was a prominent early settler.

Lapaz [ləˈpæz], town in Marshall County (B-6).

Laid out in 1873 and formerly spelled LaPaz. Apparently named for the capital of Bolivia or the city in western Mexico. The present spelling was adopted in 1893.

Lapaz Junction [ləˌpæz ˈjəŋkˌshən], village in Marshall County (B-6).

Established about 1876 nearly a mile east of Lapaz at a railroad junction, hence the name.

Lapel [ləˈpel], town in Madison County (G-8).

Platted in 1876 and allegedly so named because when the railroad was built through here a strip of land was left between it and the Pendleton Turnpike in the shape of a lapel. A former spelling was Lapell.

Lapland [ˈlæpˌlænd], village in Montgomery County (H-5).

A post office was established here in 1885. Apparently named for the region in northern Europe.

LaPorte [ləˈpōrt] County (B-5).

Organized in 1832 and called LaPorte, "the door." The French had used the name because a natural opening through the forest here served as a gateway to the north.

LaPorte [ləˈpōrt], county seat, third class city in LaPorte County (B-5).

Settled in 1830, laid out in 1833, and named for LaPorte County.

Larwill [ˈlarˌwil], town in Whitley County (C-8).

Laid out in 1854 and formerly called Huntsville, for Truman Hunt, owner of some of the land on which the town was located. The present name honors two engineers, William and Joseph Larwill, who supervised the building of a railroad here.

Lattas Creek [ˈlædəs ˌkrēk], stream in Greene County.

About 16 miles long, this stream flows southeast to West Fork White River near Bloomfield. It was named for John Latta, who lived near it.

Laud [lod] (Forest), village in Whitley County (D-9).

See Forest, Whitley County.

Lauer [ˈla(u)r], village in Perry County (O-5).

Apparently named from the personal name.

Laugherty [ˈlæfərdi] (Hartford), village in Ohio County (L-10).

See Hartford.

Laughery Creek [ˈlakˌrā ˌkrēk], stream.

Nearly 50 miles long, it heads in Ripley County and flows south, then northeast, forming the boundary between Dearborn and Ohio counties, to the Ohio River at French. It was named for Colonel Archibald

Laughery, sometimes spelled Lochry, who was killed by Indians near its mouth in 1781.

Laura ['lorə], village in Jasper County (D-4).
Founded about 1897 and named by B. J. Gifford, apparently for the christian name.

Laurel ['larəl], town in Franklin County (J-10).
Founded in 1836 by James Conwell, who named it for Laurel, Delaware. Formerly called Somerset and Conwell's Mills.

Lawrence ['lar(ə)nts; 'lor-] County (L-6).
Organized in 1818 and named for Captain James Lawrence, of the U. S. frigate *Chesapeake*.

Lawrence ['larənts; 'lor-], third class city in Marion County (H-7).
Platted in 1849 and formerly called Lanesville, but since there was another town in Indiana of that name, the name was changed to Lawrence, for the local post office, itself named for Lawrence Township.

Lawrenceburg ['larənts,bərg], county seat, fifth class city in Dearborn County (K-11).
Laid out in 1802 and named by one of the proprietors, Samuel C. Vance, for his wife, whose maiden name was Lawrence.

Lawrenceburg Junction [-jəŋkshən], village in Dearborn County (K-11).
Named for nearby Lawrenceburg.

Lawrenceport ['larənts,pōrt], village in Lawrence County (M-6).
Platted in 1837 and named for an early landowner, Josiah Lawrence.

Lawrenceville ['larənts,vil], village in Dearborn County (K-10).
Laid out in 1835 by John Lawrence, and named for him.

Lawton ['lotn], village in Pulaski County (C-6).
A post office was established here in 1902. Apparently named for the personal name.

Layton ['lātn], village in Fountain County (G-3).
A post office was located here in 1891. Probably named from the personal name.

Layton Mills [,lātn 'milz], village in Decatur County (K-9).
Named for the Layton brothers who established a mill here in 1855.

Leases Corner [,lēsəz 'kornər], village in Cass County (D-6).
Named for George Lease, who had a store here.

Leavenworth ['levən,wərth], town in Crawford County (N-6).
Founded in 1818 and platted in 1819, the town was flooded in 1937, relocated on hills behind the old site, and rebuilt in 1938. It was named for the proprietors, Seth and Zebulan Leavenworth.

Lebanon ['lebənən], county seat, fifth class city in Boone County (G-6).

88

Platted in 1832 and named for the biblical mountain noted for its cedars. Tall hickory trees on the prairie here suggested the name to the county commissioners.

Lee [lē], village in White County (D-4).

Established in 1883 as a grain market by John Lee, president of the Indianapolis, Delphi, and Chicago Railroad and named for him.

Leesburg ['lēz͵bərg], town in Kosciusko County (C-8).

Named for Levi Lee, who laid out the town in 1835.

Leesville ['lēz͵vil], village in Lawrence County (L-6).

Laid out in 1818 and named by founders for their home, Lee County, Virginia.

Leipsic ['lēpsik], village in Orange County (M-6).

Laid out in 1851 and called Lancaster. Leipsic was the post office name, apparently so named from the German city.

Leisure ['lāzhər; 'lēzh-], village in Madison County (F-8).

A post office was established here in 1888. Named for a prominent family here.

Leiters Ford [͵laitərz 'fōrd], village in Fulton County (C-6).

Originally called Hunter's Ford, for the Hunter family, early settlers. In 1872 it was renamed Leiter's Ford, for the Leiter family who bought property here. In 1893 the spelling was changed to Leiters Ford.

Lemon Creek ['lemən ͵krēk], stream in Greene County.

About 7 miles long, this stream flows northeast to Eel River about 2 miles north of Worthington. It was named for William Lemon, who settled on it.

Lena ['lēnə], village in Parke County (L-4).

Laid out in 1870. The name is of uncertain origin, although legends say for an Indian maiden or a white girl captured by Indians.

Leo ['lēō], village in Allen County (C-10).

Platted in 1849 and called Hamilton, for one of the platters, James Hamilton. Later renamed for St. Leo's Church, which was named for Pope Leo XII.

Leopold ['lēə͵pōld], village in Perry County (O-6).

Founded in 1842 and named for King Leopold of Belgium.

Leota [lē'ōdə], village in Scott County (M-8).

A post office was located here in 1884. Named for the christian name of a woman who lived here. Never officially laid out.

Leroy ['lē͵roi], village in Lake County (C-4).

Platted in 1875 and originally called Cassville, for Dr. Levi Cass, who owned land near here. The post office, established in 1869, was called LeRoy, apparently for a personal name, until 1893 when the spelling was changed to Leroy.

Letts [lets], village in Decatur County (K-8).
Laid out in 1882 and named for the first postmaster, Allen W. Lett.

Lewis ['lūus], village in Vigo County (K-4).
Originally called Centerville, but when a post office was established in 1840 the name was changed to Lewis, probably for a personal name, because there already was a town called Centerville in the state.

Lewisburg ['lūus͵bərg], village in Cass County (E-7).
Laid out in 1835 by Lewis Bowyer, for whom it was named.

Lewis Creek [͵lūus 'krēk], village in Shelby County (J-8).
Established about 1856 and named for the nearby stream of the same name.

Lewiston ['lūus͵tən], village in Jasper County (D-4).
Platted in 1901 by Benjamin J. Gifford, who named the town.

Lewisville ['lūus͵vil], town in Henry County (H-9).
Laid out in 1829 and named for the founder, Lewis Freeman.

Lewisville ['lūus͵vil], village in Morgan County (J-5).
Named for an influential pioneer family here.

Lexington ['leksiŋ͵tən], village in Carroll County (F-6).

Founded in 1835 and apparently named for the Battle of Lexington.

Lexington ['leksiŋ͵tən], village in Scott County (M-8).
Laid out in 1810 and named for Lexington, Massachusetts, apparently because of the famous battle there.

Liber ['laibər], village in Jay County (F-10).
Platted in 1853 and named for Liber College, which was located here.

Liberty ['libərdē], county seat, town in Union County (J-10).
Platted in 1822 and probably named for Liberty, Virginia, home of some early settlers.

Liberty Center [͵libərtē 'sentər], village in Wells County (E-9).
Laid out in 1878 and so named because of its location near the center of Liberty Township.

Liberty Mills [͵libərdē 'milz], village in Wabash County (D-8).
Platted in 1847. The first part of the name is inspirational and the second part is descriptive of the early mills here around which the town was built.

Libertyview ['libərdē͵vyū], village in Porter County (C-5).
Laid out in 1909. The name is commendatory.

Lick Creek ['lik 'krik], stream in Orange County.
This tributary of Lost River was

90

named for French Lick, a spring on one of its branches.

Liggett ['ligit; -ət] village in Vigo County (J-3).

Probably named for early settlers named Liggett.

Ligonier [ˌligən'ir; -'nir], fifth class city in Noble County (B-8).

Platted in 1835 and named for Ligonier, Pennsylvania.

Limberlost Creek ['limbər‚lost ‚krēk], stream.

About 18 miles long, it heads in Jay County and flows northeast into the State of Ohio, then northwest to the Wabash River about 1 mile east of Geneva in Adams County. Limberlost was the name of a post office at Geneva, 1842–74, and a swamp, formerly called Loblolly. According to local legend, the name of the swamp was changed in the early days to Limber Lost when an athletic young man, "Limber Jim" Mc-Dowell, went bear hunting in the swamp and was lost for three days. The legendary quality of this widely accepted explanation is obvious, though, as variant stories have arisen, such as the following: "A man named James Miller, while hunting along its banks, became lost. After various fruitless efforts to find his way home, in which he would always come around to the place of starting, he determined he would go on a straight course, and so, every few rods would blaze a tree. While doing this he was found by his friends who were hunting him. Being an agile man, he was known as 'limber Jim,' and after this, the stream was called 'Limberlost.' " The stream takes its name from the swamp.

Limedale ['laim‚dāl], village in Putnam County (J-5).

Laid out in 1864 and called Greencastle Junction. In 1873 when a post office was established it was renamed Limedale for the limestone quarries and lime kiln here.

Lincoln ['liŋkən], village in Cass County (E-7).

Laid out in 1852 and named for Theodore Lincoln, who surveyed part of the town.

Lincoln City [ˌliŋkən 'sitē], village in Spencer County (O-4).

Laid out in 1872 on land that once belonged to Abraham Lincoln's father, Thomas Lincoln, and named for the Lincoln family.

Lincolnville ['liŋkən‚vil], village in Wabash County (E-8).

Platted in 1876 and named for Abraham Lincoln.

Linden ['lindən], town in Montgomery County (G-5).

Laid out in 1852 and apparently named for the tree.

Linkville ['liŋk‚vil], village in Marshall County (B-6).

Laid out in 1866 and named for M. J. Link, one of the founders. Formerly called Linksville.

Linn Grove ['lin 'grōv], village in Adams County (E-10).

Laid out around 1857 and originally called Buena Vista, a popular name in Indiana commemorating an American victory in the Mexican War. The present name apparently is for the linden tree, linn being an alternate name for it.

Linnsburg ['linz‚bərg], village in Montgomery County (G-5).
Laid out in 1870 and named for Asbury Linn, prominent local merchant and farmer.

Linton ['lintn], fifth class city in Greene County (L-4).
Settled in 1816 and platted in 1857. Earlier called New Jerusalem, but the name was changed to Linton in honor of a Terre Haute man, Colonel William C. Linton, congressional candidate.

Linwood ['lin‚wud], village in Madison County (G-8).
Originally called Funk's Station, for a man instrumental in establishing the railroad station here. The present name is for the tree.

Lisbon ['liz‚bən], village in Noble County (B-9).
Laid out in 1847 and apparently named for the city in Portugal.

Little Baugo Creek ['lidəl 'bogō ‚krēk], stream in Elkhart County.
Named for Baugo Creek, q.v., of which it is a tributary.

Little Calumet River ['lidəl ‚kælyə-'met ‚rivər], stream.
Heads in LaPorte County and flows west through Porter and Lake counties to the Grand Calumet

River in Cook County, Illinois. See Grand Calumet River.

Little Pipe Creek [‚lidəl 'paip ‚krik], stream in Miami County.
See Big Pipe Creek.

Little Point ['lidəl ‚point], village in Morgan County (J-5).
Founded in 1829. A post office was established in 1876. Probably the name is descriptive.

Little Raccoon Creek [‚lidəl ‚ræ'kūn ‚krēk], stream.
About 30 miles long, it heads in Montgomery County and flows southwest through Parke County to Big Raccoon Creek, q.v., near Jessup.

Little Shawnee Creek [lidəl 'shonē ‚krēk], stream in Fountain County.
A tributary of Big Shawnee Creek, q.v.

Little Vermillion River ['lidəl ‚vər-'milyən ‚rivər], stream in Vermillion County.
Heads in Illinois and flows to the Wabash River near Newport. See Big Vermillion River.

Little York [‚lidəl 'york], town in Washington County (M-7).
Laid out in 1831 and so named because the settlers were from the State of New York.

Livonia ['lai'vōn‚yə], town in Washington County (M-6).
Laid out in 1819 and originally called Bethel, for a local church. The present name probably is for

the former Baltic province in Russia.

Lizton ['liz͵tən], town in Hendricks County (H-6).

Platted in 1851 by Jesse Veiley and named New Elizabeth for his wife. The railroad shortened the name to Lizton.

Lochiel [͵lō'kēl], village in Benton County (E-4).

Called Kaarland in 1882 when a post office was established, the name was changed to Lochiel in 1883, for "the head of the clan Cameron." "Lochiel," the title of the chief of the Camerons, is perhaps most familiar in Thomas Campbell's poem, "Lochiel's Warning," of which Donald Cameron of Lochiel is the subject.

Locke [lak], village in Elkhart County (B-7).

Laid out in 1865 and named for Locke Township, which was named for the first settler, Samuel Lockwood.

Lockport ['lak͵pōrt], village in Carroll County (E-6).

Laid out in 1836 on the Wabash and Erie Canal and named for the locks here.

Locust Point [͵lōkəs(t) 'point] (Bridgeport), village in Harrison County (N-7).

See Bridgeport.

Lodi ['lō͵dai] (Waterman), village in Parke County (E-3).

See Waterman.

Logan ['lōgən], village in Dearborn County (K-10).

Formerly called Logan Cross Roads. The name is for the township in which it is located. A post office called Logan was established in 1836.

Logansport ['lōgənz͵pōrt], county seat, fourth class city in Cass County (E-6).

Named in 1828 for Captain Logain, a Shawnee, whose Indian name was *Spemica Lawba,* "High Horn." He was killed in 1812 while serving with the U. S. Army.

Lomax ['lōmæks], village in Starke County (C-5).

Founded in 1882 and named for the owner of the land.

London ['ləndən], village in Shelby County (J-7).

Platted in 1852 and named for London, England.

Lonetree ['lōn'trē], village in Greene County (K-4).

Founded around 1860 and named for a single oak tree that stood near the original site.

Long Beach ['loŋ ͵bēch], town in LaPorte County (A-5).

The name is descriptive but probably commendatory as well.

Long Lake ['loŋ 'lāk], lake in Porter County.

Located 4 miles north of Valparaiso, this 65-acre lake was named for its long, cigar-like shape.

Long Run ['loŋ ˌrən], village in Switzerland County (M-10).

A post office was established here in 1874. Named for the nearby stream of the same name.

Loogootee [ˌlō'gōₔē], fifth class city in Martin County (M-5).

Platted in 1853 by Thomas Gootee. The name was coined from two personal names: Lowe, honoring the engineer of the first train through the town, and Gootee, for the founder and owner of the land where the town was built.

Lorane [ˌlō'rān; lə-], village in Whitley County (C-9).

Formerly called Steam Corners and Buzzards Glory, the former name for steam-powered sawmills near here and the latter allegedly for an incident. A traveler crossed a stream near here and stopped all night with the Lord family. "The next morning, he said he crossed the river Jordan, went through Glory, and stayed all night with the Lord, and from that time on the little place was called Glory. Someone added the name Buzzard. Why, no one knows." The present name seems to be a phonetic spelling of Lorraine, the French province. A former spelling was Lorain. The post office was established as Loran in 1851.

Loree [lə'rā; 'lorē], village in Miami County (E-7).

Founded in 1888 and named for a railroad official.

Losantville [lə'sænt,vil] (Bronson), town in Randolph County (G-10).

Platted in 1851 and originally called Hunt's Cross Roads, for land-owner Howard Hunt, who platted the town. Losantville, established as a post office in 1854, is a corruption of Losantiville, the original coined name of Cincinnati. "L" stands for Licking Creek, "os" is Latin for mouth, and "anti" is Greek for opposite. These were combined with the generic -ville to identify "the town opposite the mouth of Licking Creek." The alternate name, Bronson, apparently comes from a personal name.

Lost Creek ['lost ˌkrēk], stream in Vigo County.

This stream derives its name from the fact that at times it sinks and flows underground.

Lost River ['lost 'rivər], stream.

Heads in Washington County and flows west through Orange County and Martin County to East Fork White River near the southern boundary of Martin County. The stream is so named because it sinks and runs underground for several miles and rises again.

Lottaville ['latə,vil], village in Lake County (B-3).

A railroad station was established here in 1879 and called Redsdale, although the post office was named Lottaville, apparently for the personal name.

Lovett ['ləvət], village in Jennings County (L-8).

Platted in 1855 and named for a prominent railroad official.

94

Lowell ['lō(ə)l], town in Lake County (C-3).

Settled in 1836, laid out in 1853 and named for Lowell, Massachusetts.

Lucerne [lu'sərn], village in Cass County (D-6).

Laid out in 1883, the town was called Altoner and the post office Nebo, both of which were renamed Lucerne in 1891. Apparently named for the lake or city in Switzerland.

Luray [lu'rā], village in Henry County (G-9).

Laid out in 1836. The settlement was first called Virginia, as the settlers came from there. The present name is for Luray, Virginia.

Lydick ['laidik], village in St. Joseph County (A-6).

Established about 1851 and originally called Warren Center by the railroad for the township. Besides Warren Center, the post office has been called Lindley and Sweet Home. The present name is for a member of the local Milliken family.

Lyford ['laifərd], village in Parke County (H-3).

Platted in 1892 and named for W. H. Lyford, vice-president of the railroad through here.

Lyles [lailz], village in Gibson County (N-2).

Known as the Cherry Grove Vicinity before the Civil War. After the war a Negro named Lyles bought land here, other Blacks settled, and the name was changed to Lyles Station.

Lynn [lin], town in Randolph County (G-10).

Laid out in 1847 and probably named for the personal name.

Lynnville ['lin‚vil], town in Warrick County (N-4).

Platted in 1839 by John Lynn and named for him.

Lyons ['lai‚ənz], town in Greene County (L-4).

Platted in 1869 and named for Squire Joe Lyon, treasurer and auditor of the county.

Lyonsville ['lai‚ənz‚vil], village in Fayette County (H-10).

Formerly called Lyons Station, the town probably was named for Abraham Lyons, who settled here about 1808.

M

Mace [mās], village in Montgomery County (G-5).

Originally called Frederickville, for Frederick Long, who laid out the town in 1839–40. The present name probably is for the personal name.

Mackey ['mækē], town in Gibson County (N-3).

Founded around 1882 and named for O. J. Mackey, local railroad entrepreneur.

Macy ['māsē], town in Miami County (D-7).
Laid out in 1860 and originally called Lincoln, probably for Abraham Lincoln. The present name apparently is for the personal name.

Madison ['mædəsən] County (G-8).
Organized in 1823 and named for James Madison, fourth President of the U. S.

Madison ['mædəsən], county seat, fourth class city in Jefferson County (M-9).
First settled in 1805, the site was purchased in 1809 by Colonel John Paul, a Revolutionary War soldier, who platted the town and named it for President James Madison.

Magee [mə'gē], village in LaPorte County (B-5).
The name probably comes from the personal name.

Magley ['mæglē], village in Adams County (D-10).
Founded in 1882 and named for Jacob Magley, the first station agent of the town.

Magnet ['mægnət], village in Perry County (O-6).
Formerly called Rono, allegedly for a dog, the name was changed to Magnet in 1896 by the Post Office Department. Stewart says the name might be commendatory, suggesting the settlement will attract people.

Magnolia [mæg'nōl͵yə], village in Crawford County (N-6).
Platted in 1838. The name, usually for the tree, is common in the U. S. and possibly is a transfer from a southern state.

Mahon ['mā͵han], village in Huntington County (D-9).
Platted in 1853 by Archibald Mahon and named for the Mahon family, which was prominent in the development of the community.

Majenica [mə'jenəkə] (Kelso), village in Huntington County (E-9).
Kelso, apparently for the personal name, was the name of the post office established here in 1830. Platted in 1856 and named for the Miami chief *Man-ji-ni-kia,* "Big Frame."

Malden ['moldən], village in Porter County (C-4).
Established about 1902 and called Hayden, for an early settler, but since there was already a Hoosier town of that name, it was renamed Malden for the city in Massachusetts.

Manchester ['mænchestər], village in Dearborn County (K-10).
Settled in 1818 and named for the township in which it is located.

Manhattan [͵mæn'hætn], village in Putnam County (J-5).
Founded in 1829 and named for Manhattan Island, New York.

Manilla [mə'nelə], village in Rush County (J-8).

Settled in 1824, laid out in 1836, and originally called Wilmington, for the city in North Carolina, home of settlers. Apparently the present name is for the Philippine city.

Mansfield ['mænz͵fēld], village in Parke County (H-4).

Formerly called Dickson's Mills, for Francis Dickson, co-owner of a mill built here in 1821. It was platted in 1852, and probably the present name comes from Mansfield, Ohio.

Mansfield Reservoir ['mænz͵fēld 'rezə(r)͵vor; -voi] (Raccoon Lake), lake in Parke County.

See Raccoon Lake.

Manson ['mænsən], village in Clinton County (G-6).

Platted in 1874 and named for General Mahlon D. Manson.

Manville ['mæn͵vil], village in Jefferson County (L-9).

Formerly called Buena Vista in 1847 when a post office was established. In 1858 the name was changed to Manville, honoring an early settler.

Maples ['māpəlz], village in Allen County (D-10).

Platted in 1853 and named for an early settler, Lewis S. Maples.

Maple Valley [͵māpəl 'vælē], village in Henry County (H-8).

Established in 1879. Probably the name is commendatory as well as descriptive.

Maplewood ['māpəl͵wud], village in Hendricks County (H-6).

A post office called Progress was established here in 1880. In 1881 the name was changed to Maplewood for a dense maple forest on the site of the settlement.

Marco ['markō], village in Greene County (L-4).

First settled in 1816 and laid out in 1868. The present name comes from a nearby mail station. Apparently the name was coined from the names of two early residents, March and Coker. Some say it was named for Marco Polo, though.

Mardenis [͵mar'dēnəs], village in Huntington County (D-9).

Known first as Miner's Switch and then as Union Station, the name was changed to Mardenis for William R. Mardenis, who settled here in 1870 and became the local railroad agent.

Marengo [mə'rāŋgō; -reŋgō], town in Crawford County (N-6).

Platted in 1837 and named by Joseph Thornton of Leavenworth for one of Napoleon's victories over the Austrians in 1800 at Marengo, Italy.

Maria Creek [mə'rēə ͵krēk], stream.

Heads in Sullivan County and flows southwest to the Wabash River about 5 miles north of Vincennes. Apparently the name comes from the French name of the stream, *Rivière St. Marie,* which appears on early maps.

Mariah Hill [mə͵rēə 'hil; mə'raiə], village in Spencer County (N-5).

Laid out in 1860 for the trustees of a Catholic church around a church on a hill and named Maria Hill for devotional reasons and its situation.

Marietta [ˌmerēˈetə], village in Shelby County (J-8).
Laid out in 1855. Probably the name is a transfer from Ohio.

Marion [ˈmerēˌən] County (H-7).
Organized in 1882 and named for General Francis Marion, officer in the American Revolution.

Marion [ˈmerēˌən], county seat, second class city in Grant County (E-8).
Settled by Martin Boots, John Ballinger, and David Branson in 1826. When Grant County was formed in 1831, Boots and Branson donated land for the county seat, and when the town was laid out it was called Marion, for General Francis Marion, cavalry officer in the Revolution.

Marion [ˈmerēˌən], village in Shelby County (J-8).
Platted in 1820 and named for General Francis Marion.

Marion Heights [ˌmerēən ˈhaits], village in Vigo County (J-3).
Apparently named for Marion McQuilton, who was a large landowner here.

Markland [ˈmarklənd], village in Switzerland County (L-10).
Laid out in 1874 by Charles Markland and named for him.

Markle [ˈmarkəl], town in Huntington and Wells counties (D-9).
Platted around 1836 and originally called Tracy. Apparently the present name comes from the personal name.

Markleville [ˈmarkəlˌvil], town in Madison County (G-8).
Laid out in 1852 by John Markle, for whom it was named.

Marshall [ˈmarshəl] County (C-6).
Organized in 1836 and named for John Marshall, Chief Justice of the U. S. Supreme Court, 1801–35.

Marshall [ˈmarshəl], town in Parke County (H-4).
Platted in 1878 and named for Mahlon W. Marshall, who donated land for a railroad station here.

Marshfield [ˈmarshˌfēld], village in Warren County (F-3).
Platted in 1857 and named for Marshfield, Massachusetts, home of Daniel Webster.

Martin [ˈmartn] County (M-5).
Organized in 1820 and named for Major John P. Martin of Newport, Kentucky.

Martinsburg [ˈmartnzˌbərg], village in Washington County (N-7).
Laid out in 1818 by Dr. Abner Martin, for whom it was named.

Martinsville [ˈmartnzˌvil], county seat, fifth class city in Morgan County (J-6).
Laid out in 1822 and named for John Martin, senior member of the

board of commissioners who located the county seat here.

Martz [marts], village in Clay County (K-4).

Named for Arthur Martz, who founded the town in 1827. An alternate name has been Middlebury, a name arbitrarily selected from a book. Apparently residents called the town Middlebury, although Martz was the official post office name.

Mary Delarme Creek [ˌmerē ˌdel-'arm ˌkrēk], stream in Allen County.

The name of this tributary of the Maumee River is a corruption of the French name, *Marais de l'Orme,* "Elm Swamp."

Marysville ['merēzˌvil], village in Clark County (M-8).

Founded in 1871 and named for Miss Mary Kimberlain, resident of the county.

Matamoras [ˌmætə'morəs], village in Blackford County (E-9).

Organized in 1875. Apparently named for the Mexican city taken by American troops in the Mexican War.

Matthews ['mæthˌyūz], town in Grant County (F-9).

Founded in 1833 and apparently named for the personal name.

Mauckport ['makˌpōrt], town in Harrison County (O-7).

Platted in 1827 and named for the founder, Frederick Mauck.

Maumee River ['momē 'rivər], stream.

About 100 miles long, it is formed by the junction of the St. Marys and St. Joseph rivers at Ft. Wayne and flows northeast to Lake Erie. The name is a corruption, although close to the Indian pronunciation, of *Me-ah-me,* of which Miami is a form. Formerly it was called Ottawa River, for the Indian tribe that lived here. See Miami County.

Mauzy ['mozē], village in Rush County (J-9).

Originally called Griffin Station for a local family. A post office called Mauzy was established in 1884. The present name honors the Mauzy family, local landowners.

Maxinkuckee ['mæksnˌkəkē], village in Marshall County (C-6).

Named for Lake Maxinkuckee, q.v.

Maxville ['mæksˌvil], village in Randolph County (G-10).

Formerly Macksville, it was laid out about 1832 by Robert McIntyre, and apparently named for him.

Maxville ['mæksˌvil], village in Spencer County (O-5).

Laid out in 1841 and probably named for James McDaniel, proprietor.

Maxwell ['mæksˌwel], village in Hancock County (H-8).

Surveyed in 1881 and first called Junction. Soon after the name was changed to Maxwell in honor of a man involved in building the railroad here.

Mays [māz], village in Rush County (H-9).

Originally called May's Station, for a resident, it was laid out in 1884.

Maysville ['māz‚vil], village in Daviess County (M-4).

Laid out in 1834 and apparently named for the personal name.

Maywood ['mā‚wud], village in Marion County (H-7).

Originally called Beeler's Station, for a local miller, the town was laid out in 1873 by John and Clay Campbell, who apparently named the town for Maywood, Illinois.

McCordsville [mə'kordz‚vil], village in Hancock County (H-7).

Laid out in 1865 and named for a prominent local family. An early settler was Elias McCord.

McCormicks Creek [mə‚kormiks 'krēk], stream in Owen County.

Located in southeastern Owen County, this stream was named for John McCormick, who owned land at its mouth.

McCoy [mə'koi], village in Decatur County (K-9).

Platted in 1871 and apparently named for the personal name.

McCoysburg [mə'koiz‚bərg], village in Jasper County (D-4).

Established in 1877 and named for Alfred McCoy, local landowner.

McCutchanville [mə'kəchən‚vil], village in Vanderburgh County (O-3).

Established about 1845 and named for Samuel McCutchan, first postmaster.

McGrawsville [mə'groz‚vil], village in Miami County (E-7).

Founded in 1867 by Nelson McGraw and named for him.

McKinley [mə'kinlē], village in Washington County (M-7).

A post office was established here in 1891 and allegedly named for William McKinley, who became President in 1897.

McVille [mək'vil], village in Greene County (K-5).

Founded in 1836 by John McHaley who first called it McHaleysville but then shortened it to McVille.

Mecca ['mekə; 'mekē], village in Parke County (H-3).

Platted in 1890. A church near here was nicknamed the Arabian Church, for its location on a dry, sandy hill. Each spring when the roads became passable, the residents near the church came to the store of Alexander McCune, who remarked that the Arabians were coming on their annual visit to Mecca, hence the name for the Arabian city. Formerly called Mecca Mills. A local legend offers another explanation of the name: "Mecca is a town, and it was first settled about the early 1840's. In 1898 they built a tile plant, and so they needed workers, and they needed cheap workers, so they sent over to the Near East and got these Moslems, in that general area. They lived there outside town, and when they got paid, they'd come to town and say it was almost like coming to Mecca, and so they called the town Mecca."

Mechanicsburg [mə'kæniks‚bərg], village in Boone County (G-6).

Platted in 1835. A common commendatory name, allegedly it remembers the manual skills of many early settlers.

Mechanicsburg [mə'kæniks‚bərg], village in Decatur County (K-9).

Laid out in 1846. Probably the name is commendatory.

Mechanicsburg [mə'kæniks‚bərg], village in Henry County (G-8).

Laid out in 1858 and so named because there were "so many mechanics representing different trades living there." The name probably is commendatory as well as descriptive.

Medaryille [mə'derē‚vil] town in Pulaski County (D-5).

Platted in 1853 by Carter Hathaway who named it for Joseph Medary, Ohio statesman.

Medford ['med‚fərd], village in Delaware County (G-9).

Platted in 1901 and originally called Phillips, for the founder Clarissa Phillips. The present name might be for the town in Maine.

Medora [mə'dōrə], town in Jackson County (L-7).

Laid out in 1853 and commonly believed to be named for the first three notes of the scale—do, re, mi

—although the order was changed. Probably the name comes from Lord Byron's poem, "The Corsair."

Mellott ['melət; ‚mə'lat], town in Fountain County (G-4).

Platted in 1882 by John B. and Syrena C. Mellott, for whom it was named.

Meltzer ['meltsər], village in Shelby County (J-8).

Established in the 1870's around a country store owned by John Meltzer and named for him.

Memphis ['mem‚fus], village in Clark County (M-8).

Founded in 1852 and probably named for Memphis, Tennessee, since early settlers came from that area.

Mentone ['men‚tōn; ‚men'tōn], town in Kosciusko County (C-7).

Platted in 1882 and probably named for the city on the Mediterranean in France, although one source says for Mennonites who settled here in 1885.

Mentor ['men(t)ər], village in Dubois County (N-5).

Platted in 1881.

Merom ['mirəm], town in Sullivan County (L-3).

Laid out in 1817 and actually named for the biblical lake, although local legend says that the town received its name from Indians who, coming here for liquor, said, "Me rum!"

Merom Station [‚mirəm 'stāshən], village in Sullivan County (L-3).

Named for the nearby town of Merom, as the railroad passed through here instead of through Merom.

Merrillville ['merə(l)ˌvil], fourth class city in Lake County (B-3).
First called Centreville, but known by the present name since 1848 when a post office was established. Named for Dudley Merrill, local storekeeper.

Messick ['mesik], village in Henry County (G-9).
Founded in 1882 and named for the Messick family who lived here many years.

Metamora [ˌmetə'mōrə], village in Franklin County (J-10).
Platted in 1838 and named for J. A. Stone's play of the same name.

Metea ['mētēə; -d̲-], village in Cass County (D-6).
Laid out in 1853 and named for the Potawatomi chief *Mi-ti-a,* "Kiss Me."

Metz [mets], village in Steuben County (B-11).
Platted in 1855 and named for Metz, France, home of some of the settlers.

Mexico ['meksēˌkō], village in Miami County (E-7).
Laid out in 1834 and named for the country, apparently because of sympathy for the Mexican struggle for independence.

Miami [ˌmai'æmē] County (E-7).
Organized in 1834 and named for the Miami nation of Indians, who once inhabited the area. Early French chroniclers wrote the name *Oumiamiouek* and *Oumiamiak,* apparently a corruption of *Wemiamik,* literally "all beavers" but figuratively "all friends," the Delaware name for the Miamis.

Miami [ˌmai'æmē], village in Miami County·(E-7).
Platted in 1849 and named for the Miami nation.

Michaels ['maikəlz], village in Grant County (F-8).
A post office called Michael was established here in 1892. Apparently named for the personal name, as William Michael was the first postmaster.

Michiana Shores [ˌmishi'ænə 'shōrz], town in LaPorte County (A-5).
Located on Lake Michigan; the name is coined from the first four letters of Michigan and the last four letters of Indiana.

Michigan City [ˌmishigən 'sid̲ē], second class city in LaPorte County (A-5).
Founded in 1831 on Lake Michigan in Michigan Township as the terminus of the Michigan Road, so the name is a local transfer.

Michigantown ['mishēgənˌtaun], town in Clinton County (F-6).
Founded in 1830 and named for the Michigan Road that passes through it, which for a time was the most important north-south highway in Indiana.

102

Middlebury ['mid̠əl̩berē], town in Elkhart County (A-8).

Platted in 1835 and named for Middlebury Township, which was named for Middlebury, Vermont, home of the first settler.

Middlefork ['mid̠əl̩fork], village in Clinton County (F-6).

In 1836 a post office called Middle Fork was established here. The spelling was changed to Middle-fork in 1893. Named for a nearby stream of the same name.

Middletown ['mid̠əl̩taun], village in Allen County (D-10).

Platted in 1851. Apparently the name is locational, for its position between Ft. Wayne and Decatur.

Middletown ['mid̠əl̩taun], town in Henry County (G-9).

Laid out in 1829 and so named because of its location between New Castle and Anderson.

Middletown ['mid̠əl̩taun], village in Shelby County (J-8).

Platted in 1829. Apparently the name is locational.

Midland ['mid̩lænd], village in Greene County (K-4).

Platted in 1901 by the Midland Coal Company. The name Midland apparently comes from the town's location midway between Sullivan and Worthington on an old mail route.

Midway ['mid̩wā], village in Spencer County (O-4).

Founded about 1854. The name is locational, although accounts vary as to what it is midway between.

Mier ['miər], village in Grant County (E-8).

Laid out in 1848 and named for the Mexican town which was on General Scott's route to Mexico City during the Mexican War.

Mifflin ['miflən], village in Crawford County (N-6).

Established about 1851. The name ultimately comes from the personal name, especially General Thomas Mifflin of the Revolution who was governor of Pennsylvania, 1790–99. Several eastern towns bear this name, so it may be a transfer.

Milan ['mailən], town in Ripley County (K-10).

Laid out in 1831 and apparently named for the Italian city.

Milford ['milfərd], town in Decatur County (J-8).

Originally called Needmore, it was platted in 1835. The present name is for a mill built at a ford here.

Milford ['milfərd], town in Kosciusko County (B-8).

Laid out in 1836 and allegedly named for a ford at a mill here on Turkey Creek.

Milford Junction [-jəŋkshən], village in Kosciusko County (B-8).

Named for nearby Milford.

Mill Creek [ˌmil 'krēk; krik], stream.

Water mills for sawing wood and

grinding flour were essential and numerous in Indiana during the nineteenth century, and this is reflected in the names of several streams named Mill Creek in the state. Invariably these streams, as the one in Jackson County, are so named for one or more mills on them.

Mill Creek ['mil ˌkrik], village in LaPorte County (B-6).

Platted in 1834 and named for a nearby stream of the same name.

Millersburg ['milərzˌbərg], town in Elkhart County (B-8).

Laid out in 1855 and named for Solomon Miller, on whose land the town was built.

Millersburg ['milərzˌbərg], village in Hamilton County (G-7).

Laid out in 1860 and named for Peter Miller, co-founder.

Millersburg ['milərzˌbərg], village in Orange County (M-6).

Named for Greenup Miller, who established the first store here in 1833.

Millersburg ['milərzˌbərg] (Canal), village in Warrick County (O-3).

Platted in 1852 and named for Phillip Miller, early settler, and his descendants. Since there are other towns of the same name in Indiana, the post office was called Canal, for its location on the Wabash and Erie Canal.

Millersville ['milərzˌvil], village in Marion County (H-7).

Founded in 1838 and formerly called Brubaker's Mill. The present name probably comes from the milling industry once here.

Millgrove [ˌmil'grōv], village in Blackford County (F-9).

Laid out in 1867 and so named because in 1866 a mill was built here in a shady grove.

Millhousen ['milˌhauzn], town in Decatur County (K-9).

Settled in 1838 by Maximilian Schneider, who named it for his hometown in Germany.

Milligan ['miləgən; 'milē-], village in Parke County (H-4).

Originally called South Waveland, a locational name. The present name is for an early local merchant, Joseph Milligan. A railroad station was established here in 1878.

Milltown ['milˌtaun], town in Crawford and Harrison counties (N-6).

Platted in 1827, the settlement originally was called Leavenworth's Mill because Zebulon Leavenworth had a mill here. The present name comes from the mill.

Millville ['milˌvil], village in Henry County (H-9).

Laid out in 1831 and named for a nearby mill.

Milners Corner [ˌmilnərz 'kornər], village in Hancock County (H-8).

Unplatted, but it has been a center of business since about 1850. A post office was established here in 1868. Named for a local family, probably for Henry Milner, an early merchant.

104

Milroy ['mil,roi], village in Rush County (J-9).

Laid out in 1831 and named for Samuel Milroy, speaker of the Indiana House, who signed the act creating Rush County.

Milton ['miltn], town in Wayne County (H-10).

Laid out in 1824 and so named because there were several mills here. Possibly the name was influenced by Milford Meeting, a society of Friends established here in 1819.

Milton ['miltən; -tn] (Guionsville), village in Ohio County (L-10).

See Guionsville.

Mineral City [,minərəl 'sidē], village in Greene County (L-5).

Formerly called Fellows' Mill and Mineral. The post office established here was called Mineral City in 1877. The present name was applied by the railroad and is descriptive, either of coal or mineral springs here.

Mishawaka [,mishə'wokə], second class city in St. Joseph County (A-7).

According to local legend the town was named for an Indian princess who died in 1818, but actually the name is a corruption of the Potawatomi *m'seh-wah-kee-ki,* "country of dead trees," referring to a deadening, generally where trees are girdled with axes as a first step toward clearing a forest. Apparently there was a tract of dead timber here. It was laid out in 1833.

Mississinewa River [,mi(si)'sinə,wa ,rivər], stream.

Heads in the State of Ohio and flows northwest through Randolph, Delaware, Grant, Wabash, and Miami counties to the Wabash River near Peru. The name is a corruption of the Miami name *Na-mah-chis-sin-wi,* which literally means "an ascent" but as applied to the river means "much fall in the river." Formerly the name was written *Mas-sis-sin-e-way.*

Mitchell ['michəl], fifth class city in Lawrence County (M-6).

Land near here was settled as early as 1813, but the town wasn't platted until 1852. It was named for O. M. Mitchell, a construction engineer for the Ohio and Mississippi Railroad, which was built here in 1856.

Mixerville ['miksər,vil], village in Franklin County (J-11).

Named for William Mixer, who platted the town in 1846.

Modesto [mə'destō], village in Monroe County (K-6).

A post office was established here in 1892. This Spanish name meaning "modest" is found in California dating from 1870 and most likely is a transfer.

Modoc ['mōdak], town in Randolph County (G-10).

Platted around 1882 and named for the Indian tribe. Supposedly the name is the Shasteeca word for "enemy." Local legend says the name was suggested by a picture of a Modoc chief on a cigar box.

Moffett ['mafət], village in Jasper County (D-4).
Probably named from the personal name.

Mohawk ['mō͵hok], village in Hancock County (H-8).
Platted in 1883 and named for the Iroquois tribe. Probably a corruption from *Maugwawogs,* "man-eaters." According to local legend, there was once a flight of hawks overhead, and some residents ran out and called, "More hawks, more hawks!"

Mongo ['maŋ͵gō], village in Lagrange County (A-9).
From *Mon-go-quin-ong,* "Big Squaw," the Potawatomi name for the Elkhart River. The town was platted with that name in 1840, but later it was shortened to Mongo.

Monitor ['manətər], village in Tippecanoe County (F-5).
A settlement was located here about 1823. In 1864 a post office was established and allegedly named for the Union ironclad *Monitor,* which fought the Confederate *Merrimack* on March 9, 1862.

Monmouth ['man͵məth], village in Adams County (D-10).
Platted in 1836 and named for Monmouth, New Jersey, by Quaker settlers.

Monon ['mō͵nan], town in White County (D-5).

A post office was established here in 1838 and named Monon for the township in which it was located. When the town was platted in 1853, it assumed the name of the post office. The name Monon comes from a Potawatomi word equivalent in usage to the southern "tote."

Monoquet [mə'nə͵kwət], village in Kosciusko County (C-8).
Laid out in 1834 and named for a Potawatomi chief.

Monroe [mən'rō] County (K-6).
Organized in 1818 and named for James Monroe, fifth President of the U. S.

Monroe [mən'rō], town in Adams County (E-10).
Platted in 1847 and named for the fifth President of the U.S., James Monroe.

Monroe [͵man'rō], village in Tippecanoe County (F-5).
Platted in 1832 and probably named for President James Monroe. A post office was established as Huntersville, for the personal name, in 1836, but the post office name was changed to Monroe in 1840.

Monroe City [mən͵rō 'sid̲ē], town in Knox County (M-3).
Laid out in 1856 and apparently named for Monroe Alton, proprietor. Formerly called Nashville and Lively Dale.

Monroe Reservoir [mən'rō 'rez-ə(r)͵vor; -voi], lake.
This 10,750-acre lake is located

in Brown County and Monroe County, for which it was named.

Monroeville [mən'rō͵vil], town in Allen County (D-11).

Settled in 1841, incorporated in 1865, and named for Monroe Township.

Monrovia [mən'rōvē͵ə], village in Morgan County (J-6).

Laid out in 1834; the name is a Latinized form of Monroe Township, in which the village is located.

Montclair [͵mant'kler], village in Hendricks County (H-6).

Settled in 1879. The name probably was borrowed from an eastern city for its commendatory value.

Monterey [͵mantə'rā], town in Pulaski County (C-6).

Laid out in 1849 and formerly called Buena Vista. The name was changed to Monterey, site of a battle in the Mexican War, when it was found there was already a town of the former name in Indiana.

Montezuma [͵mantə'zūmə], town in Parke County (H-3).

Settled in 1821 and named by early settlers for the last Aztec emperor of Mexico. Platted in 1849.

Montgomery [͵mant'gəm(ə)rē] County (G-5).

Organized in 1823 and named for General Richard Montgomery, Revolutionary War officer who was killed in the Battle of Quebec in 1775.

Montgomery [mənt'gəmrē], town in Daviess County (M-4).

Named for Valentine Montgomery, who platted the town in 1865.

Monticello [͵mantə'selō], county seat, fifth class city in White County (E-5).

Laid out in 1834 and named for Thomas Jefferson's home.

Montmorenci [͵mantmə'rentsē], village in Tippecanoe County (F-4).

Platted in 1838. The post office first was called Bringham's Groves, for the first postmaster, John Bringham. The present name is for the commune in France, perhaps via the river in Quebec or the town in South Carolina.

Montpelier [͵mant'pēl͵yər], fifth class city in Blackford County (E-9).

Platted in 1837 by Abel Baldwin, who, with other early settlers, came from Vermont and named the town for the Vermont city.

Moody ['mūdē], village in Jasper County (D-4).

Named for Granville Moody, who founded the village in 1893.

Moonville ['mūn͵vil], village in Madison County (G-8).

Laid out in 1835 by Zimri Moon and named for him.

Moore [mōr], village in Dekalb County (B-10).

A post office was established as Moore's Station in 1875. In 1882 the name was changed to Moore.

Named for G. S. Moore, an early settler.

Moorefield ['mōr͵fēld], village in Switzerland County (L-10).
Laid out in 1834 and named for the Moore family who owned land here.

Mooreland ['mōr͵lənd], town in Henry County (G-9).
Laid out in 1882 and named for the proprietor, Miles M. Moore.

Moores Hill [͵mōrz 'hil], town in Dearborn County (K-10).
Founded in 1828, platted in 1838, and originally called Moore's Mill, for Adam Moore, who owned a mill here. A mistake was made when the town applied for a post office, and the name became Moores Hill.

Mooresville ['mōrz͵vil], town in Morgan County (J-6).
Laid out in 1824 by Samuel Moore, proprietor and early settler, and named for him.

Moran [mə'ræn], village in Clinton County (F-6).
Laid out in 1873 and named for a railroad official.

Morgan ['morgən] County (J-6).
Organized in 1822 and named for General Daniel Morgan, who served under Arnold at Quebec in 1775–76 and defeated Tarleton at Cowpens in 1781.

Morgantown ['morgən͵taun], town in Morgan County (J-6).

Laid out in 1831 and perhaps named for a pioneer family named Morgan but most likely for the county.

Morocco [mə'rakō], town in Newton County (D-3).
Laid out in 1851 and apparently named for the country in North Africa, although according to local legend the town was named for a stranger's boots, which were topped with red morocco leather.

Morris ['morəs], village in Ripley County (K-10).
Originally called Springdale, the town was laid out in 1858 and named Morris, for George Morris, a resident.

Morrison Creek [͵morəsən 'krēk], stream in Sullivan County.
This tributary of Busseron Creek was named for Lt. Morrison, who was killed here by Indians in 1815.

Morristown ['mor(ə)s͵taun; mar-], town in Shelby County (H-8).
Laid out in 1828 by Rezin Davis and Samuel Morrison and named for Morrison.

Morton ['mortn], village in Putnam County (H-5).
Settled as early as 1825, and a post office was established in 1855. Generally thought to have been named for Oliver Perry Morton, governor of Indiana, 1861–67, but the name here seems to be older than Morton's prominence.

Moscow ['mas͵kō], village in Rush County (J-9).

108

Laid out in 1832 and apparently named for the Russian city.

Mt. Auburn [ˌmaunt 'obərn] (Blackhawk), village in Shelby County (J-7).

Platted in 1837, established as a post office in 1838, and originally called Black Hawk, for the Sauk chief. In 1844 the name was changed to Mt. Auburn to avoid confusion with the other town called Blackhawk in Indiana. Apparently the name is commendatory.

Mt. Auburn [ˌmaunt 'obərn], town in Wayne County (H-10).

Platted in 1864. Probably the name is commendatory.

Mt. Ayr [ˌmaunt 'er], town in Newton County (D-4).

Laid out in 1882 by Louis Marion, who named it for his home, Mt. Airy, North Carolina. Previous spellings have been Mt. Airy and Mt. Ayer.

Mt. Carmel [ˌmaunt 'karməl], town in Franklin County (J-11).

First laid out in 1832 and named for the local Mt. Carmel Presbyterian Church.

Mt. Carmel [ˌmaunt 'karməl], village in Washington County (M-6).

Laid out in 1837 and apparently named for the biblical mountain.

Mt. Comfort [ˌmaunt 'kəmfərt], village in Hancock County (H-7).

Platted in 1885 and named for the post office established here in the 1840's. The origin of the post office name is unknown, although the name has commendatory value.

Mt. Etna [ˌmaunt 'etnə], town in Huntington County (E-8).

Founded in 1839 and named for the volcano in Sicily.

Mt. Healthy [ˌmaunt 'helthē], village in Bartholomew County (K-7).

Laid out in 1851 and supposedly so named because it is located on high ground and "free of miasmatic vapors."

Mt. Liberty [ˌmaunt 'libərdē], village in Brown County (K-7).

A post office was established here in 1877. Apparently the name is commendatory.

Mt. Meridian [ˌmaunt mə'ridēˌin], village in Putnam County (J-5).

Laid out in 1833 and called Carthage. When the post office was established in 1835, the Post Office Department renamed it Mt. Meridian because there was another town named Carthage in the state.

Mt. Olive [ˌmaunt 'aliv; -əv], village in Martin County (L-5).

Apparently named for the biblical Mount of Olives.

Mt. Olympus [ˌmaunt ə'limpəs], village in Gibson County (N-3).

Originally called Ennes, for a pioneer blacksmith, William Ennes. Samuel Kelly, a schoolteacher, gave the town its present name from the home of the Greek gods.

Mt. Pisgah [ˌmaunt 'pisˌgē; 'pizgə], village in Lagrange County (B-9).

A post office was established here in 1848. Named for the biblical mountain.

Mt. Pleasant [ˌmaunt 'plezənt], village in Cass County (D-6).

Laid out in 1836 and probably selected for its commendatory value.

Mt. Pleasant [ˌmaunt 'plezənt] (Hazel), village in Delaware County (G-9).

Laid out in 1837 and probably named for the nearby Mt. Pleasant United Brethren Church.

Mt. Pleasant [ˌmaunt 'plezənt], village in Martin County (M-5).

Laid out in 1826. The name is commendatory. According to tradition, "The people who settled Mt. Pleasant came there from a place called Hindostan Falls whence they had been forced to leave on account of a plague which infested that vicinity. The settlement of Mt. Pleasant is located on a hill and the surroundings were a very agreeable change to the first settlers over the plague-ridden Hindostan they had left. Hence the name."

Mt. Sinai [ˌmaunt 'sain(ē)ai], village in Dearborn County (K-10).

Named for the Mt. Sinai Methodist Episcopal Church built here prior to 1836.

Mt. Sterling [ˌmaunt 'stərliŋ], village in Switzerland County (L-10).

Laid out in 1816 on a hill and named for the Sterling family.

Mt. Summit [ˌmaunt 'səmət], town in Henry County (G-9).

Platted in 1854 and surrounded by hilly farmland, the town is situated on one of the higher elevations in the county, from which it received its name.

Mt. Tabor [ˌmaunt 'tābər], village in Monroe County (K-5).

Platted in 1828 and apparently named for the biblical mountain.

Mt. Vernon [ˌmaunt 'vərnən], county seat, fifth class city in Posey County (O-2).

Settled by Andrew McFadden about 1800 and formerly known as McFadden's Bluff and McFadden's Landing. Platted in 1816. The present name is for Washington's home.

Mt. Vernon [ˌmaunt 'vərnən], village in Wabash County (E-8).

Platted in 1847 and named for George Washington's home.

Mt. Zion [ˌmaunt 'zaiˌən], village in Wells County (E-9).

Platted in 1895 and named for a church around which the village was built.

Muddy Fork Silver Creek [ˌmədē ˌfork 'silvər ˌkrēk], stream in Clark County.

The name is descriptive. See Silver Creek.

Mulberry ['məlˌberē; mol-], town in Clinton County (F-5).

Platted in 1858 and allegedly named for a tall mulberry tree here.

Muncie ['mən(t)sē], county seat, second class city in Delaware County (G-9).

Settled as early as 1818 and platted in 1827. Formerly called Munseetown or Muncey Town because so many Delawares of the Munsee clan lived here. Sometimes spelled Monsy and Monthee, the original was *Min-si* or *Min-thi-u,* "people of the stony country."

Munster ['mənstər], town in Lake County (B-3).

Settled in 1855 and named for one of the first settlers, Eldert Munster.

Murray ['mərē], village in Wells County (E-9).

Settled in 1829 and laid out in 1839. Originally called New Lancaster. The Post Office Department changed the name to Murray.

Muscatatuck River [məs'kætətək 'rivər; -tek-], stream.

About 53 miles long, it heads in Jefferson County and flows west through Jennings, Scott, Washington, and Jackson counties to the East Fork White River, about 4 miles south of Medora. The name comes from the Delaware name of the stream, *Mosch-ach-hit-tuk,* "Clear River."

Muskelonge Lake ['məskə,lənj ,lāk], lake in Kosciusko County.

This 32-acre lake is located ½ mile south of Warsaw. The name comes from the Ojibwa name, *Maskinonge,* existing in various dialectical forms and meaning "the great pike."

N

Nabb [næb], village in Clark County (M-8).

Platted in 1855 and named for a railroad superintendent, General Nabb.

Napoleon [nə'pōl,yən], town in Ripley County (K-9).

Laid out in 1820 and named for Napoleon Bonaparte.

Nappanee [,næpə'nē], fifth class city in Elkhart County (B-7).

Founded in 1874. Ultimately the name comes from the Missisauga *na-pa-ni,* "flour." The Hoosier town gets its name from the Canadian town Napanee, which received its name from a gristmill there.

Nashville ['næsh,vil], county seat, town in Brown County (K-7).

Founded in 1836 and called Jacksonburg. When a post office was established in 1837 the name was changed to Nashville, for Nashville, Tennessee.

Nashville ['næsh,vil], village in Hancock County (H-8).

Laid out on December 30, 1834, by John Kennedy and Daniel Blakeley. Perhaps named for Nashville, Tennessee.

Natchez ['næchəz], village in Martin County (M-5).

A post office was established here in 1844. Apparently a transfer name from the city in Mississippi, so named from the Indian tribe.

Navilleton [nə'vil͵tən], village in Floyd County (N-7).

Founded about 1845. The name probably comes from the personal name.

Nead [nēdz], village in Miami County (E-7).

A post office was established here in 1894. Named for Samuel Nead, an early settler.

Nebraska [nə'bræskə], village in Jennings County (K-9).

Platted in 1856 and apparently named for the Nebraska Territory, established in 1854.

Needham ['nēdəm], village in Johnson County (J-7).

Platted in 1866 and named for the proprietor, Noah Needham. The post office here originally was called Needham's Station.

Needmore ['nēd͵mōr], village in Brown County (K-6).

A post office was located here in 1872. One local anecdote says that either a storekeeper or boss of a threshing crew said that he had never seen a community that needed more, so the town became known as Needmore.

Needmore ['nēd͵mōr], village in Lawrence County (L-6).

Settled in 1873 and, according to local legend, was named by Aunt Lou Goodman "during the Cleveland administration, who said the people were always needing more bread and meat than they had."

Needmore ['nēd͵mōr], village in Vermillion County (J-3).

Platted in 1904. This is a widespread name, with at least five Hoosier settlements and eight Kentucky communities bearing the name. Stewart calls the name a "humorous derogatory" suggesting that "the place needs more of everything."

Nevada [nə'vædə], village in Tipton County (F-7).

Laid out in 1852 and named by Sylvester Turpen, county recorder, supposedly "after a town in Mexico." Perhaps named for the mountain range, for which the territory ceded by Mexico in 1848 was named.

Nevada Mills [nə͵vādə 'milz], village in Steuben County (A-10).

Originally called Millville, for local sawmills. A landowner here named Dean had lived in Nevada County, California, during the Gold Rush and suggested the name Nevada. When a post office was established in 1867, Mills was added to distinguish it from another Hoosier town named Nevada.

New Albany [͵nū 'olbənē], county seat, second class city in Floyd County (N-8).

112

Platted in 1813 by Joel, Abner, and Nathaniel Scribner, who named it for the capital of their native state, Albany, New York.

New Alsace [͵nū 'ælsəs], village in Dearborn County (K-10).
Apparently named for the region and former province in France, as the first settler, Anthony Walliezer, who came here in 1833, was a native of France. Laid out in 1837.

New Amsterdam [͵nū 'æmstər͵dæm], town in Harrison County (O-6).
Platted in 1815 and apparently named for the Dutch city, perhaps influenced by the former name of New York.

Newark ['nū͵ərk], village in Greene County (K-5).
Founded around 1860 and named for Newark, Ohio, home of early settlers.

New Augusta [͵nū ə'gəstə], village in Marion County (H-7).
Platted in 1852 and originally called Holsbrook, although the railroad depot was called Augusta, for the nearby town. When the town assumed the name of the railroad station, New was added to distinguish it from the neighboring town.

New Bath ['nū ͵bæth], village in Franklin County (J-11).
Platted in 1815 on the Chesapeake and Ohio Railroad and named for Bath Township, in which it is located. See Old Bath.

New Bellsville [͵nū 'belz͵vil], village in Brown County (K-7).

Settled in the 1830's and named by settlers from Bellsville, Ohio.

Newbern ['nūbərn], village in Bartholomew County (K-8).
Laid out in 1832 and named for New Bern, North Carolina, home of Aaron Davis, one of the founders.

Newberry ['nūberē], town in Greene County (L-4).
Originally called Slinkards Mills, 1823–30, the town was first platted in 1830 and apparently named for Newberry, South Carolina, although one source says the town was laid out in 1842 by M. Newberry.

New Boston [͵nū 'bostən], village in Harrison County (O-7).
Apparently named for the English town via Massachusetts.

New Boston [͵nū 'bostən] (Huff), village in Spencer County.
Laid out in 1851. Apparently named for Boston, Massachusetts. The post office was called New Boston from 1852 until 1868. Huff, probably for the personal name, distinguishes it from the other Hoosier village named New Boston.

New Britton [͵nū 'britn], village in Hamilton County (G-7).
Laid out in 1851 and a post office was established in 1856. Appears as New Britain in one county history, so there is a possibility it was named for the country.

New Brunswick [͵nū 'brənzwik], village in Boone County (G-6).
Platted in 1850. Apparently a transfer name from an eastern state.

Newburgh ['nūbərg] town in Warrick County (O-3).

First laid out in 1817 by John Sprinkle and called Sprinklesburg, for him, although it also was known locally as Mt. Prospect. An adjoining town was laid out in 1829 and called Newburgh. In 1837 the two towns were consolidated and called Newburgh.

New Burlington [ˌnū 'bərliŋtən], village in Delaware County (G-9).

Platted in 1837 on the Burlington Pike and probably named for it.

New Carlisle [ˌnū ˌkar'lail], town in St. Joseph County (A-6).

Founded in 1835 by Richard R. Carlisle, traveler and adventurer, for whom it was named.

New Castle ['nū ˌkæsəl], county seat, third class city in Henry County (H-9).

Originally platted in 1823 and named by Ezekiel Leavell, an early settler, for his home, New Castle, Kentucky.

New Chicago [ˌnū shu'kagō], town in Lake County (B-4).

A post office was established here in 1907. Named for the nearby city in Illinois. See East Chicago.

New Columbus [ˌnū kə'ləmbəs] (Ovid), village in Madison County (G-8).

See Ovid.

New Corydon [ˌnū 'korədən], village in Jay County (E-11).

Platted in 1844 and named for Corydon, Indiana, q.v.

New Durham [ˌnū 'durəm] (Pinhook), village in LaPorte County (B-5).

See Pinhook, LaPorte County.

New Farmington [ˌnū 'farmiŋtən], village in Jackson County (L-8).

Laid out in 1852. The name probably is a transfer from an eastern state selected for its commendatory value.

New Frankfort [ˌnū 'fræŋkˌfərt], village in Scott County (M-8).

Formerly called Woostertown, it was platted in 1838 and named by settlers from Kentucky for the capital of their native state.

New Goshen [ˌnū 'gōshən], village in Vigo County (J-3).

Laid out in 1853. The name Goshen is fairly popular in the U. S. and comes from the biblical land. The adjective New distinguishes this village from the city in Elkhart County.

New Harmony [ˌnū 'harmənē], town in Posey County (O-2).

Settled in 1814 by George Rapp and associates and named for Harmonie, Pennsylvania, site of their first settlement. In 1825 it was sold to Robert Owen, who renamed it New Harmony.

New Haven ['nū 'havən], fifth class city in Allen County (D-10).

Platted in 1839 and named for New Haven, Connecticut.

New Hope ['nū 'hōp], village in Owen County (K-5).

Established about 1870 and

named for a church here when the village was founded.

New Lancaster [ˌnū ˈlæŋkəstər], village in Tipton County (G-7).
Settled about 1845. The name comes from the English county and town, probably via an eastern state.

Newland [ˈnūlənd], village in Jasper County (D-4).
Laid out in 1906 on reclaimed marshlands, hence the name.

New Lebanon [ˌnū ˈlebənən], village in Sullivan County (L-3).
Settled around 1827 by Methodists and named for the biblical mountains. Since there was another town named Lebanon in Indiana, New was added. A post office was established here in 1836.

New Liberty [ˌnū ˈlibərdē], village in Washington County (M-8).
Liberty is a common name in the U. S. and probably was borrowed for its commendatory value.

New Lisbon [ˌnū ˈlizbən], village in Henry County (H-9).
Platted in 1833 and named for the town in eastern Ohio. Originally called Jamestown, commonly Jimtown, for one of the original proprietors, James Donaldsen.

New Lisbon [ˌnū ˈlizbən], village in Randolph County (F-11).
Platted in 1848. The name comes from the city in Portugal, perhaps via an eastern state.

New London [ˌnū ˈləndən], village in Howard County (F-6).

Laid out in 1845. Probably named for the city in Connecticut, perhaps via Ohio.

New Marion [ˌnū ˈmerēˌən], village in Ripley County (L-9).
First called Marion, but because there was already a town of that name in Indiana, the name was changed to New Marion in 1832, the year it was laid out. Apparently named for Francis Marion.

New Market [ˈnū ˌmarkət], village in Clark County (M-8).
Laid out in 1839 and allegedly so named because market wagons assembled here.

New Market [ˈnū ˌmarkət], town in Montgomery County (G-5).
Platted in 1872. Allegedly, when a gristmill here burned, another mill was rebuilt south of the first one and other businesses followed it. The new site was called New Market.

New Maysville [ˌnū ˈmāzˌvil], village in Putnam County (H-5).
Laid out around 1826 by Robert Biddle who named it for Maysville, Kentucky.

New Middletown [ˌnū ˈmidəlˌtaun], town in Harrison County (O-7).
Laid out in 1860 and formerly called Middletown.

New Mount Pleasant [ˌnū ˌmaunt ˈplezənt], village in Jay County (F-10).
Laid out in 1838, the town formerly was called Mount Pleasant, for a Quaker meeting house in Ohio.

New Otto ['nū 'atō], village in Clark County (M-9).

See Old Otto.

New Palestine [ˌnū 'pæləsˌtēn], town in Hancock County (H-7).

Laid out in 1838. The post office was known as Sugar Creek, the railroad station as Palestine, and the town as New Palestine. Because of these three names and the fact that there was already a Palestine in Kosciusko County, confusion resulted, and the post office and railroad station were renamed New Palestine in 1889.

New Paris [ˌnū 'perəs], village in Elkhart County (B-8).

Founded in 1838, the town was named for the French city. Early settlers were from Alsace-Lorraine.

New Pekin ['nū 'pēkən], town in Washington County (M-7).

Established about 1852 as a railroad station near the village of Pekin, for which it was named.

New Pennington [ˌnū 'piniŋtən], village in Decatur County (K-9).

Laid out in 1851 by Eli Pennington and named for him.

New Philadelphia [ˌnū 'filə'delfēə], village in Washington County (M-7).

Laid out in 1837 and named for Philadelphia, Pennsylvania.

New Pittsburg [ˌnū 'pitsˌbərg], village in Randolph County (F-10).

Platted in 1856 and named for Pittsburgh, Pennsylvania.

New Point ['nū ˌpoint], town in Decatur County (K-9).

Laid out in 1859 and formerly called Crackaway. A post office established in 1838 was called Rossburg, but the name was changed to New Point in 1870. Probably the name is descriptive.

Newport ['nūˌpōrt], county seat, town in Vermillion County (H-3).

Established in 1828 and perhaps named for Newport, Delaware.

New Providence [ˌnū 'pravədənts], town in Clark County (M-7).

Laid out in 1817. Probably the name was borrowed for devotional reasons.

New Richmond [ˌnū 'richˌmən(d)], town in Montgomery County (G-4).

Platted in 1830 by Samuel Kincaid, who named it for his hometown, New Richmond, Ohio.

New Ross ['nū ˌros], town in Montgomery County (G-5).

New Ross Post Office originally was established about a mile from Valley City, founded about 1841. In 1868 the post office was moved to Valley City, which then assumed the post office name. New Ross was named by local innkeeper George Dorsey for the English town, Ross, scene of an English battle.

New Salem [ˌnū 'sāləm], village in Rush County (J-9).

Laid out in 1831. Salem is a very popular name in the U. S. and probably was borrowed for its commendatory value.

New Salisbury ['nū 'salzˌberē], village in Harrison County (N-7).

116

Platted in 1839 by John Kepley and named for his home, Salisbury, North Carolina.

New Santa Fe ['nū ˌsæntə 'fā], village in Miami County (E-7).
Platted in 1902 and named for another town, Santa Fe, in the same county.

Newton ['nūtn] County (D-3).
Organized in 1859 and named for Sgt. John Newton, who served under Marion in the Revolutionary War.

Newton ['nūtn] (Bretzville), village in Dubois County (N-5).
See Bretzville.

Newton Stewart ['nūtn 'stūˌərt], village in Orange County (N-5).
Laid out in 1839 by William and Henry Stewart, who named it Newton Stewart. Allegedly, to their own name they added the name of their birthplace in Ireland.

Newtonville ['nūtnˌvil], village in Spencer County (O-5).
Laid out in 1865 and named for the Newton family, early local merchants. One of the founders was Bezaleel Newton.

Newtown ['nūˌtaun], town in Fountain County (G-4).
Platted in 1829 and established as a post office in 1831. Apparently the name is descriptive.

New Trenton ['nū 'trentn], village in Franklin County (K-10).
Laid out in 1816 and probably named for Trenton, New Jersey, perhaps via another state.

New Unionville ['nū 'yūnyənˌvil], village in Monroe County (K-6).
Established about 1906 and named for nearby Unionville, q.v.

Newville ['nūˌvil], village in Dekalb County (C-11).
Platted in 1837 and formerly called Vienna, though the post office was called Newville Post Office for its location in Newville Township.

New Washington ['nū 'woshiŋtən], village in Clark County (M-9).
Laid out in 1815, and a post office was established in 1824.

New Watson ['nū 'watsən], village in Clark County (N-8).
Established about a mile southeast of Watson, now Old Watson, q.v., and named for it.

New Waverly ['nū 'wāvərˌlē], village in Cass County (E-7).
Laid out in 1855. Probably named for Scott's Waverly novels with the adjective New added to distinguish it from the town in Morgan County.

New Winchester ['nū 'winchestər], village in Hendricks County (H-5).
Laid out in 1832. Perhaps named for the English town via an eastern state.

Nine Mile ['nain 'mail], village in Allen County (D-9).
A locational name, for the town is about 9 miles southwest of Ft. Wayne.

Nineveh ['ninəvə], village in Johnson County (J-7).

Settled about 1830 in Nineveh Township, which was named for nearby Nineveh Creek.

Nineveh Creek ['ninəvə 'krēk], stream.

Heads in Johnson County and flows southwest through Bartholomew County to Driftwood River 8 miles north of Columbus. Although the name appears biblical, allegedly it was first named Nineveh's Defeat, for Nineveh Berry who fell into the stream and nearly drowned while carrying a deer's carcass across the stream. A number of streams allegedly have been named for men who fell in them and were nearly drowned. For instance, see Beanblossom Creek.

Noble ['nōbəl] County (B-9).

Organized in 1836 and named for Noah Noble, governor of Indiana, 1831–37, when the county was organized.

Noble ['nōbəl], village in Jay County (F-11).

Named for Noble Township, which was named for Noah Noble, Indiana governor.

Noblesville ['nōbəlz,vil], county seat, fifth class city in Hamilton County (G-7).

Laid out in 1823 and probably named for James Noble, first U. S. Senator from Indiana. Local legend, however, says the town was named by one of the founders for his fiancée, Lavinia or Kathleen Noble. A typical oral account is: "John Conner and James Polk founded the town of Noblesville in 1823. At that time Polk was engaged to marry a woman from Indianapolis by the name of Kathleen Noble. Polk built a new home for his bride in the center of his newly discovered town. He planted a garden of vegetables in an outline which spelled out her name. He thought that this would symbolize his great love for Miss Noble. However, Miss Noble was not pleased. Instead, she was greatly enraged and insulted by the vegetable garden. Thus she broke her engagement to Polk. Sometime later a couple passing through the territory came to the Polk cottage, which was deserted, and saw the garden which he had planted. The man turned to the woman and asked, 'What is the name of this town?' His wife replied that this must be Noblesville because the garden said so."

Nora ['nōrə], village in Marion County (H-7).

In 1871 Peter Lawson named the post office here Nora for the town in southern Sweden.

Normal ['norməl], village in Grant County (F-8).

Never laid out, a post office was established as Slash in 1852. In 1880 the name was changed to Normal.

Normanda [,nor'mændə], village in Tipton County (F-7).

Laid out in 1849, and a post office was established in 1852.

Norman Station ['normən 'stāshən], village in Jackson County (L-6).

118

Founded in 1889 by John A. Norman, for whom it was named.

Norris ['norəs] (Harristown), village in Washington County (M-7). See Harristown.

Norristown ['norəsˌtaun], village in Shelby County (J-8).
Laid out in 1851 and named for Dr. James M. Norris, prominent physician.

North Belleville ['north 'belˌvil], village in Hendricks County (H-6).
The name is locational as the village was established on the railroad north of Belleville.

North Branch Garrison Creek [ˌnorth ˌbrænch 'gerəsən ˌkrēk], stream in Fayette County.
See Garrison Creek, for which it was named.

Northfield ['northˌfēld], village in Boone County (G-6).
A post office was established as Georgetown, for the first postmaster, George Shirts, in 1832. In 1834 when the village was laid out the name was changed to Northfield.

North Fork Salt Creek [ˌnorth ˌfork 'solt ˌkrēk], stream.
See Salt Creek.

North Grove ['north 'grōv], town in Miami County (E-7).
Platted in 1854 by William North and presumably named for the North family, as many of its citizens were of that name.

North Judson ['north 'jədˌsən], town in Starke County (C-5).

A post office was established in 1860, and the town was laid out in 1861. Perhaps a transfer name from one of the communities named Judson south of here.

North Landing ['north 'lændiŋ], village in Ohio County (L-11).
Founded in 1831 by R. F. North, for whom it was named. Originally it was called Grant's Creek, for a nearby stream, then North, and in 1865 North's Landing.

North Liberty ['north 'libərdē], town in St. Joseph County (B-6).
Founded in 1836. The name is locational, as it is located in the northern part of Liberty Township.

North Manchester ['north 'mænˌchestər], town in Wabash County (D-8).
Laid out in 1837 and formerly called Manchester, presumably for the city in England, perhaps via New England.

North Salem ['north 'sāləm], town in Hendricks County (H-5).
Laid out in 1835 and a post office was established in 1839. Probably a transfer name from southern Indiana or a southern state.

North Vernon ['north 'vərnən], fifth class city in Jennings County (L-8).
Platted in 1854 north of the older town of Vernon; hence, the name is locational.

North Webster ['north 'webˌstər], town in Kosciusko County (C-8).
Settled in 1841 and named for Malcolm Webster, landowner.

Nortonsburg ['nortnz͵bərg], village in Bartholomew County (K-8).

Never platted, the town was named for the Norton family, who operated a general store here. In 1886 a post office was established with Ephraim B. Norton as first postmaster.

Norway ['nor͵wā], village in White County (E-5).

Laid out in 1845 and named for the Scandinavian country, home of several settlers and the founder. Originally called Mt. Walleston.

Nottingham ['nadiŋ͵hæm], village in Wells County (E-10).

Platted in 1895 and named for the township in which it is located.

Nulltown ['nəl͵taun], village in Fayette County (J-10).

Founded in 1847 and named for the Null brothers who had a mill here. The original post office name was Ashland, which was changed to Null's Mills in 1848 and finally Nulltown in 1895.

Numa ['nūmə], village in Parke County (J-3).

Platted in 1836. The origin is uncertain, although some residents believe it is an Indian name. The name may be classical, for the traditional second king of Rome.

Nyesville ['naiz͵vil], village in Parke County (H-4).

Platted in 1871 by the Sand Creek Coal Company and named for its president, William H. Nye.

O

Oak [ōk] (Thornhope), village in Pulaski County (D-6).

See Thornhope.

Oakford ['ōk͵fərd] (Fairfield), village in Howard County (F-7).

Laid out in 1849 as Fairfield. Since there was already a town of that name in Indiana, the post office was called Oakford. Apparently both names are commendatory.

Oak Forest ['ōk 'forəst], village in Franklin County (J-10).

A post office was established here in 1848. Apparently the name is

commendatory as well as descriptive.

Oakland City ['ōklən(d) 'sidē], fifth class city in Gibson County (N-3).

Platted in 1856 and originally called Oakland, for oak groves on the town site.

Oaklandon [͵ōk'lændən], village in Marion County (H-7).

Platted in 1849 and originally called Oakland, for the numerous oak trees here. The name was changed to distinguish it from another town named Oakland.

Oaktown ['ōk‚taun], town in Knox County (L-3).

Formerly called Oak Station, it was laid out in 1867. Apparently the name is descriptive.

Oakville ['ōk‚vil], village in Delaware County (G-9).

Laid out in 1873 and called Pleasant Hill. The Post Office Department would not accept the name, so it was changed to Oakville. Both names seem to be commendatory.

Ober ['ōbər], village in Starke County (C-6).

Platted in 1889 and named for Ober Heath, pioneer resident.

Occident ['aksi‚dent; 'aksə-], village in Rush County (H-9).

Originally called Tail Holt, it was renamed when the post office was established in 1882.

Ockley ['aklē], village in Carroll County (F-5).

Laid out in 1884 and locally thought to be an Indian name of unknown origin.

Odell [‚ō'del; 'ō‚del], village in Tippecanoe County (F-4).

Named for Major John W. O'Dell, of the War of 1812 and the Black Hawk War. Soon after he arrived here in 1831 a settlement, O'Dell's Corners, sprang up. In 1871 a post office was established, and the name became Odell.

Odon ['ōdn], town in Daviess County (L-4).

Laid out in 1846. Earlier names were Clark's Spring, Clark's Prairie,

and Clarksburg, for George Rogers Clark; the present name comes from the Norse god, Odin.

Ogden ['agdən], village in Henry County (H-9).

Platted in 1829 and named for an engineer who worked on the construction of the National Road.

Ogden Dunes ['agdən 'dūnz], town in Porter County (B-4).

Established in 1925 and named for Francis A. Ogden, who once owned the land, and the dunes here.

Ohio [ō'hai‚ə; -ō] County (L-10).

Organized in 1844, the county is bordered on the east by the Ohio River, for which it was named.

Ohio River [ō'hai‚ə 'rivər; -ō], stream.

This river forms the entire southern boundary of Indiana. The name is Iroquois and means "beautiful." In 1680, LaSalle wrote of the river: "the Iroquois call it Ohio, and the Ottawas *Oligh-in-cipau.*"

Old Bargersville ['ōld 'bargərz‚vil], village in Johnson County (J-7).

Laid out in 1850 by Jefferson Barger, for whom the town was named. Formerly called Bargersville, q.v.

Old Bath [‚ōld 'bæth], village in Franklin County (J-10).

Originally called Colter's Corner but renamed Bath, for the township in which it is located, when a post office was established around 1840. The township was named for nearby medicinal springs. Now called Old

121

Bath to distinguish it from New Bath, q.v.

Oldenburg ['ōldən͵bərg], town in Franklin County (J-9).

Founded by German immigrants in 1837 who named the town for their birthplace in Germany.

Old Milan ['ōld 'mailən], village in Ripley County (K-10).

Laid out by David Brooks in 1854, just across the railroad from South Milan, and named Brooklin, for Brooks. The present name is for nearby Milan, q.v.

Old Otto ['ōld 'atō], village in Clark County (M-9).

A post office called Otto was established in 1864. Named for Judge Otto. New Otto is located about ½ mile west of Old Otto.

Old St. Louis [͵ōld ͵sānt 'lūus], village in Bartholomew County (K-8).

Laid out in 1836 by Lewis Reed and Abraham Zeigler and formerly called St. Louis, presumably for Lewis Reed. Old was added to distinguish it from nearby St. Louis Crossing, q.v.

Old Tip Town ['ōl(d) 'tip ͵taun], village in Marshall County (C-7).

Platted in 1850 as Tippecanoe Town, named for the river on which it is located. When it was bypassed by the railroad (see Tippecanoe), it was referred to as Old Tippecanoe Town, of which the present name is a variant form.

Old Watson ['ōld 'watsən], village in Clark County (N-8).

Laid out in 1876 and called Watson. The present name distinguishes it from nearby New Watson, q.v.

Olean [͵ōlē'æn], village in Ripley County (L-9).

Laid out in 1857 and named for Olean, New York, home of settlers.

Omega [͵ō'megə], village in Hamilton County (G-7).

A post office was established here in 1870. Named for the last letter in the Greek alphabet. According to local anecdote, the name was selected when a post office was established because the former name, Dogtown, was not acceptable; hence, "it was the last of 'Dogtown.'"

Ontario [͵an'terēō], village in Lagrange County (A-9).

Laid out in 1837 and named for the lake.

Onward ['onwərd], town in Cass County (E-7).

Laid out in 1869 and named for the post office here. Apparently the name is commendatory, but local legend says it comes from a remark local citizens made after loafing at the local store: "I must now plug onward."

Oolitic [ō'lidik; ū-], town in Lawrence County (L-6).

Platted in 1888 and named for the oolitic texture of its limestone.

Ora ['ōrə], village in Starke County (C-6).

Named for Ora Keller, son of the man who laid out the town in 1882.

Orange ['or(ə)nj; 'orinj] County (M-6).

Organized in 1816 and named for Orange County, North Carolina, from which early settlers came.

Orange ['or(i)nj; 'orənj], village in Fayette County (J-9).

Laid out in 1824 and named for Orange Township.

Orangeville ['or(ə)nj͵vil], village in Orange County (M-6).

Laid out in 1849 and named for the county in which it is located.

Orestes [o'restəs], town in Madison County (F-8).

Founded about 1876 and named for Orestes McMahan, son of the first postmaster.

Oriole ['ōrē͵ōl], village in Perry County (N-6).

Formerly known as Chestnut City, for the chestnut trees here; the name was changed to Oriole, for the bird, by the Post Office Department when a post office was established here in 1890.

Orland ['ōrlənd], town in Steuben County (A-10).

Settled in 1834 by Vermonters and called The Vermont Settlement. Later called Millgrove, but as there was another town of that name in Indiana, the name was changed to Orland. Allegedly the postmaster opened a hymnbook and named the town for the title of the first hymn he saw.

Orleans [͵or͵lēnz], town in Orange County (M-6).

Founded in March 1815, two months after Jackson's victory at New Orleans, for which it was named.

Ormas ['orməs], village in Noble County (C-8).

Laid out in 1856 and named for Ormas Jones, a resident.

Orrville ['or͵vil], village in Knox County (M-2).

A post office was established here in 1891. Probably named for the Orr family, prominent in county history. Edgar J. Orr was postmaster in 1904.

Osceola [͵ōsē'ōlə], town in St. Joseph County (B-7).

Originally called Bancroft's Mill, it was laid out in 1837 and named for the famous Seminole chief, whose name comes from *os-y-o-hul-la,* a ceremonial drink.

Osgood ['az͵gud], town in Ripley County (K-9).

Laid out in 1857 and named for the head surveyor of the railroad built here.

Ossian ['osē͵ən], town in Wells County (D-10).

Laid out in 1846 and named for Ossian Hall, County Old, Scotland, home of some of the early settlers.

Oswego [͵as'wēgō], village in Kosciusko County (C-8).

Laid out in 1837 and named for the town in New York. This Iroquoian name, meaning "flowing out," is appropriate, for the Hoosier town is located at the outlet of Tippecanoe Lake.

Otis ['ōdis; -us], village in LaPorte County (B-5).

A railroad station was established here in 1852. First called Salem Crossing, then LaCroix, then Packard, for Congressman Jasper Packard. Packard suggested the present name. The name was changed to Otis in 1872.

Otisco [ō'tiskō], village in Clark County (M-8).

Founded in 1854 and apparently named for Otisco Lake in New York.

Otterbein ['adər,bain; -bən], town in Benton County (F-4).

Platted in 1872 and named for Otterbein Brown, an early settler. William Otterbein Brown was the first postmaster and first schoolteacher.

Ottwell ['at,wel], village in Pike County (N-4).

Laid out in 1855 and called Pierceville until 1864. Formerly spelled Otwell. Apparently the name is from the personal name.

Ovid ['ōvəd] (New Columbus), village in Madison County (G-8).

Laid out in 1834 and called New Columbus, a name the town still shares. When the post office was established in 1837, it was called Ovid to avoid confusion with Columbus, Indiana. New Columbus possibly is for Columbus, Ohio. Ovid probably is for the classical poet, perhaps via New York.

Owasco [,ō'was,kō], village in Carroll County (F-5).

Laid out in 1884. The name, borrowed from the New York lake, is Iroquois and means "floating bridge."

Owen ['ō,ən] County (K-5).

Organized in 1819 and named for Colonel Abraham Owen of Kentucky, who was killed in the Battle of Tippecanoe.

Owen ['ō,ən], village in Clark County (N-9).

Named for Owen Township, which was named for John Owens, a county commissioner.

Owensburg ['ō,ənz,bərg], village in Greene County (L-5).

First platted in 1842 and named for Silbern Owens, a local blacksmith, who, with Lilbern Owens, laid out the town.

Owensville ['ō,ənz,vil], town in Gibson County (N-2).

Platted in 1817 and named for Thomas Owen, famous Kentuckian.

Oxford ['aksfərd], town in Benton County (F-4).

A popular American place name coming from the English town and university. When this town was organized in 1843, Judge David McConnell suggested the name, hoping that it might become an educational center. A local folk explanation says that Pine Creek was crossed at a ford here by wagons drawn by oxen. It was originally called Milroy, for a local commissioner, then Hartford, for the city in Connecticut.

Oxonia [ˌaks'ōnē͵ə] (Hitchcock), village in Washington County (M-7).
See Hitchcock.

P

Packerton ['pækərtən], village in Kosciusko County (C-8).
Platted about 1882 by John C. Packer and named for him.

Palestine ['pæləs͵tain] (Wynn), village in Franklin County (J-10).
See Wynn.

Palestine ['pæləs͵tain], village in Kosciusko County (C-7).
A post office established in 1830 was called Tipicanunk, a form of Tippecanoe. In 1839 the name was changed to Palestine for the biblical region.

Palmer ['po(l)mər; 'pa-], village in Lake County (B-4).
Named for Dennis Palmer, who platted the town in 1882.

Palmyra [ˌpæl'mairə], town in Harrison County (N-7).
Founded in 1810 by Hays McCallan and called McCallan's Crossroads, for him. In 1836 the town was laid out again and called Carthage. In 1839 lots were added, and the name was changed to Palmyra, apparently for the ancient city allegedly built by Solomon.

Paoli [ˌpā'ōlə; -ē], county seat, town in Orange County (M-6).

Platted in 1816 and named for Pasquale Paoli (1725–1807), a Corsican patriot and general, perhaps via Paoli, Pennsylvania, or Paoli Ashe, son of Samuel Ashe, governor of North Carolina and friend of Pasquale Paoli. According to one local legend, the name comes from a Swede named Oley who operated a toll road. People traveling along the road had to "pay Oley."

Paragon ['perə͵gan], town in Morgan County (J-6).
Founded in 1852. Apparently, the name is commendatory.

Paris ['perəs], village in Jennings County (L-8).
Laid out in 1829. Presumably named for the city in France.

Paris Crossing ['perəs 'krosiŋ], village in Jennings County (L-8).
Located along the railroad about a mile northwest of Paris, for which it was named.

Park [park], village in Greene County (L-5).
Originally called Parker, for settlers of that name. A post office established in 1866 was named Park.

Parke [park] County (H-4).

Organized in 1821 and named for Benjamin Parke, territorial congressman and judge.

Parker City ['parkər 'sidē], town in Randolph County (G-9).

Platted in 1851 and formerly called Morristown, probably for a local family. An early settler was Thomas W. Parker, and the present name perhaps honors him or his family.

Parkersburg ['parkərz͵bərg], village in Montgomery County (H-5).

A post office was established here in 1834, and the town was platted in 1835. Named for Nathaniel Parker, first postmaster, although for a few years after platting, the town was called Faithville, for Thomas Faith, co-founder.

Parr [par], village in Jasper County (D-4).

Platted in 1895 and named for Judge Simon Parr Kenton, who donated land for a railroad depot and switch here.

Parrottsville ['perəts͵vil] (Jacksons), village in Tipton County (F-7).

See Jacksons.

Patoka [pə'tōkə], town in Gibson County (N-3).

Settled in 1789 and platted in 1813, it was named for the Patoka River. Former names were Smithville, for John Smith, an early settler, and Columbia.

Patoka River [pə'tōkə 'rivər], stream.

About 100 miles long, it heads in Orange County and flows west through Crawford, Dubois, Pike, and Gibson counties to the Wabash River just south of the mouth of White River. The name is Miami for "Comanche," who often were held as slaves by the Illinois and Miamis. In French chronicles they are called *Padocquia* or *Padouca*.

Patricksburg ['pætriks͵bərg], village in Owen County (K-4).

Laid out in 1851 by Patrick Sullivan and named for him.

Patriot ['pātrē͵ət], town in Switzerland County (L-11).

Laid out in 1820 and named Troy, for Troy, New York. The present name is inspirational. One local anecdote says the name comes from "the Patriots," veterans of the Revolution who settled here, while a more likely account says that when the name was changed from Troy, town leaders wanted to rename the town Washington for the greatest patriot, but since there already were several towns of that name in Indiana, they settled for Patriot.

Patton ['pætn], village in Carroll County (E-5).

Laid out in 1883 by H. Patton, for whom the town was named.

Paxton ['pæks͵tən], village in Sullivan County (L-3).

Platted in 1868 and named for a nearby railroad station, which was established several years earlier.

126

Paynesville ['pānz͵vil], village in Jefferson County (M-9).

Named for Miller Payne, an early settler.

Peabody ['pē͵badē͟], village in Whitley County (D-9).

A post office was established here in 1883. Named for local businessman James Peabody.

Pecksburg ['peks͵bərg], village in Hendricks County (H-6).

Platted in 1853 and named for the first president of the Vandalia Railroad.

Peerless ['pir͵lus], village in Lawrence County (L-6).

Platted in 1891 and named for the Peerless Quarry here.

Pekin ['pēkin], village in Washington County (M-7).

Laid out in 1831 and apparently named for the city in China.

Pelzer ['pelzər], village in Warrick County (O-4).

A post office was located here in 1898. Named for the Pelzer family, who were early residents.

Pembroke ['pem͵brōk], village in Newton County (D-4).

Perhaps named for the Welsh county or town via an eastern state.

Pence [pents], village in Warren County (F-3).

Named for Frank R. Pence, who founded the town about 1902.

Pendleton ['pen(d)əl͵tən], town in Madison County (G-8).

Platted in 1830 by Thomas Pendleton, for whom it was named.

Penntown ['pen͵taun], village in Ripley County (K-10).

Laid out in 1837 and originally called Pennsylvaniaburg, as most of the settlers were from Pennsylvania. The present name is an abbreviated form of the earlier name.

Pennville ['pen͵vil], town in Jay County (F-10).

Established around 1836 and named for Penn Township, which was named for William Penn.

Pennville ['pen͵vil], village in Wayne County (H-10).

Laid out in 1836 and formerly called New Lisbon, Camden, and Penn, apparently for William Penn, as this was a Quaker meeting center.

Peoga [͵pē'ōgə], village in Brown County (J-7).

A post office was established here in 1898. The origin is uncertain, but some villagers have claimed that Peoga is an Indian word for "village."

Peoria [͵pē'ōrē͵ə], village in Franklin County (J-11).

A post office was located here in 1850. An alternate name of this village has been Ingleside. Peoria is from the name of a subtribe of the Illinois Indians, first applied to the city in Illinois.

Peoria [͵pē'ōrē͵ə], village in Miami County (E-7).

Platted in 1849. According to local legend, settlers passed through here on the way to Peoria, Illinois, and were so pleased with the locale that they stayed and named the place for their destination.

Peppertown ['pepər‚taun], village in Franklin County (J-10).

Platted in 1859 and named for an early settler, August Pepper.

Perkinsville ['pərkənz‚vil], village in Madison County (G-8).

Laid out in 1837 and named for William Parkins, an early settler. When the plat was recorded an error was made, however, and the name became Perkinsville.

Perry ['perē] County (O-5).

Organized in 1814 and named for Commodore Oliver Hazard Perry, who defeated the British in the Battle of Lake Erie in 1813.

Perrysburg ['perēz‚bərg], village in Miami County (D-7).

Platted in 1837 and presumably named for a resident or friend of the founders.

Perrysville ['perēz‚vil], town in Vermillion County (G-3).

Laid out in 1826 and named for Commodore O. H. Perry by James Blair, who served under Perry in the War of 1812.

Pershing ['pərshiŋ], village in Fulton County (D-6).

Named for the World War I General, J. J. Pershing.

Pershing ['pərzhiŋ] (East Germantown), town in Wayne County (H-10).

Laid out in 1827 and named Georgetown, for the proprietor, George Shortridge. In 1832 it was renamed Germantown, for German settlers from Pennsylvania, although the post office was called East Germantown to distinguish it from another Germantown in Indiana. In 1918, during World War I, the name was changed to Pershing, for General J. J. Pershing, since there was so much bitterness against Germany then.

Perth [pərth], village in Clay County (J-4).

Laid out in 1870 by Michael McMillan and named for Perth, Scotland, birthplace of the proprietor's ancestors.

Peru ['pē‚rū], county seat, fourth class city in Miami County (E-7).

Laid out in 1838 as Miamisport, for the Miami Indians. Apparently the present name is for the country in South America.

Petersburg ['pētərz‚bərg], county seat, fifth class city in Pike County (M-3).

Laid out in 1817 and named for Peter Brenton, an early settler and principal donor of land.

Peterson ['pēdər‚sən], village in Adams County (E-10).

Founded in 1870 and named for Smith Peterson of nearby Decatur.

Petersville ['pētərz‚vil], village in Bartholomew County (K-8).

For Peter S. Blessing, who laid out the town in 1874.

Petroleum [pə'trōl̩yəm], village in Wells County (E-10).

Laid out in 1894 in the midst of an oil field, for which it was named.

Pettit ['petət], village in Tippecanoe County (F-5).

A post office was established here in 1854. Pettit was the family name of early settlers, so the name comes from a local personal name.

Phenix ['fēniks], village in Wells County (E-10).

Established as a post office in 1889. Phenix, a variant spelling of Phoenix, is for the mythological bird. The name has been fairly popular in the U. S., so there is a possibility of borrowing from another state.

Philadelphia [ˌfilə'delˌfēˌə], village in Hancock County (H-8).

Laid out in 1838 and named for Philadelphia, Pennsylvania.

Philomath ['fai'lōməth], village in Union County (H-10).

Organized in 1833. The name is Greek for "lover of learning," apparently so named because Western Union Seminary was located here.

Phlox [flaks], village in Howard County (F-7).

Established by Quakers around 1847 and apparently named for the flower.

Pickamick River ['pikəˌmik 'rivər], stream.

See Iroquois River.

Pickard ['pikərd], village in Clinton County (F-6).

Laid out in 1844 and named for Joseph Pickard, local miller. Formerly called Pickard's Mill.

Pierceton ['pirsˌtən], town in Kosciusko County (C-8).

Laid out in 1852 and named for President Franklin Pierce. The post office first was called Deed's Creek and later Princeton.

Pierceville ['pirsˌvil], village in Ripley County (K-10).

A post office was established here in 1854. Named for the local Pierce family.

Pigeon River ['pijən 'rivər], stream.

Heads in Steuben County and flows northwest through Lagrange County to the St. Joseph River in Michigan. The name comes from the Potawatomi name, *Wabememe,* "White Pigeon."

Pike [paik] County (N-4).

Organized in 1817 and named for General Zebulon Montgomery Pike, who was killed in 1813 while commanding the attack on York, Canada.

Pikes Peak ['paiks 'pēk], village in Brown County (K-7).

A post office was established here in 1868. According to local legend, an early settler, James Ward, hearing of the gold rush, set out in a prairie schooner which carried the sign "Pikes Peak or Bust." When he arrived at Madison, however, he became homesick, so he purchased enough supplies to open a store and returned to Brown County. When his customers visited his store they would say, "Guess I'll go over to Pikes Peak for supplies," and the settlement became known as Pikes Peak.

Pikeville ['paik₁vil], village in Pike County (N-4).

Laid out in 1859 and named for Pike County.

Pilot Knob ['pailət 'nab], village in Crawford County (N-6).

A post office was located here in 1850. Named for a nearby peak of the same name.

Pimento [₁pai'ment₁ō], village in Vigo County (K-3).

Laid out in 1852. Formerly called Hartford, but renamed by the Post Office Department because there was already a Hartford, Indiana. Apparently the name comes from the sweet pepper, usually spelled "pimiento."

Pine [pain], village in St. Joseph County (B-6).

Allegedly so named for the tree but more likely for a local family name.

Pine Village ['pain 'vilij], town in Warren County (F-4).

Platted in 1851. A trading post here first was called Pine Village, allegedly for a lone pine tree that stood on the creek bluff here. The town is located on Big Pine Creek, though, and it is possible the name comes from the stream name.

Pinhook ['pin₁huk], (New Durham), village in LaPorte County (B-5).

Settled around 1830 and platted in 1847. First called New Durham, for New Durham Township, which was named for Durham, Greene County, New York. It was nicknamed Pinhook, which became the official name. According to local legend, "a woman entered a store in the town and left with a package of pins, having failed to pay for them." Another account says citizens of a nearby rival town gave New Durham its nickname. Probably the name is descriptive of roads converging here.

Pinhook ['pin₁huk], village in Lawrence County (L-6).

First settled about 1818. According to local legend, the town "received its name through the sale of pins [liquor?] in an illegal manner. No person in the community had a permit to sell whiskey by the drink. But in order to evade the law, one of the early merchants of the little community is said to have hit upon the idea of selling a customer a bent pin to use for a fishhook and giving him a drink of whiskey as a premium. Hence the name Pinhook." Another anecdote says, "Pinhook's name is related to the making of fish hooks from pins in earlier days." A third oral account probably explains the name: "Pinhook, it was thought, was named from a peculiar twist in the road at the little village."

Pinola [₁pin'ōlə], village in LaPorte County (B-5).

Allegedly named for pine trees on the townsite.

130

Pittsboro ['pits‚bərō; -burō], town in Hendricks County (H-6).

Settled in 1830 and originally called Pittsburg.

Pittsburg ['pits‚bərg], village in Carroll County (E-5).

Laid out in 1836 by Merkle, Kendall, and Co. and probably named for Pittsburgh, Pennsylvania.

Plainfield ['plān‚fēld], town in Hendricks County (H-6).

Laid out in 1839. Named by Quaker settlers, "the plain people." Presumably the name is commendatory.

Plainfield ['plān‚fēld], village in St. Joseph County (A-6).

Laid out in 1833. Probably the name was selected for its commendatory value.

Plainville ['plān‚vil], town in Daviess County (L-4).

Formerly called Stump Town because the timber had been cut and only stumps remained, the town was laid out in 1855. It received its present name for the level terrain here.

Plano ['plānō], village in Morgan County (J-5).

A post office was located here in 1889. The name is Spanish for "plain" or "level" and presumably is a transfer from a western state.

Plato ['plā‚tō], village in Lagrange County (B-9).

A post office was established here in 1890. Apparently named for the ancient Greek philosopher.

Plattsburg ['plæts‚bərg], village in Washington County (M-7).

A post office was located here from 1844 until 1845. The name may be a transfer from New York or Ohio.

Pleasant ['plezənt], village in Switzerland County (L-10).

Settled in 1817 but never platted. Named for the township in which it is located.

Pleasant Lake [‚plezənt 'lāk], lake in Steuben County.

The name of this 53-acre lake comes from the Indian name, *Nipcondish,* "Pleasant Waters."

Pleasant Lake [‚plezənt 'lāk], village in Steuben County (B-10).

Originally laid out in 1846 and named for the nearby lake of the same name.

Pleasant Mills [‚plezənt 'milz], village in Adams County (E-11).

Laid out in 1846. The name combines the subjectively descriptive "Pleasant" with the objectively descriptive "Mills," derived from the fact that it had the only gristmill in the area.

Pleasant Plain [‚plezənt 'plān], village in Huntington County (E-9).

Laid out in 1875 as Nixville, but the post office was named Pleasant Plain, which soon became the name of the village. The name is subjectively descriptive: "Old settlers say that the name was adopted because of the beautiful location of the place."

Pleasant Ridge [ˌplezənt 'rij], village in Jasper County (E-4).

Established around 1870 and so named for the pleasant view and ridges here.

Pleasant Valley [ˌplezənt 'vælē], village in Martin County (M-5).

Platted in 1850. Presumably the name is subjectively descriptive.

Pleasant View [ˌplezənt 'vyū], village in Shelby County (H-7).

The post office originally was called Wrights, for the first postmaster, Jordan Wright, then Doblestown, for William Doble, who platted a town by that name in 1837. Pleasant View, a commendatory name, began as a trading post in 1835 and was platted in 1836.

Pleasantville ['plezəntˌvil], village in Sullivan County (L-4).

Platted in 1864 by William Pleasant O'Haver and named for him.

Plevna ['plevˌnə], village in Howard County (F-7).

Originally called Pleasantville, then Pomeroy, after a local politician. A post office established here in 1879 was called Plevna, probably for the Bulgarian city of the same name.

Plummer ['pləmər], village in Greene County (F-4).

A post office was established here in 1889. Named for Thomas Plummer, early resident and member of the first board of county commissioners.

Plummers Creek [ˌpləmərz 'krēk], stream in Greene County.

This stream in southwest Greene County was named for Thomas Plummer, who lived nearby.

Plum Tree ['pləm ˌtrē], village in Huntington County (E-9).

Once called Yankee Town. The preesnt name, applied to a post office here in 1876, apparently comes from a large wild plum tree on the townsite at its founding.

Plymouth ['pliməth], county seat, fifth class city in Marshall County (C-6).

Platted in 1834 and apparently named for Plymouth, Massachusetts.

Poe [pō], village in Allen County (D-10).

Platted in 1848 by William Essig and named Williamsport for him. Poe was the old post office name, the origin of which is unknown.

Point Isabel ['point 'izəbel], village in Grant County (F-8).

Never laid out, the town was named for the Ohio town of the same name. A post office was established here in 1859.

Poison Creek ['poizən ˌkrēk], stream in Perry County.

This tributary of the Ohio River was named for the prevalence of milk sickness in the area.

Poland ['pōlənd], village in Clay County (J-4).

Founded in 1841 and named for James Alexander Poland, the settlement's first blacksmith.

132

Poling ['pōliŋ], village in Jay County (F-10).

Formerly called Polingtown, it was named for a local family. A post office called Poling was established in 1887. In 1888 William Poling was postmaster.

Poneto [pə'nētō], town in Wells County (E-9).

Platted in 1871 and formerly called Worthington, for a railroad superintendent. Since there was another Hoosier town of that name, confusion resulted, and allegedly residents coined Poneto because it did not resemble the name of any other town in the U. S.

Popcorn ['pap̬korn], village in Lawrence County (L-5).

Settled about 1880 and named for a nearby stream, Popcorn Creek. Of course, there are local legends explaining this unusual name. One goes: "A family came to visit from Vincennes to a family in Perry Township. The two families were always arguing about who raised the best corn. The man from Vincennes said, 'Your corn is popcorn compared to what we grow.' That's how Popcorn got its name."

Poplar Grove ['paplər 'grōv], village in Howard County (E-6).

Settled around 1847 and named for a large grove of poplars on the town site.

Portage ['pōrtij], fourth class city in Porter County (B-4).

Named for Portage Township, which was named for Portage County, Ohio.

Porter ['pōrtər] County (B-4).

Organized in 1836 and named for Commodore David Porter, commander of the *Essex* in the War of 1812.

Porter ['pōrtər], town in Porter County (B-4).

Founded about 1850 and named for the county. Henry Hageman founded a town near here in 1872 and named it Hageman, although the railroad station was called Porter and the post office, a mile from Hageman, was called Porter Post Office.

Portersville ['pōrtərz͵vil], village in Dubois County (M-4).

Established about 1818 and said to be named for a relative of one of the town proprietors, Arthur Harbison.

Portland ['pōrt͵lənd], county seat, fifth class city in Jay County (F-10).

Laid out in 1837 and named for Portland, Maine, hometown of Daniel W. McNeal, who platted the town.

Portland Mills ['pōrt͵lən(d) 'milz], village in Putnam County (F-10).

Established about 1821 and originally called Upper Raccoon, then Portland. Mills was added to distinguish it from another Portland in Indiana. A gristmill was built here in 1825.

Port Mitchell [͵pōrt 'michəl], village in Noble County (C-9).

Laid out in 1838 and apparently named for a local miller or one of his family.

133

Posey ['pōzē] County (O-2).

Organized in 1814 and named for General Thomas Posey, officer in the Revolution and governor of Indiana Territory, 1813–16.

Poseyville ['pōzē͵vil], town in Posey County (N-2).

Laid out in 1840 and named for Posey County. Called Palestine until 1852.

Pottersville ['patərz͵vil], village in Owen County (K-5).

Laid out in 1858. Apparently named for the personal name.

Powers ['pau͵ərz], village in Jay County (F-10).

Platted in 1868 and named for Andrew Powers, Jr., who laid out the town.

Prairie City ['prerē 'sidē], village in Clay County (J-4).

Laid out in 1869 by Absalom B. Wheeler and so named because it borders on what was already known as Wheeler's Prairie or Clay Prairie.

Prairie Creek ['prerē ͵krēk], stream in Daviess County.

Heads in eastern Daviess County and flows southeast across the county to West Fork White River at the Daviess-Knox county line near Maysville. The name is descriptive of the landscape through which the stream flows. Although prairie is a generic, it has become a rather common specific for streams in Indiana. There are small streams in Boone, Delaware, and Vigo counties called Prairie Creek and a small stream in Howard and Grant counties called Prairie Run.

Prairie Creek ['prerē ͵krēk], village in Vigo County (K-3).

Laid out in 1831 as Middleton. The post office name was Prairie Creek, though, for the nearby stream of the same name.

Prairieton ['prerēt͵n; -͵tən], village in Vigo County (J-3).

Laid out in 1837. Formerly called Hoggatt's Store, as Moses Hoggatt and his son, Robert, owned a store here. The post office was Honey Creek. The present name is for its location on the Honey Creek prairie.

Preble ['prebəl], village in Adams County (D-10).

Platted in 1884 and named for Preble Township, which was organized in 1838.

Prescott ['pres͵kat; -kət], village in Shelby County (J-8).

A post office called Prescott, apparently for the personal name, was established here in 1860, and the town was laid out in 1867.

Pretty Lake ['pritē 'lāk], lake in Marshall County.

Located 4 miles west of Plymouth, this lake covers 97 acres. Its name is subjectively descriptive.

Priam ['prai͵əm] (Trenton), village in Blackford County (F-9).

See Trenton.

Princeton ['prints͵tən], county seat, fifth class city in Gibson County (N-3).

Founded in 1814 and named for Captain William Prince, an early settler who became a representative in Congress.

Progress ['pra͵gres], village in Delaware County (G-9).
A post office was established here in 1900. Presumably the name is commendatory.

Prospect ['pra͵spekt], village in Orange County (M-5).
Established about 1836. The name probably was selected for its commendatory value.

Prosperity [͵pras'perətē], village in Madison County (G-8).
A post office was located here from 1853 until 1875. Apparently this is a commendatory name.

Providence ['pravə͵dens; -dənts], village in Johnson County (J-7).
Platted in 1837 and first called Union Village, as it is located in Union Township. The present name probably was applied for devotional reasons.

Pulaski [pu'læs͵kai; -kē] County (D-5).
Organized in 1840 and named in honor of Count Casimir Pulaski, a Polish general killed in the attack on Savannah in 1779 while fighting with the Americans in the Revolution.

Pulaski [pu'læs͵kai], village in Pulaski County (D-5).
Laid out in 1855 and named for the county.

Pumpkin Center [͵pəmpkin 'sentər], village in Orange County (M-6).
According to local legend, the name is for a local farmer's pumpkin patch, supposedly the largest in the state. The farmer grew enormous pumpkins, too: ". . . One year he grew a pumpkin that weighed 107 pounds. I know 'cause my uncle told me about it when I was little. Well, anyway, this old guy was so proud of his pumpkins that one day he put this sign up that said 'Duncan's Pumpkin Center of the World.' Well, folks thought this was real funny, and they started just calling his place Pumpkin Center, and that's what people call it to this day, and that's all I'm saying."

Pumpkin Center ['pəŋkin 'sentər], village in Washington County (M-7).
This name is found in nearby Orange county, too, as well as in South Dakota, where the name was humorously applied "to denote a place excessively rural and isolated."

Purcell ['pərsəl], village in Knox County (M-3).
Named for Andrew Purcell, on whose farm a railroad station and post office, established in 1871, were located. Formerly Purcell Station and Purcells.

Putnam ['pət͵nəm; 'pət͵mən] County (H-5).
Organized in 1822 and named for General Israel Putnam, officer in the American Revolution.

135

Putnamville [ˈpət͵nəm͵vil; ˈpət͵mən-], village in Putnam County (J-5).

Laid out in 1831 and named for the county in which it is located.

Pyrmont [ˈpir͵maunt], village in Carroll County (F-5).

First known as Wildcat Corner. The post office formerly was called Featherhuff's Mills, with John Featherhuff as the first postmaster. In 1866 the name was changed to Pyrmont, apparently for the German principality, Waldeck-Pyrmont.

Q

Quaker [ˈkwākər], village in Vermillion County (H-3).

First called Quaker Point, for Quakers who settled here. In 1866 the name became Quaker Hill, and in 1894 the name was changed to Quaker.

Quakertown [ˈkwākər͵taun], village in Union County (J-10).

Originally called Millboro, for the grist and woolen mills here. The present name, applied to a post office established in 1866, is for the Quakers who lived here. The first settler was Nathan Henderson, a Quaker, who came here before 1826.

Queensville [ˈkwēnz͵vil], village in Jennings County (K-8).

A post office named Queensville was established in 1847, and the village was laid out in 1848.

Quercus Grove [͵k(w)ərkəs ˈgrōv], village in Switzerland County (L-10).

Sometimes called Bark Works, the town was settled in 1816 by Daniel D. Smith and others, who ground and packed oak bark to send to England for dyes, hence the name Quercus Grove, i.e., "Oak Grove."

Quincy [ˈkwinsē], village in Owen County (J-5).

Laid out in 1853, and a post office was established in 1854.

R

Raber [ˈrābər], village in Whitley County (D-9).

A post office was established here in 1884. Named for Samuel Raber, pioneer resident.

Raccoon [͵ræˈkūn], village in Putnam County (H-5).

Laid out in 1880 and called Lockridge for R. Z. Lockridge, local landowner. The present name comes from the railroad station here, named for nearby Big Raccoon Creek.

Raccoon Lake [ˌræˈkūn ˈlāk] (Mansfield Reservoir), lake in Parke County.

This 2060-acre lake at Raccoon Lake State Recreational Area was named Raccoon for the stream it was built on. The name Mansfield Reservoir is for the nearby town.

Radioville ['rādēōˌvil], village in Pulaski County (C-5).

Founded in 1934.

Radley ['rædˌlē], village in Grant County (F-8).

Originally called Elliotville, for a local family name. When a post office was established in 1899, it was called Radley, also for a personal name.

Radnor ['rædnər], village in Carroll County (F-5).

A post office was established here in 1883. Thought to be an Indian name of unknown meaning, but more likely it is for the county in Wales, perhaps via Pennsylvania.

Raglesville ['rægəlzˌvil], village in Daviess County (L-4).

Laid out in 1837 and probably named for John Ragle, the first postmaster.

Ragsdale ['rægzˌdāl], village in Knox County (M-3).

A post office was established here in 1917. Probably named for the Ragsdale family, prominent in county history.

Rainsville ['rānzˌvil], village in Warren County (F-3).

Platted in 1833 by Isaac Rains and named for him. Rains settled here in 1832 and built a mill.

Raintown ['rānˌtaun], village in Hendricks County (H-6).

Established about 1870 and named for Hiram Rain, who had a sawmill here.

Raleigh ['ralē], village in Rush County (H-9).

Platted in 1847 and named for Raleigh, North Carolina, home of some of the settlers.

Ramsey ['ræmˌzē], village in Harrison County (N-7).

Named for H. C. Ramsey, who laid out the town in 1883.

Randolph ['rænˌdo(l)f] County (G-10).

Organized in 1818 and probably named for Thomas Randolph, territorial attorney general who was killed in the Battle of Tippecanoe, although some sources say for Randolph County, North Carolina.

Randolph ['rænˌdo(l)f], village in Randolph County (F-10).

Formerly Randolph Station, it was laid out in 1867 and named for the county in which it is located.

Range Line ['rānj 'lain], village in Lake County (C-4).

So named for its location on the survey line.

Raub [rab], village in Benton County (E-3).

Laid out in 1872 by A. D. Raub, for whom it was named.

Raymond ['rāmən(d)], village in Franklin County (J-11).
Platted in 1903 and probably named for the personal name.

Rays Crossing ['rāz 'krosiŋ], village in Shelby County (J-8).
Originated as a station point in the early 1870's and named for the Ray family.

Raysville ['rāz₁vil], village in Henry County (H-9).
Laid out in 1832 and named for James R. Ray, fourth governor of Indiana.

Red Cloud ['red 'klaud], village in Knox County (M-3).
A post office was established here by 1875. Perhaps the name comes from the famous Sioux chief, Red Cloud, for whom other settlements in the U. S. were named.

Reddington ['rediŋ₁tən], village in Jackson County (L-8).
Laid out in 1837 and named for Redding Township, in which it is located.

Redkey ['red₁kē], town in Jay County (F-10).
Originally laid out in 1854. First called Half Way, for a nearby stream, but platted as Mt. Vernon. James Redkey platted an addition in 1867, and it was renamed for him. Locally it has been called Lick Skillet, Grab All, and Buzzard's Roost, allegedly for the scanty

meals served sawmill hands at a local boarding house.

Reed [rēd], village in Delaware County (G-9).
Platted as Reed's Station in 1877 by William Reed and named for him.

Reelsville ['rēlz₁vil], village in Putnam County (J-4).
Laid out in 1852 by John Reel and named for him. He settled here in 1826.

Reiffsburg ['raifs₁bərg], village in Wells County (E-10).
Platted by John Reiff in 1851 and named for him.

Remington ['remiŋ₁tən], town in Jasper County (E-4).
Laid out in 1860 and formerly called Carpenter's Creek and Carpenter's Station, for a nearby stream. In 1861 the present name was adopted for a merchant who established a general store here that year but remained only a few months.

Reno ['rēnō], village in Hendricks County (H-5).
Platted 1870. The name is found in several states and usually honors the American general Jesse Lee Reno, who was killed in the battle of South Mountain, Maryland, in 1862.

Rensselaer [₁ren(t)sə'lir], county seat, fifth class city in Jasper County (D-4).
Named for James Van Rensselaer, a merchant from New York

who founded the town in 1837 and operated a gristmill here.

Retreat [ˌrēˈtrēt], village in Jackson County (L-8).
Established by 1850. Apparently the name is commendatory suggesting withdrawal and seclusion.

Rexville [ˈreksˌvil], village in Ripley County (L-9).
A post office was located in 1870. Named for the Rex family who lived here.

Reynolds [ˈrenəldz], town in White County (E-5).
Named for Benjamin Reynolds, who founded the town about 1854.

Rhodes [rōdz], village in Vermillion County (J-3).
Platted in 1903 by the Brazil Block Coal Co.

Riceville [ˈraisˌvil], village in Crawford County (N-5).
Founded around 1882 and named for Wash Rice, a prominent businessman.

Richland [ˈrichˌlænd], village in Rush County (J-9).
Laid out in 1854 and named for the township in which it is located. The township was named for the quality of the soil here.

Richland Center [ˌrichlənd ˈsentər], village in Fulton County (C-6).
A post office was established here in 1878 and named for Richland Township, in which it is located.

Richland City [ˌrichlənd ˈsidē], village in Spencer County (O-4).

Laid out in 1861 and so named for the rich farmland here.

Richland Creek [ˈrichlənd ˈkrēk], stream in Greene County.
This branch of Beech Creek in northeastern Greene County was named for the good farmland along it.

Richmond [ˈrichˌmənd], county seat, second class city in Wayne County (H-10).
Platted in 1816 and named Smithville, for the proprietor, John Smith. An adjoining town was laid out in 1818 by Jeremiah Cox and called Coxborough, for him. Later in 1818 the two towns were incorporated together as Richmond. The name was selected from several suggested names for its commendatory idea of richness of soil.

Richvalley [ˈrichˈvælē], village in Wabash County (E-7).
Settled around 1827 by Jonathan Keller and called Keller's Station, for him. The present name describes the fertility of surrounding farmlands.

Riddle [ˈridəl], village in Crawford County (N-6).
A post office was established here in 1892. Named for a Civil War veteran, Colonel Riddle.

Ridgeville [ˈrijˌvil], town in Randolph County (F-10).
Originally platted in 1837 and re-platted in 1853. The name is descriptive of the townsite on slightly elevated land.

Ridgeway ['rij͵wā], village in Howard County (F-6).

A post office was located here in 1879. Named for the Ridgeway family, local store owners.

Rigdon ['rigdən], village in Madison County (F-8).

Laid out in 1851, the town first was named Independence, but the post office was called Rigdon, for Dr. Prior Rigdon, an early settler.

Riley ['railē; -lā], town in Vigo County (J-3).

Platted in 1836 as Lockport because of its location on the Wabash and Erie Canal. The post office was named Riley, for the township it is in, by the Post Office Department because there is another Lockport, Indiana.

Rileysburg ['railēz͵bərg], village in Vermillion County (G-3).

A post office was established here in 1887 and called Rileysburgh, apparently for the personal name. In 1893 the spelling was changed to Rileysburg. The village was platted in 1904.

Ripley ['riplē] County (K-9).

Organized in 1818 and named for General Eleazar Wheelock Ripley, officer in the War of 1812.

Rising Sun [͵raisiŋ 'sən], county seat, fifth class city in Ohio County (L-11).

Platted in 1814. "The name was suggested by the grandeur of the sunrise over the Kentucky hills above the town of Rabbit Hash, across the river." Local legend offers another explanation: "That's how Rising Sun got its name. They was going down the river [Ohio River], and the sun was a comin' up, an' they said, 'Look at the rising sun.' And that's right about along where Rising Sun is, an' that's how they named it. The Indians give Rising Sun its name."

Rivare [ri'ver] (Bobo), village in Adams County (D-11).

Platted in 1883. The railroad name was Rivare, apparently a corruption of Antoine Rivard, an Indian who was awarded the only reservation in the county. The post office was named Bobo, for a circuit judge.

River ['rivər] (Lancaster), village in Huntington County (E-9).

See Lancaster.

River Deshee [͵rivər də'shē], stream in Knox County.

Flows southwest to the Wabash River. The name apparently is a corruption of the French name, *Rivière du Chien,* "Dog River," which appears on early maps.

Riverside ['rivər͵said], village in Fountain County (F-4).

Platted in 1857 and named for its location on the Wabash River.

Riverton ['rivər͵tən], village in Sullivan County (L-3).

Laid out in 1887 and so named because of its location on the Wabash River.

Roachdale ['rōch͵dāl], town in Putnam County (H-5).

A post office was established here in 1880. First called Langsdale, for the editor of the Greencastle *Banner,* it was renamed Roachdale for the railroad station here, which was named for Judge Roach, director of the Monon Railroad.

Roann [͵rō'æn], town in Wabash County (D-7).

Platted in 1853. Only legends explain the origin of this name. One version says: "During a time of high water, a girl by the name of Ann was in a boat on the river. As she was attempting to get back to shore, the current was swiftly carrying her downstream. Suddenly she was whirled into a place where the current was not so strong, and her father, who had been watching, helpless to aid, called, 'Row, Ann, row, Ann!' So from this the town is said to have received the name." More likely, the town was named for Roanne, France.

Roanoke ['rō(ə)n͵ōk], town in Huntington County (D-9).

A sawmill built here in 1845 was called Roanoke Mills. A post office established in 1846 was called Roanoke. The name comes from the Virginia Indians and refers to their shell money.

Roanoke Station [͵rōnōk 'stāshən], village in Huntington County (D-9).

Established as a railroad station about a mile southeast of Roanoke, for which it was named.

Roberts ['rabərts], village in Fountain County (F-4).

Founded in 1883 and named for a resident, J. H. Roberts.

Rob Roy ['rab ͵roi], village in Fountain County (F-4).

Platted in 1828, it was named in 1826 for the Scottish outlaw, Rob Roy, by John Foster, who was fond of Scott's novels.

Rochester ['ra͵chestər], county seat, fifth class city in Fulton County (C-7).

Laid out in 1835 and probably named for Rochester, England, perhaps via Rochester, New York. There was a mill owner here named Rochester, too.

Rock Creek ['rak ͵krēk], village in Huntington County (E-9).

A variant name has been Rock Creek Center, from its location in the center of Rock Creek Township, established in 1842 and named for Rock Creek, a nearby stream with a rocky bed.

Rockfield ['rak͵feld], village in Carroll County (E-6).

Platted in 1856, the town is located in Rock Creek Township, so possibly there was a transfer of part of the name; however, it is commonly held that the town was so named because of the rocky soil here.

Rockford ['rak͵fərd], village in Jackson County (L-8).

Laid out in 1830 and so named because it is located "at a point where the bed of the White River is composed of slate rock, forming a good ford."

Rockford ['rak,fərd] (Barbers Mills), village in Wells County (E-9).

Platted in 1849 and formerly called Barbers Mills, as Hallett Barber had a sawmill here. The alternate name, Rockford, is descriptive of a ford on Rock Creek.

Rock Hill ['rak 'hil], village in Spencer County (O-4).

Named for an outcrop of rock at the site of an elementary school here.

Rocklane ['rak'lān], village in Johnson County (J-7).

Settled around 1843 and originally called Clarksburg. Locally thought to be so named for the rocky soil.

Rockport ['rak,pōrt], county seat, fifth class city in Spencer County (O-4).

Established in 1817, the site was called Hanging Rock by settlers because of a projecting rock formation, which also was known as Lady Washington's Rock, once here. The rock formation gave the town its present name.

Rockville ['rak,vil], county seat, town in Parke County (H-4).

Laid out in 1823 and named for a large rock, now on the courthouse lawn.

Rogersville ['rajərz,vil], village in Henry County (G-9).

Platted in 1837 by Joseph Rogers and John Colburn and named for Rogers.

Roll [ral], village in Blackford County (E-9).

A post office was established here in 1881. Named for Mathias Roll, an early settler.

Rolling Prairie ['rōliŋ 'prerē], village in LaPorte County (A-5).

Platted in 1853 as Portland. The present name, descriptive of the undulating terrain, was adopted by the post office and railroad.

Rome [rōm], village in Perry County (O-6).

Laid out in 1818 and originally called Washington, for President Washington, but since there were other towns of that name, the name was changed to Franklin, for Benjamin Franklin, the same year. It was named Rome, for the classical city, in 1819.

Rome City ['rōm 'sitē], town in Noble County (B-9).

Founded about 1837 when Sylvan Lake was made. According to one anecdote, both French and Irish workers were employed on the dam, and the French were given the best quarters. When the Irish demanded better living conditions, the superintendent of construction led the French against the Irish. The Irish were told to "do as the Romans do," and called their camp Rome. When the town was platted in 1839 on the campsite, it was called Rome City.

Romney ['ram,nē], village in Tippecanoe County (F-5).

Founded in 1831 and first called Columbia. The present name is for Romney, West Virginia, home of some of the settlers.

Romona [rəˌmōnə], village in Owen County (K-5).

Laid out in 1819 by Adam Brinton and called Brintonville. The present name is for Helen Hunt Jackson's popular novel, *Ramona,* and was adopted, though misspelled, following its publication in 1884.

Roseburg [ˈrōzˌbərg], village in Union County (J-10).

Named for the Rose family. General John B. Rose came here in 1817 and helped organize the county.

Rosedale [ˈrōzˌdāl], town in Parke County (J-3).

Named in 1860 by railroad officials for Chauncey Rose, prominent early settler and promoter and stockholder of a railroad.

Roseland [ˈrōzˌlænd], town in St. Joseph County (A-7).

Allegedly so named because of the numerous wild roses in the vicinity; however, the Rose family was important in county history.

Roselawn [ˈrōzˈlon; -lan], village in Newton County (C-3).

Laid out in 1882 and apparently named for two of the founders, Orlando and Bell Rose.

Ross [ros; ras], village in Lake County (B-3).

Founded about 1857 and named for William Ross, an early settler.

Rossburg [ˈrosˌbərg], village in Decatur County (K-9).

Laid out in 1836 and probably named for the personal name.

Rosston [ˈrosˌtən], village in Boone County (G-6).

A post office was established here in 1886. Named for the Ross brothers whose farm adjoined the town.

Rossville [ˈrosˌvil], town in Clinton County (F-6).

Platted in 1834 and named for John Ross, an early county associate judge.

Roundgrove [ˈraun(d)ˈgrōv], village in White County (E-4).

A post office was established here in 1878. Named for Round Grove Township, in which it is located.

Royal Center [ˈroi(ə)l ˈsentər], town in Cass County (D-6).

Laid out in 1846 and named for Royal Center, New York.

Royalton [ˈroilˌtən], village in Boone County (H-6).

Established in 1832 and formerly called Rodmans; the name was changed to Royalton in 1838.

Royerton [ˈroi(y)ərtən], village in Delaware County (F-9).

Named for John Royer, who established the town in 1870.

Rugby [ˈrəgbē], village in Bartholomew County (K-8).

A post office was established in 1884 and apparently named for the English town.

Runnymede ['rənē͵mēd], village in LaPorte County (C-5).

Apparently named for the meadow in England where the Magna Charta was granted in 1215.

Rural ['rurəl; -ol], village in Randolph County (G-10).

Established around 1870 and sometimes called Wood's Station, apparently for Joseph Wood who lived here. The present name comes from the local post office.

Rush [rəsh] County (J-9).

Organized in 1822 and named for Dr. Benjamin F. Rush, physician, soldier in the Revolution, and a signer of the Declaration of Independence.

Rush Creek Valley ['rəsh ͵krēk 'vælē], village in Washington County (M-7).

A post office was established here in 1871. Named for the stream on which it is located.

Rushville ['rəsh͵vil], county seat, fifth class city in Rush County (J-9).

Founded in 1822 as the seat of Rush County, for which it was named.

Rusk [rəsk], village in Martin County (M-5).

Settled in 1836 and named for either two Rusk brothers, doctors in the Civil War, who were born here, or Jeremiah McLain Rusk, congressman and Secretary of Agriculture.

Russellville ['rəsəl͵vil], town in Putnam County (H-4).

Laid out in 1829 and named for Russell Township, in which it is located.

Russiaville ['rūshə͵vil], town in Howard County (H-4).

Laid out in 1845. The name is a corruption of Richardsville, the French name of *Pin-je-wah,* a Miami chief. Richardsville generally was pronounced as Rusherville and sometimes written accordingly. See Howard County.

Rutland ['rət͵lənd], village in Marshall County (C-6).

A post office named Cavender, for postmaster Edward Cavender, was established here in 1883. In 1884 the name was changed to Rutland. Perhaps named for the English county via an eastern state.

Rye [rai] (Toto), village in Starke County (C-5).

See Toto.

S

St. Bernice [͵sānt ͵bər'nēs], village in Vermillion County (H-3).

A post office named Jones, for local landowner Philip Jones, was located here in 1862. In 1867 the post office name was changed to St. Bernice, and in 1905 the village was platted as St. Bernice.

St. Croix ['sānt 'kroi; -'kraks], village in Perry County (N-6).

Founded in 1855 by Father Dion, who named it St. Croix, French for "Holy Cross."

St. Henry ['sānt 'henrē], village in Dubois County (N-5).

A post office was established as St. Henry in 1870 and the village was platted in 1874. Perhaps named for a congregation organized at Henryville in 1862. Henry Hogg, for whom it was possibly named, was a local Benedictine priest.

St. James ['sānt 'jāmz], village in Gibson County (N-3).

A post office was established here in 1878. Named for the St. James Roman Catholic Church here.

St. Joe ['sānt 'jō], town in Dekalb County (C-10).

Laid out in 1875 and named for nearby St. Joseph River.

St. John ['sānt 'jan], town in Lake County (B-3).

Settled in the 1830's. Earlier called Western Prairie and Prairie West. Laid out in 1881 and named for the township, which was named for John Hack, the first German to settle here. Saint was added for euphony.

St. Joseph ['sānt 'jōzəf] County (B-6).

Organized in 1830 and named for the St. Joseph River.

St. Joseph ['sānt 'jōzəf], village in Floyd County (N-8).

Located near the Clark-Floyd county line, this German Catholic community was settled around 1846, and the first church was built in 1853. The settlement first was called St. Joseph's Hill, for devotional reasons and for the hilly countryside.

St. Joseph ['sānt 'jōzəf], village in Vanderburgh County (O-2).

Named for St. Joseph's Catholic Church, built here in 1841.

St. Joseph River ['sānt 'jōzəf 'rivər], stream.

Heads in Michigan and flows southwest through Elkhart County to South Bend in St. Joseph County, then northwest into Michigan again. The Potawatomi name was *Sahg-wah-se-be*, "Mystery River." The present name, for the Virgin Mary's husband, was applied by Catholic explorers.

St. Louis Crossing ['sānt ˌlūus 'krosiŋ], village in Bartholomew County (K-8).

Laid out in 1864 on the railroad west of St. Louis, for which it was named. See Old St. Louis.

St. Marks ['sānt 'marks], village in Dubois County (N-5).

Platted in 1872. Apparently a devotional name.

St. Marys ['sānt 'merēz] (Haymond), village in Franklin County (K-10).

A post office was established here in 1861 and called Haymond, probably for a personal name. The alternate name, St. Marys, is for a Catholic church here.

145

St. Marys ['sānt 'merēz], village in Vigo County (J-3).

Originally Thrall's Station. St. Mary of the Woods parish was established here in 1837, and the village was named for it.

St. Maurice ['sānt 'morəs], village in Decatur County (J-9).

Laid out in 1859 around a Catholic church, for which it was named.

St. Meinrad ['sānt 'main͵ræd; -rəd], village in Spencer County (O-5).

Settled in 1836, laid out in 1861, and named for the Catholic monastery here.

St. Omer ['sānt 'omər], village in Decatur County (J-8).

Laid out in 1834. Apparently named for St.-Omer in France.

St. Paul ['sānt 'pol], town in Decatur and Shelby counties (J-8).

Founded in 1853 and first called Paultown, for the first settler, Jonathan Paul. Laid out in Decatur County in 1854 by John Paul, Jonathan's son, but the additions are in Shelby County.

St. Peter ['sānt 'pēdər], village in Franklin County (K-10).

Established in 1853 as a German Catholic settlement and named for a church here.

St. Philips ['sænt 'filəps; sānt-], village in Posey County (O-2).

German Catholic settlers built their community around their church. A post office was established as St. Philip in 1872.

St. Thomas ['sānt 'taməs], village in Knox County (M-3).

A post office was established here in 1896. Probably named for the St. Thomas Church, one of the oldest in the county, that once served as a place of election.

St. Wendel ['sænt 'wendəl; sānt-], village in Posey County (O-2).

A post office called St. Wendels was established in 1852. Supposedly named for Wendel Wasman, early settler who was the principal donor for the construction of a Catholic church here.

Salamonia ['sælə'mōnē; -mōn͵yə], town in Jay County (F-11).

Originally called Lancaster, it was platted in 1839. Renamed for the Salamonie River.

Salamonie River ['sælə͵mōnē 'rivər], stream.

Heads in Jay County and flows northwest through Blackford, Wells, Huntington, and Wabash counties to the Wabash River near Lagro. The name is a corruption of the Miami name, *On-sah-la-mo-nee,* which was their name for bloodroot. Actually the word means "yellow paint," as the Indians made a yellow dye from the bloodroot. The Miami chief LaGros, who lived opposite the mouth of the river, had the same name, so the stream may have been named for him or he for the stream.

Salem ['sāləm] (Steele), village in Adams County (E-11).

Platted in 1866 and named for Salem, Massachusetts. The alternate name comes from Major George W. Steele, an Indiana congressman.

Salem ['sāləm], county seat, fifth class city in Washington County (M-7).

Platted in 1814 and named for Salem, North Carolina.

Salem Center ['sāləm 'sentər], village in Steuben County (B-10).

Established in 1843 and named for the township in which it is located.

Saline City ['sālēn 'sid̠ē; sə'lēn], village in Clay County (J-4).

Laid out in 1870 and called Saline, for a salt lick here in pioneer days. In 1872 the name was changed to Saline City.

Salt Creek ['solt ˌkrēk], stream.

Heads at the outlet of Monroe Reservoir in Monroe County and flows south through Lawrence County to East Fork White River 4 miles southwest of Bedford. The North Fork Salt Creek, at the inlet of the reservoir, heads in Brown County. Salt springs were located and worked near the stream; hence, the name is descriptive.

Saltillo ['sælˌtilō; ˌsæl'tilō], town in Washington County (M-6).

Platted in 1849 and named for the Mexican city occupied by U. S. troops in the Mexican War.

Saluda [sə'lūdə], village in Jefferson County (M-9).

A post office was established in 1828. Named for Saluda Township, in which it is located. The name ap-

pears in other states and originally was an Indian name applied to a river and meaning "river of corn."

Samaria [sə'merēˌə], village in Johnson County (J-7).

Platted in 1852 and first called Newburg. The post office here once was called Musselman, for the postmaster. The present name comes from the biblical city.

Sandborn ['sænˌbərn], town in Knox County (L-4).

Laid out in 1868 and named for a civil engineer on the Indianapolis and Vincennes Railroad.

Sand Creek ['sæn(d) 'krēk], stream.

About 50 miles long, it heads in Decatur County and flows southwest through Jennings County to East Fork White River east of Jonesville. The name is a translation of the Indian name, *Laque-ka-ou-e-nek,* "water running through sand."

Sandcut Farms ['sæn(d)kət 'farmz], village in Vigo County (J-3).

Formerly called Sand Cut and Sandcut, it was established about 1927 and apparently named for the sandy soil.

Sanders ['sændərz], village in Monroe County (K-6).

Platted in 1892 and named for one of the oldest residents, Billy Sanders.

Sandford ['sæn(d)fərd], village in Vigo County (J-3).

A post office established here in 1840 was called New Market. In 1855 the post office name was

147

changed to Sandford. The village was laid out in 1854.

Sandusky ['sænˌdəskē], village in Decatur County (J-9).

Laid out in 1882. The name probably comes from the city, county, river, and bay in Ohio.

Sandytown ['sændēˌtaun], village in Vermillion County (H-3).

So named for the sandy soil here.

San Jacinto [ˌsæn ˌjə'sintō], village in Jennings County (L-9).

Probably named for the San Jacinto River in Texas, site of the famous battle in which Sam Houston defeated Santa Anna in 1836 and decided the independence of Texas.

San Pierre ['sæn 'pi(ə)r; Pē'er], village in Starke County (C-5).

Laid out in 1854 and originally called Culvertown, while the post office formerly was named Pierre, allegedly for a French-Canadian named Pierre who started a saloon here.

Santa Claus ['sæntə ˌkloz], town in Spencer County (O-5).

Platted in 1846. The suggested name was Santa Fe; however, there was already a Santa Fe in Indiana, so Santa Claus jocularly was suggested as an alternative since it was around Christmas. The name has given rise to several local legends which attempt to explain it. One story goes: "Santa Claus Land is located at Highway 162 and 245 in southern Indiana. It was founded by German pioneers on Christmas Eve in 1852 during a village meeting to find a name for their settlement. Snow was very deep, and travel was almost impossible. When all of the settlers arrived, they began proposing names, but none suited them, when all of a sudden the door was swung open, and there stood a man dressed in a Santa Claus costume. They were all pretty drunk and ready for anything, so one of them suggested it be named Santa Claus and thus it was named Santa Claus, Ind."

Santa Fe ['sæntə 'fā], village in Miami County (E-7).

Platted in 1845 and formerly known as Old Santa Fe to distinguish it from New Santa Fe in the same county. Apparently the name is a transfer from a western state.

Saratoga [ˌserə'tōgə], town in Randolph County (F-10).

Platted in 1875 and probably named for Saratoga, New York, perhaps suggested by the name on a railroad car. Several local legends have arisen to explain the name. One story goes: "While looking for a name the postmaster was in Albright's general store when in bounced a beautiful redheaded girl. Her name was Sara Loller. When asked if she would like to have a town named after her she said yes, whereupon Mr. Albright suggested toga be added to her name and the town called Saratoga."

Sardinia [ˌsar'dēnēˌə], village in Decatur County (K-8).

Laid out in 1865. The post office formerly was called Big Creek. The present name probably comes from the Mediterranean island, but according to local anecdote: "Sardinia was so named because old Frank Gaston gave a big sardine supper, free, one time in order to get people to trade at his store. After that, everyone called the town Sardinia. It was called Big Creek at one time, but I don't know at what period in history that was. While there was a post office still here some lady wrote and wanted to know if Sardinia was connected in any way to Sardinia Island in the Mediterranean Sea. Em Sherman and I [Mrs. Raymond Hern] were appointed to do the research to find out, and though we tried and tried, we could not find any connections."

Sassafras ['sæsə‚fræs], village in Perry County (N-5).

A post office established here in 1916 was called Saffaras. In 1957 the name was changed to Sassafras, apparently for the tree.

Saturn ['sæt‚ərn], village in Whitley County (D-9).

A post office was established here in 1857. Named by postmaster James Broxon, probably for the planet since the Clerk-Maxwell theory about its rings was in the news that year.

Scalesville ['skālz‚vil], village in Warrick County (N-4).

A post office was established here in 1879. Named for the Scales family, prominent in the early history of the county. William Scales was the first postmaster.

Schererville ['shirə‚vil], town in Lake County (B-3).

Named for Nicholas Scherer, who platted the town in 1866.

Schneider ['snaidər], town in Lake County (C-3).

A post office called Schneider was established in 1902. Named for a large landowner here.

Schnellville ['shnel‚vil], village in Dubois County (N-5).

Platted in 1865 by Henry Schnell, for whom it was named.

Schooner Creek ['skūnər 'krēk], stream in Brown County.

About 8 miles long, it flows west to North Fork Salt Creek near the Brown-Monroe county line. It was named for a man named Schoonover who settled on it around 1820.

Scipio ['sipēō], village in Franklin County (J-11).

Platted in 1826. The post office was called Philanthropy, apparently a commendatory name. Scipio is for one of the classical Roman statesmen, perhaps via New York.

Scipio ['sipēō], village in Jennings County (K-8).

Laid out in 1817 and named by William Clapp for one of the noted Roman generals.

Scircleville ['sərkəl‚vil], village in Clinton County (F-6).

Named for George Addison Scircle, who platted the town in 1873.

Scotland ['skat͵lənd], village in Greene County (L-5).

Platted in 1835 and named by Scots for their homeland.

Scott [skat] County (M-8).

Organized in 1820 and named for General Charles Scott, officer in the Revolution and governor of Kentucky.

Scottsburg ['skats͵bərg], county seat, fifth class city in Scott County (M-8).

Laid out in 1871 and not named for the county in which it is located but for Thomas Scott, president of the Jeffersonville, Madison, and Indianapolis Railroad.

Scottsburg Reservoir ['skats͵bərg 'rezə(r)͵voi], lake in Scott County.

This 83-acre lake is located 1 mile southwest of Scottsburg, for which it was named.

Scottsville ['skats͵vil], village in Floyd County (N-7).

Laid out in 1853, the town presumably was named for Moses and John Scott, who settled here in 1812.

Seafield ['sē͵fēld], village in White County (E-4).

Platted in 1863 and named for a storekeeper named Sea, whose store was near the townsite.

Sedalia [sə'dāl͵yə], village in Clinton County (F-6).

Laid out in 1872. The name was coined in 1857 by the founder of a Missouri town and then spread eastward to several states.

Sedan [si'dæn; su-], village in Dekalb County (B-10).

In 1854 a post office called Iba was established here. In 1871 the name was changed to Sedan, apparently for the French city.

Seelyville ['sēlē͵vil], town in Vigo County (J-4).

A post office was established here in 1867, and the town was laid out in 1871. Named for Jonas Seely, first postmaster, who laid out the town.

Sellersburg ['selərz͵bərg], town in Clark County (N-8).

Laid out in 1846 by John Hill and Moses W. Sellers and named for Sellers.

Selma ['selmə], town in Delaware County (N-4).

Platted in 1852 and a post office was established in 1853. Apparently named for the personal name.

Selvin ['selvən], village in Warrick County (N-4).

Laid out in 1839 and originally called Taylorsville, for the proprietor, George Taylor. The name was changed to Selvin in 1881 when the post office name was changed from Polk Patch.

Servia ['sərvē͵ə], village in Wabash County (D-8).

Platted in 1856 and named for the former European kingdom. The post office formerly was New Madison.

Sevastopol [sə'væstə͵pūl; -pul], village in Kosciusko County (C-7).

Settled around 1838, platted in 1856, and named for the Russian city.

Sexton ['seks,tən], village in Rush County (H-9).

Laid out in 1882 by Martha J., Francis M., and Rebecca Hamilton and named Hamilton for them. Since there was another Hamilton in the state, the name was changed to Sexton, apparently for the post office here.

Seymour ['sē,mōr], fourth class city in Jackson County (L-7).

Founded in 1852 and named for Henry C. Seymour, superintendent of construction of the Ohio and Mississippi Railroad.

Shadeland ['shād,lənd], village in Tippecanoe County (F-5).

Platted in 1824. Apparently the name is commendatory.

Shakamak Lake ['shækəmæk 'lāk], lake.

Located in Shakamak State Park, this 56-acre lake received its name for the Delaware name of nearby Eel River, q.v., which was *Shack-a-mak,* "slippery fish."

Shanghai ['shæŋ,hai], village in Howard County (F-6).

A post office was established here in 1858. According to local anecdote, it was named for Shanghai chickens owned by a resident here.

Shannondale ['shænən,dāl], town in Montgomery County (G-5).

Platted in 1857 and named for Nathan Shannon, first postmaster.

Sharon ['sherən], village in Carroll County (E-6).

Laid out in 1868 by Benjamin Duncan. Perhaps the name is inspirational, either commendatory or biblical.

Sharpsville ['sharps,vil], town in Tipton County (F-7).

Platted in 1850 and named for its founder, E. M. Sharp, who came here in 1831.

Shelburn ['shelbərn], town in Sullivan County (K-3).

Laid out in 1855 by Paschal Shelburn and named for him. He settled here in 1818.

Shelby ['shelbē] County (J-8).

Organized in 1822 and named for Isaac Shelby, officer in both the Revolution and War of 1812 and governor of Kentucky, 1792–96 and 1812–16.

Shelby ['shelbē], village in Lake County (C-3).

Platted in 1886 by William R. Shelby, for whom it was named.

Shelbyville ['shelbē,vil], county seat, fourth class city in Shelby County (J-8).

Platted in 1822 and named for Shelby County.

Shepardsville ['shepərdz,vil], village in Vigo County (J-3).

Settled in 1920 and named for a local mine owner.

Sheridan ['sherədən], town in Hamilton County (G-7).

Laid out in 1860 and first called Millwood. Several years later the name was changed to Sheridan, allegedly for P. H. Sheridan, Union officer during the Civil War.

Shideler ['shaid͵lər], village in Delaware County (F-9).
Platted by Isaac Shideler in 1871 and named for him.

Shipshewana ['ship͵she'wanə], town in Lagrange County (A-8).
Platted in 1888 and named for Shipshewana Lake.

Shipshewana Lake ['ship͵she'wanə 'lāk], lake in Lagrange County.
This 202-acre lake is located 1 mile west of the town of Shipshewana. It was named for a Potawatomi Indian, *Cup-ci-wa-no,* "Vision of a Lion."

Shirkieville ['shərke͵vil], village in Vigo County (J-3).
Founded in 1921 and named for the owner of a nearby mine.

Shirley ['shər͵le], town in Hancock and Henry counties (H-8).
Platted in 1890 and named for Joseph A. Shirley, division superintendent of the Ohio, Indiana, and Western Railway.

Shoals [shōlz], county seat, town in Martin County (M-5).
Settled in 1816 and so named because of its location at a shoals, a ford or shallow place, in White River. Formerly called Daugherty's Shoals, for William Daugherty, early settler, and a shallow ford on White River.

Siberia [͵sai'bire͵ə], village in Perry County (N-5).
Named Sabaria in 1869 by Father Isidore Hobi in honor of the birthplace of St. Martin of Tours. Apparently the Post Office Department thought the name had been misspelled and changed it to Siberia in 1885.

Sidney ['sid͵ne], town in Kosciusko County (C-8).
Settled in 1834 and, according to tradition, named for Sidney, Ohio, home of early settlers, but more likely named by railroad officials for the Sidney family, from whom land was purchased.

Silver Creek ['silvər ͵krēk], stream.
Heads in Clark County and flows south to the Ohio River 1 mile east of New Albany. Traditionally this name has been associated with a local legend of an Indian silver mine near the stream; however, the stream probably was so named because of its comparative clearness due to its gravelly bottom. The West Fork, much muddier, is called Muddy Fork.

Silver Lake ['silvər 'lāk], town in Kosciusko County (D-7).
Settled in 1860 and named for the nearby lake of the same name.

Silverville ['silvər͵vil], village in Lawrence County (L-5).
Platted in 1855. The name comes from the erroneous belief that silver ore could be found here. A local tradition is that the town is so named because early settlers bought the land with silver dollars.

152

Silverwood ['silvər‚wud], village in Fountain County (G-3).

Platted in 1881 and apparently named for nearby Silver Island. The Wabash and Erie Canal passed through the county forming, with the Wabash River, an island called Silver Island because Indians supposedly had hidden silver at this spot.

Simpson ['simpsən], village in Huntington County (D-9).

Platted in 1885 and originally called Roche's Station, apparently for a local personal name. In 1886 a post office called Simpson, probably for a personal name, was established here.

Sims [simz], village in Grant County (F-8).

A post office was established here in 1881. Named for Sims Township, in which it is located.

Sitka ['sitkə], village in White County (E-5).

Established in 1880 and apparently named for Sitka, Alaska.

Six Points ['siks ‚points], village in Hendricks County (H-6).

Probably so named because a railroad and two roads intersect here.

Skelton ['skeltn], village in Gibson County (N-2).

Laid out in 1911 and named for J. W. Skelton, an early settler.

Sleeth [slēth], village in Carroll County (E-5).

A post office was located here in 1880. Named for W. H. Sleeth, who donated land to the town.

Sloan [slōn], village in Warren County (F-3).

A post office was established in 1914. Named for the Sloan family here.

Smartsburg ['smarts‚bərg], village in Montgomery County (G-5).

A post office called Smartsburgh was established in 1886. The spelling was changed to Smartsburg in 1892. One source says it was named "after the smartweed along the creek," but probably for Dr. Smart, a pioneer physician.

Smedley ['smed‚lē], village in Washington County (M-7).

A post office was established here in 1884. Named for the first merchant, Morgan Smedley. The first postmaster was Henry Smedley.

Smithfield ['smith‚fēld], village in Delaware County (G-9).

A post office was established and the village laid out in 1830. Apparently named for a personal name.

Smithland ['smith‚lənd], village in Shelby County (J-8).

Laid out by Hezekiah Smith in 1851 and named for him.

Smiths Crossing ['smi(th)s 'krosiŋ], village in Decatur County (K-9).

Laid out in 1859 and named for William Stewart Smith who lived here for several years.

Smithson ['smi(th)‚sən] (Wheeler), village in White County (E-5).

A post office was established here around 1880 and named Smithson for Lt. Bernard G. Smith, veteran of the Civil War and son of Abel T. Smith, prominent citizen who came here in 1846. Wheeler was the name of a flag station on the railroad and honors Hiram Wheeler, who built a tile factory here in 1879.

Smith Valley ['smith 'vælē], village in Johnson County (J-7).

Settled in 1869 and originally called Smith's Valley, for one of the early settlers, William K. Smith.

Smithville ['smith‚vil], village in Monroe County (L-6).

Platted in 1851 and named for George Smith, who owned some of the land where the town is located and was co-founder.

Smothers Creek ['smoṯhərz ‚krēk], stream in Daviess County.

About 23 miles long, it flows southwest to the West Fork White River at the Daviess-Knox county line. It was named for an early settler named Smothers.

Smyrna ['smərnə], village in Decatur County (K-9).

A post office was established here in 1846. This name is fairly popular in the U. S. and comes from the seaport in Asia Minor noted as the alleged birthplace of Homer and as one of the seven cities addressed by John in Revelation; hence, the name is probably biblical.

Snow Hill ['sno 'hil], village in Randolph County (G-10).

Formerly called Mt. Pleasant and Vinegar Hill. Allegedly the present name, applied to a post office here in 1859, is for "the snow which gathered on the mound in winter." The name also is found in England and in other states.

Solitude ['salə‚tud], village in Posey County (O-2).

A post office was located here from 1858 until 1917. Apparently the name is descriptive.

Solsberry ['salz‚berē], village in Greene County (K-5).

Laid out in 1848 and named for Solomon Wilkerson, town organizer and builder of the first house.

Somerset ['səmər‚set], village in Wabash County (E-8).

Founded in 1816 and platted in 1844. Originally called Springfield and Twin Springs, for two nearby springs. A popular notion is that the present name is for an Indian chief; however, it is more likely that the present name is for the English county, perhaps via New England.

Somerville ['səmər‚vil], town in Gibson County (N-3).

Laid out in 1853 and originally named Summitville, because it is on high ground. The present name was applied by the Post Office Department, probably to avoid confusion with another Summitville in Indiana.

South Bend ['sauth 'bend], county seat, second class city in St. Joseph County (A-6).

The founder, Alexis Coquillard,

154

named the place Big St. Joseph Station, but settlers called it The Bend or South Bend, for its location on the St. Joseph River, where the river turns north from a westward course. Colonel Lathrop M. Taylor opened a trading post here and in 1827 renamed the settlement St. Joseph's. In 1829 the name was changed to Southold. It officially became South Bend in 1830 and was laid out in 1831.

South Bethany ['sauth 'bethənē], village in Bartholomew County (K-7).

Laid out in 1849 and called Bethany, for the village in the New Testament, perhaps via a local church.

South Boston ['sauth 'bostən], village in Washington County (M-7).

Originally called Boston, for the city in Massachusetts. South was added to the name to distinguish it from another Boston, Indiana. A store was opened here as early as 1834.

South Gate ['sauth ˌgāt], village in Franklin County (K-10).

A post office was established here in 1839, and the village was platted in 1850.

South LaPorte ['sauth lə'pōrt], village in LaPorte County (B-5).

The name is locational, as the village is located south of the city of LaPorte.

South Martin ['sauth 'martn], village in Martin County (M-5).

A post office was established in 1861. So named because the village is in the southern part of Martin County.

South Milford ['sauth 'milˌfərd], village in Lagrange County (B-9).

A post office was established in 1848, and the village was laid out in 1856 in southern Milford Township; hence, the name is locational.

Southport ['sauthˌpōrt], fifth class city in Marion County (H-7).

Platted in 1852, and, according to local legend, it is an incident name. An old sailor who was riding through here in a stagecoach around 1835 said, as the coach slowed down, "She's laying to—she can't weather the first port south. Run up the sails, boys." Since there was also a Northport (see Valley Mills) in Marion County when Southport was platted, the name is probably locational, suggested by Northport.

South Raub ['sauth 'rab], village in Tippecanoe County (F-5).

Platted in 1822 and named for a local family. Apparently South was added to the name to distinguish it from Raub, in Benton County.

South Salem ['sauth 'sāləm], village in Randolph County (G-11).

Platted in 1849 by David Polly and formerly called Pollytown for him. Formerly named Salem.

South Wanatah ['sauth 'wanəˌta], village in LaPorte County (B-5).

Founded in 1859. The name is locational. See Wanatah.

Southwest ['sauth'west], village in Elkhart County (B-7).

A locational name, for the village is southwest of Goshen, the county seat.

South Whitley ['sauth 'hwit₁lē], town in Whitley County (D-8).

Originally called Springfield, it was platted and a post office was established in 1838. The post office was called Whitley, for the county. In 1842 the name was changed to South Whitley, as the town is located in the southern part of the county.

Spades [spādz], village in Ripley County (K-10).

Formerly called Spades' Depot, for early settler Jacob Spades, the village was laid out in 1855.

Sparksville ['sparks₁vil], village in Jackson County (L-7).

Founded around 1812 by and named for Stephen Sparks, who established a ferry, called "Sparks' Ferry," here. The town was platted in 1857.

Sparta ['spardē; -də], village in Dearborn County (K-10).

A post office was established here in 1846. Named for the township in which it is located.

Spartanburg ['spartn₁bərg], village in Randolph County (G-11).

Founded in 1832 and originally called Newberg. A post office established in 1842 was named Spartanburg.

Spearsville ['spirz₁vil], village in Brown County (K-7).

Named for William Spears, who founded the town around 1835.

Speed [spēd], village in Clark County (N-8).

For W. S. Speed, who founded a cement plant here.

Speedway ['spēd₁wā], fourth class city in Marion County (H-6).

So named because it is the home of the Indianapolis Motor Speedway; it was laid out in 1912.

Speicherville ['spaikər₁vil] (Spiker), village in Wabash County (D-8).

Platted in 1881 and named for the proprietor, Christian Speicher. Formerly called Speicher, hence the alternate name, Spiker.

Spencer ['spen₁sər] County (O-4).

Organized in 1818 and named for Captain Spier Spencer, who was killed in the Battle of Tippecanoe.

Spencer ['spen₁sər], county seat, town in Owen County (K-5).

Established in 1820 and named for Captain Spier Spencer of Kentucky, who was killed in the Battle of Tippecanoe.

Spencerville ['spensər₁vil], village in DeKalb County (C-10).

Settled around 1834 and named for Isaac Spencer, brother-in-law of R. Dawson, who laid out the town.

Spiceland ['spais₁lənd], town in Henry County (H-9).

156

Platted in 1850 and named for "the abundance of spice brush that grew in that neighborhood."

Spiker ['spaikər] (Speicherville), village in Wabash County (D-8).
See Speicherville.

Sponsler ['span͵slər], village in Greene County (L-4) .
Founded in 1889 and named for William Sponsler who owned land here when a railroad stop was established.

Spraytown ['sprā͵taun], village in Jackson County (L-7).
Named for the first merchant, whose name was Spray. The post office was first called White Creek.

Springboro ['spriŋ͵bərō], village in White County (E-5).
Established around 1830 and named for a nearby stream, Spring Creek.

Springersville ['spriŋərz͵vil], village in Fayette County (H-10).
Laid out in 1840 when a post office was established. Probably named for the personal name.

Springfield ['spriŋ͵fēld], village in Posey County (O-2).
Laid out about 1817. Probably the name is a transfer from another state.

Spring Lake ['spriŋ 'lāk], town in Hancock County (H-8).
William Dye made a spring-fed artificial lake here in 1884–85, and the area, a picnic grounds, was called Dye's Grove. The area became known as Spring Lake, for the lake, and was platted in 1912.

Springport ['spriŋ͵pōrt], town in Henry County (G-9).
Laid out in 1868 and named for springs located near the railway depot here.

Springville ['spriŋ͵vil], village in LaPorte County (A-5).
Laid out in 1833 and named for a large spring here.

Springville ['spriŋ͵vil], village in Lawrence County (L-5).
Platted in 1832 and named for a nearby stream, Spring Creek.

Squirrel Creek ['skwər(ə)l ͵krēk], stream.
About 11.2 miles long, it heads in Miami County and flows southeast to the Eel River at Stockdale in Wabash County. It was named for a Potawatomi chief, *Niconga,* "Squirrel."

Stanford ['stænfərd], village in Monroe County (K-5).
Platted in 1838 and said to be named for the home of early settlers, Stanford, North Carolina; however, current maps and gazetteers do not show such a place name there. Apparently the name is a transfer, though, perhaps from England or Kentucky.

Star City ['star 'sidē], village in Pulaski County (D-6).
Laid out in 1859 and called Scarboro, but the citizens did not like

157

the name and petitioned to change the name to Star City in 1861.

Starke [stark] County (C-5).

Organized in 1850 and named for General John Stark, who served with Rogers' Rangers in the French and Indian War and was a distinguished officer in the Revolution.

Staser ['stāsər], village in Vanderburgh County (N-3).

A post office was located here in 1892. Named for the Staser family, prominent citizens of Scott Township. The first German to settle here was Frederick Staser.

State Line City ['stāt 'lain 'sid̲ē], town in Warren County (G-3).

Platted in 1857 and so named because the Indiana-Illinois state line intersects the town.

Staunton ['stontn], town in Clay County (J-4).

Founded in 1851 by Lewis Bailey and originally called Highland, for the alleged elevation, but when a post office was established, the name was changed to Staunton, for Staunton, Virginia, hometown of the founder.

Steam Corner ['stēm 'kornər], village in Fountain County (G-4).

A post office was established here in 1851. A steam sawmill here gave the village its name.

Stearleyville ['stərlē͵vil], village in Clay County (J-4).

Named for George Stearley, on whose land it was founded in 1891.

Steele [stēl] (Salem), village in Adams County (E-11).

See Salem, Adams County.

Stendal ['stæn͵dāl; 'stendəl], village in Pike County (N-4).

Laid out in 1869 and named by Rev. W. Baumeister for his native city in Germany.

Steuben ['stūbən] County (A-10).

Organized in 1837 and named for Baron Friedrich Wilhelm August Heinrich Ferdinand von Steuben, a Prussian general who served with the Americans in the Revolution.

Steubenville ['stūbən͵vil], village in Steuben County (B-10).

A post office was located here in 1839. Apparently this village was named for the county in which it is located.

Stevenson ['stēvən͵sən], village in Warrick County (O-3).

Originally called Armery, for Francis Armery, who, with George Goddard, platted it in 1886. The present name apparently comes from an addition, first called Stephens, for the proprietor, and later Stevenson Station, "the spelling and pronunciation being easier."

Stewartsville ['stūərts͵vil], village in Posey County (N-2).

Named for William Stewart, who laid it out in 1838. Called Paris until the post office was established in 1853.

Stilesville ['stailz͵vil], town in Hendricks County (K-5).

158

Laid out in 1828 and named for the proprietor, Jeremiah Stiles.

Stillwell ['stil͵wel], village in Laporte County (B-5).

Named for Thomas Stillwell, who settled here about 1831. A post office was established here in 1870.

Stinesville ['stainz͵vil], town in Monroe County (K-5).

Platted in 1855 and named for Eusebius Stine, a large landowner here who helped lay out the town.

Stips Hill ['stips 'hil] (Buena Vista), village in Franklin County (J-9).

See Buena Vista, Franklin County.

Stockdale ['stak͵dāl], village in Wabash County (D-7).

Laid out in 1839, and a post office was established in 1855.

Stockport ['stak͵pōrt], village in Delaware County (F-9).

A post office was established here in 1892. Perhaps so named "because it was a livestock shipping point."

Stockwell ['stak͵wel], village in Tippecanoe County (F-5).

Platted in 1850 and originally called Baker's Corner, for Reuben Baker, the original landowner. The present name honors Robert Stockwell, who, with others, bought the site from Baker.

Stone [stōn], village in Randolph County (G-10).

Established about 1870 and formerly called Clark's Post Office and Stone Station.

Stone Bluff ['stōn 'bləf], village in Fountain County (G-4).

Platted in 1873 and presumably named for its location.

Stones Crossing ['stōnz 'krosiŋ], village in Johnson County (J-7).

Settled in the early 1830's. The post office here was first called Stone's Crossing, for the Stone family, large landowners.

Story ['stōrē], village in Brown County (K-7).

Once known as Storyville, it was named for one of the first settlers, Dr. Story. According to local anecdote, however, the name is for storytelling at a local store: "There's only a general store where men used to sit and tell stories, lies." A post office called Story was established here in 1882.

Stout [staut] (Bethel), village in Delaware County (F-9).

A church was organized here in 1836, and the biblical name Bethel probably comes from it. More recently the town has been called Stout, for Isaac Stout, local merchant.

Straughn [stron], town in Henry County (H-9).

Originally called Straughn's Station, for early settler Merriman Straughn, the town was platted in 1868.

Strawtown ['stro͵taun], village in Hamilton County (G-7).

Named for Chief Straw, a Delaware Indian whose village was here, although one source says "its name is derived from a house in it thatched with straw."

Sugar Creek ['shugər ˌkrēk; -krik], stream.

About 100 miles long, it heads in Clinton County and flows southwest through Boone, Montgomery, and Parke counties to the Wabash River about 5 miles north of Montezuma. Formerly called Sugar Tree Creek, which is a translation of the Miami name, *Sa-na-min-dji si-pi-wi*.

Sullivan ['sələvən; 'sel-] County (K-3).

Organized in 1817 and named for General Daniel Sullivan, who was killed by Indians while carrying messages from Vincennes to Louisville during the Revolution.

Sullivan ['sələvən; 'sel-], county seat, fifth class city in Sullivan County (K-3).

Laid out in 1842 and named for Sullivan County.

Sulphur ['səlfər], village in Crawford County (N-6).

A post office called Sulphur Well was established in 1873. In 1895 the name was changed to Sulphur. Named for nearby sulphur springs.

Sulphur Springs ['səlfər 'spriŋz], village in Crawford County (N-6).

Apparently this is a descriptive name.

Sulphur Springs ['səlfər 'spriŋz], town in Henry County (G-9).

A post office called Sulphur Springs was located here in 1844, and the town was platted in 1853. Named for sulphur springs here.

Suman ['sūmən], village in Porter County (B-4).

Originally called Sumanville when a post office was established here in 1873 with Colonel I. C. B. Suman as postmaster, for whom it was named.

Sumava Resorts [sə'mavə ri'zorts], village in Newton County (C-3).

Founded in 1926, it was established as a recreational area.

Summit ['səmət], village in Dekalb County (B-10).

A post office was established in 1871. Allegedly so named because the site is the highest elevation on the road.

Summit ['səmut; -ət], village in Greene County (L-4).

Platted in 1889 and named for the nearby Summit Coal Mine, so named because it was surrounded by hills.

Summit Grove ['səmət 'grōv], village in Vermillion County (H-3).

Laid out in 1871 when a post office was established. Apparently the name is commendatory.

Summitville ['səmətˌvil], town in Madison County (F-8).

Platted in 1867 and so named because it is located on high ground.

Sunman ['sənˌmən], town in Ripley County (K-10).

160

Laid out in 1856 and named for Thomas Sunman, Sr., prominent citizen.

Surprise [sə'praiz], village in Jackson County (L-7).
Platted in 1897. A traditional account says acting postmaster Doc Isaacs said he was surprised the town got a railroad through it and was surprised the town got a post office, so it was called Surprise.

Surrey ['sərē], village in Jasper County (D-4).
A post office was established here in 1882. Named for the English county.

Swalls [swolz], village in Vigo County (J-4).
A post office was located here from 1891 until 1900. Probably named for David Swalls, first landowner here.

Swan [swan], village in Noble County (C-9).
Laid out in 1870 and named for Swan Township, in which it is located.

Swanington ['swaniŋtən], village in Benton County (E-4).
Once called Wyndham, the name became Swanington, for landowner William Swan, in 1886.

Swayzee ['swāzē], town in Grant County (F-8).
A post office was established here in 1881. Named for James Swayzee, who owned land here.

Sweetser ['swēt͵sər], town in Grant County (E-8).
Laid out in 1871 and named for James Sweetser, a nearby landowner.

Switz City ['swit(s) 'sid̠ē], town in Greene County (L-4).
Founded about 1869 and named for John Switz, local landowner.

Switzerland ['switsər͵lənd] County (L-10).
Organized in 1814 and named for Switzerland by Swiss settlers who came here in 1802.

Sycamore ['sikə͵mōr], village in Howard County (F-7).
Founded in 1881 and allegedly named for a large sycamore tree on the townsite.

Sylvania [͵sil'vānē͵ə], village in Parke County (G-3).
Platted in 1836, the Latinized name is descriptive of the wooded area here but probably was selected for its commendatory value.

Symonds Creek ['saimənz 'krēk], stream.
Over 10 miles long, it heads in Henry County and flows southeast to the Whitewater River about 1½ miles north of Cambridge City. Named for Nathan and Thomas Symons, who settled near its mouth.

Symons Creek ['saimənz ͵krēk], stream.
About 17 miles long, it heads in Henry County and flows southeast, then northeast, through Fayette

County to the Whitewater River about a mile southeast of Cambridge City. Named for Nathan and Thomas Symons, who settled near here.

Syracuse ['serə͵kyūz; 'sirə-], town in Kosciusko County (B-8).

Settled about 1834 and named for Syracuse, New York.

Syria ['sirē͵ə], village in Orange County (M-6).
A post office was established here in 1880. Apparently named for the Asian country.

T

Tab [tæb], village in Warren County (F-3).
Platted in 1905 by Harrison "Tab" Goodwine and named for him.

Talbot ['tælbət], village in Benton County (F-3).
Laid out in 1873 by Ezekiel M. Talbot and named for him.

Talma ['tælmə], village in Fulton County (C-7).
The post office here was called Bloomingsburg from 1851 until 1896, when it became Talma. The present name comes from a local personal name.

Tampico [͵tæm'pēkō], village in Jackson County (L-7).
Founded about 1840 when a blacksmith shop was built here. Probably named for the Mexican seaport.

Tangier ['tæn'jir], village in Parke County (H-3).
Established in 1886. County surveyor J. T. Campbell suggested naming the town for Tangier, Morocco, then in the news.

Tanner ['tænər], village in Greene County (L-5).
A post office was established here in 1888. The name honors John Riley Tanner, a prominent Republican who became governor of Illinois.

Tanners Creek ['tænərz 'krēk], stream in Dearborn County.
About 17 miles long, this stream flows southeast and then south to the Ohio River about a mile below Lawrenceburg. It was named for a defunct settlement, Tanner's Station, which was named for Rev. John Tanner, a Baptist preacher from Kentucky.

Tarry Park ['terē 'park], village in Lawrence County (L-6).
Platted in 1850 as Juliet. Formerly called Yockey, for a local family, and Red Cross Park, as Joseph Gardner donated land near here to the International Red Cross

Society. The present name is for Gardner's home.

Taswell ['tæz,wel], village in Crawford County (N-6).

Platted around 1882 and named for James Laswell, who owned the land. The name became Taswell through a clerical error.

Taylor ['tālər], village in Tippecanoe County (F-5).

Formerly called Taylor Station, for a family here.

Taylorsville ['tālərz,vil], village in Bartholomew County (K-7).

Platted in 1849 and named for Zachary Taylor, twelfth president of the U. S. The original name was Herod, for a local lawyer, but the name was changed because it became associated with the biblical Herod.

Teegarden ['tē,gardn], village in Marshall County (B-6).

Platted in 1873 and named for a landowner, Dr. Teegarden.

Tefft [teft], village in Jasper County (C-5).

Originally called Dunnville, for Nancy and Isaac Dunn, who laid out the town in 1884, but since the name was confused with Danville, the town was renamed for Mr. Dunn's brother-in-law, Dr. Tefft.

Tell City ['tel 'sidē], fifth class city in Perry County (O-5).

Settled in 1857 by Swiss, who named the town for William Tell, the Swiss legendary hero.

Temple ['tempəl], village in Crawford County (N-6).

Established in the 1880's and named for an early landowner, James Temple.

Templeton ['tempəl,tən], village in Benton County (F-4).

For William J. Tempelton, who organized the town in 1873.

Tennyson ['tenəsən], town in Warrick County (O-4).

Platted about 1882 and apparently named for Alfred, Lord Tennyson, then poet laureate of England.

Terhune ['ter,hūn; ,ter'hūn], village in Boone County (G-6).

Formerly called Kimberlin, the name was changed to Terhune in 1883, apparently for the personal name.

Terre Hall [,terə 'hol] (Hemlock), village in Howard County (F-7).

See Hemlock.

Terre Haute ['ter(ə) 'hōt; terē-; -hət], county seat, second class city in Vigo County (J-3).

A French settlement from about 1720 to 1763 and called Terre Haute, "high land." It was platted in 1816.

Terry ['terē], village in Perry County (O-5).

Probably named for the Terry family, who came to this county from Virginia in 1815.

Tetersburg ['tētərz,bərg], village in Tipton County (F-7).

163

Laid out in 1848 on the farm of Mahlon and Asa Teter and named for them.

Thales [thālz; tālz], village in Dubois County (M-5).

A post office was established here in 1879. Also known as Hickory Grove. Possibly named for the classical lyric poet.

Thayer ['thā͵ər], village in Newton County (C-3).

Laid out in 1882 and named for an early resident here.

Thornhope ['thorn͵hōp] (Oak), village in Pulaski County (D-6).

Originally called Parisville, then Rosedale, then Oak. It was laid out in 1853. Oak was the post office name.

Thorntown ['thorn͵taun], town in Boone County (G-5).

Laid out in 1831. A translation of the name of the Indian village here which was *Ka-wi-a-ki-un-gi,* "Place of Thorns," or *Ka-win-ja-ki-un-gi,* "Thorn Tree Place." Several legends attempt to explain the name. A typical one runs: "Thorntown was an Indian town. There was this Indian princess, and she was in love with a warrior. They both lived there. She was unable to marry him, though, because he was either killed in battle or her father had promised her to someone else. Anyway, she was heartbroken about the whole thing. So she went running through a woods full of thorns and briers and thick bushes that hadn't been cleared away. Somehow she got tangled up in the briers and fell, and a thorn went through her heart and killed her. Since she was so pretty and everything the people around there were broke up about it and named the place Thorntown. The name stuck and that's what it's called today."

Thurman ['thərmən], village in Allen County (C-10).

Founded in 1901 and named for a pioneer family in the area.

Tilden ['tildən], village in Hendricks County (H-6).

A post office was established here in 1880. Named for the American statesman and lawyer Samuel Jones Tilden, the Democratic candidate for President in 1876.

Tillmans ['tilmənz], village in Allen County (D-10).

Founded in 1898 and named for an early settler, John Tillman.

Tiosa [͵tai'ōsə], village in Fulton County (C-7).

Settled in 1869 and allegedly named for a Potawatomi chief, *Tiosa,* "Beaver."

Tippecanoe [͵tipēkə'nū] County (F-5).

Organized in 1826 and named for the Tippecanoe River.

Tippecanoe [͵tipēkə'nū], village in Marshall County (C-7).

Laid out in 1882 about a mile south of Tippecanoe Town (See Old Tip Town) along the Nickel Plate Railroad and called Tippecanoe Town Station. In 1886 the name was changed to Ilion, and in 1905 it became Tippecanoe.

Tippecanoe Lake [ˌtipēkə'nū 'lāk], lake in Kosciusko County.

Located at Oswego, the lake is 707 acres. It was named for the Tippecanoe River.

Tippecanoe River ['tipēkə'nū 'rivər], stream.

About 220 miles long, it heads in Kosciusko County, flows west through Marshall, Fulton, and Starke counties, then south through Pulaski, White, Carroll, and Tippecanoe counties to the Wabash River north of Lafayette. The name is a corruption of the Potawatomi *Ke-tap-e-kon-nong,* "Ketapekon town or place," an Indian town at the mouth of the stream. The Miami name of the river was *Ke-tap-kwon,* "buffalo fish," which are common in the river.

Tipton ['tipˌtən] County (F-7).

Organized in 1844 and named for General John Tipton, Hoosier soldier and U. S. Senator, 1832–39.

Tipton ['tipˌtən], county seat, fifth class city in Tipton County (F-7).

Laid out in 1839 by Samuel King, who named it Kingston. When the county was organized in 1844 and this town was selected as the county seat the name was changed to Canton. Shortly after, since there was another Hoosier town of that name, it was renamed Tipton, for Tipton County.

Tobinsport ['tōbənzˌpōrt], village in Perry County (P-5).

Settled in 1827 and named for Robert Tobin, early settler.

Tocsin ['taksən], village in Wells County (D-10).

Platted in 1884. The name means "alarm bell," and allegedly the founder, Michael Blue, thought the fame of the new town would resound through the countryside.

Toledo [tə'lēdō], village in Huntington County (E-9).

Platted in 1875 and named for the Toledo Railroad which was supposed to pass through here but did not. Variant names have been Brownville and Brown's Corners.

Topeka [tə'pēkə], town in Lagrange County (B-9).

Platted in 1843. Although commonly the word is said to mean "potatoes," it is the Shawnee word for the Jerusalem artichoke.

Toto ['tōd̲ō] (Rye), village in Starke County (C-5).

A post office called Toto was established here in 1855, and the village was platted in 1891 as Toto, supposedly an Indian word meaning "bullfrog." The alternate name is perhaps for the English borough.

Tower ['tauˌər], village in Crawford County (N-6).

A post office was located here in 1890. Named for a local family.

Tracy ['trāsē], village in LaPorte County (B-5).

165

A post office established here in 1879 was called Tracy Station. In 1882 the name was changed to Tracy. It received its name from the foreman of a railroad crew.

Traders Point ['trādərz 'point], village in Marion County (H-6).

Platted in 1864. It received its name from an Indian trading post which was located nearby.

Trafalgar [trə'fælgər; -vər], town in Johnson County (J-7).

First platted in 1851 and called Liberty. Another plat in 1853 was named Hensley Town. In 1867 a third plat was laid out and called Trafalgar, and the former names soon were abandoned. The present name comes from the British victory over the French.

Trail Creek ['trāl ˌkrik], stream in LaPorte County.

Flows north, then west, to Lake Michigan at Michigan City. The French name was *Rivière du Chemin,* which, as the English name, is a translation of the Potawatomi name, *Mi-e-we-si-bi-we. Dishmaw,* a corruption of the French, appears on early maps.

Trail Creek ['trāl 'krik], town in LaPorte County (A-5).

Incorporated in 1923 and named for a nearby stream, Trail Creek.

Travisville ['trævəsˌvil], village in Wells County (E-9).

Named for John Travis, who laid out the town in 1871.

Treaty ['trēd̲ē], village in Wabash County (E-8).

Settled in 1876 and named for nearby Treaty Creek.

Treaty Creek ['trēd̲ē 'krēk], stream in Wabash County.

About 10 miles long, it flows west and then northwest to the Wabash River near Wabash. The name comes from an Indian treaty of 1826 made near its mouth.

Tremont ['trēˌmant], village in Porter County (B-4).

Settled about 1845 and named for three large sand dunes here called Three Mountains, or Tremont. The name also has been applied to a village in Marion County.

Trenton ['trentn] (Priam), village in Blackford County (F-9).

Laid out in 1845 and named for Trenton, New Jersey. Priam is the post office name.

Trevlac ['trevˌlæk], village in Brown County (K-6).

Former names were Gold Creek, Bear Creek, and Richards before the villagers settled for Trevlac, the name of one of the founders, Calvert, spelled backwards. The post office here was established as Richards in 1881, and the name was changed to Trevlac in 1907.

Trinity ['trinətē], village in Jay County (E-11).

Named for the Holy Trinity Church, built here in 1861.

Trinity Springs ['trinətē 'spriŋz], village in Martin County (M-5).

Platted in 1837 and named for three mineral springs here.

Troy [troi], town in Perry County (O-5).

Settled in 1809, laid out in 1815, and named for the Homeric city.

Tulip ['tūlup], village in Greene County (K-5).

A post office was established here in 1884 and discontinued in 1906. Probably named for the tulip, or yellow poplar, tree rather than for the flower.

Tunker ['təŋkər], village in Whitley County (D-8).

Settled in 1839 by Dunkers (i.e., Dunkards), sometimes spelled Tunkers, and named for them.

Tunnelton ['tənəltən], village in Lawrence County (L-6).

Laid out in 1859 and named for two nearby railroad tunnels.

Turner ['tərnər], village in Clay County (J-4).

Founded in 1854 and first called Newburg, although the first post office was called Sherman. When a post office was reestablished in the 1870's, it was named Turner, for Rev. Turner of Indianapolis, who was president of the Indianapolis Mining, Coal and Coke Co. and had business interests here.

Twelve Mile ['twelv ˌmail], village in Cass County (D-7).

Established in 1852 and named for Twelve Mile Creek, which flows nearby. Folk legend offers another account of the naming and preserves a familiar superstition: "About 100 years ago there arose a small community of people who lived in Cass County, Indiana. As this small settlement gradually got bigger in size and population, they realized they had no official name to call their little establishment. Since they had to go into the nearest town, which was Logansport, for practically all their major supplies, they decided to arrive at a reasonable guess as to how far it was to Logansport, and they would name their town that number. Well, as it turned out they estimated it to be about 12½ or 13 miles into Logansport. Being the suspicious bunch of old settlers that they were, they wouldn't think of naming their town Thirteen Mile, so the only logical thing to do was to call it Twelve Mile, meaning that it was 12 miles from Logansport."

Twin Lakes ['twin 'lāks], village in Lagrange County (A-9).

Named for nearby Twin Lakes, two lakes of about equal size.

Twin Lakes ['twin 'lāks], village in Marshall County (C-6).

A post office was established here in 1887. Named for two nearby lakes that resemble each other.

Tyner ['tainər], village in Marshall County (B-6).

Platted in 1855 and named for one of the founders, Thomas Tyner. Originally called Tyner City.

167

U

Underwood ['əndər‚wud], village in Clark County (M-8).

Founded in 1879. Allegedly the name was a compromise between the suggested names of Dallas Town and Underbrush.

Union ['yūnyən] County (H-10).

Organized in 1821. The name is inspirational, suggesting a feeling of patriotism.

Union ['yūnyən], village in Pike County (M-3).

Laid out in 1867. Apparently the name is inspirational.

Union Center ['yūnyən 'sentər], village in LaPorte County (B-5).

Settled by 1835 and named for Union Township in which it is located.

Union City ['yūnyən 'sitē], fifth class city in Randolph County (G-11).

Platted in 1849. Probably the name is patriotic.

Uniondale ['yūnyən‚dāl], town in Wells County (D-10).

Platted in 1883 and named for Union Township, in which it is located.

Union Mills ['yūnyən 'milz], village in LaPorte County (B-5).

Platted in 1849, although settled as early as 1832. In 1837 the first gristmill was built here and char-

tered as Union Mills, for which the town was named.

Unionport ['yūnyən‚pōrt], village in Randolph County (G-10).

Platted in 1837 in the center of a proposed township, Union, which was never established, and apparently named for it.

Uniontown ['yūnyən‚taun], village in Jackson County (L-8).

The village was laid out in 1859. Apparently this popular name is idealistic.

Uniontown ['yūnyən‚taun], village in Perry County (N-5).

In 1858 called Foster's Ridge, for the first postmaster, Alexander Foster. The present name, applied in 1890, apparently was chosen for its inspirational quality.

Uniontown ['yūnyən‚taun], village in Wells County (D-9).

A post office was established here in 1886. Named for Union Township, in which it is located.

Unionville ['yūnyən‚vil], village in Monroe County (K-6).

Formerly called Youngs Ridge, Buzzards Roost, Fleenersburg or Flenersburg, Union, and Old Unionville (to distinguish it from New Unionville, q.v.), the village was platted in 1837. The present name comes from a Baptist congregation called "Little Union," organized in 1832.

Universal ['yūnə'vərsəl], town in Vermillion County (J-3).

Platted in 1911 and formerly called Bunsen, for the Bunsen Coal Company that operated Universal Mines No. 4 and No. 5 here. In 1912 a post office was established and named Universal, for the local mines.

Upland ['əp,lænd], town in Grant County (F-9).

Platted in 1867 with the coming of the railroad and named by railroad officials because it was the highest point between Union City and Logansport.

Upton ['əp,tən], village in Posey County (O-1).

Established as a station on the L. & N. Railroad and named for a man who lived near the station. A post office named Upton was established here in 1886.

Urbana [,ər'bænə], village in Wabash County (D-8).

Platted in 1854. The name is a common commendatory name in the U. S. In this case, allegedly the name was drawn from a hat in which the proprietors had put suggested names.

Urmeyville ['ərmē,vil], village in Johnson County (J-7).

Platted in 1866 when a post office was established. Apparently the name comes from a personal name.

Utica ['yūḏikə], village in Clark County (N-8).

Platted in 1816 and probably named for Utica, New York.

V

Valeene [,væl'lēn], village in Orange County (N-6).

Laid out in 1837 and a post office was established in 1838. Probably named for a personal name.

Valentine ['vælən,tain], village in Lagrange County (B-9).

A post office named Valentine was established here in 1869. Probably named for a personal name.

Valley City ['vælē 'siḏē], village in Harrison County (O-7).

Laid out in 1860 and named for its location in a valley.

Valley Mills ['vælē 'milz], village in Marion County (H-6).

Platted in 1839 as Northport and changed to Fremont in 1856. The present name is for postmaster Abner Mills and for the town's location in a small valley.

Vallonia [və'lōn,yə], village in Jackson County (L-7).

Platted in 1810 on the site of Fort Vallonia, which was built in

1805 and so named because of its location in a valley.

Valparaiso [ˌvælpə'rāzō], county seat, third class city in Porter County (B-4).

Platted in 1836 as Portersville. The present name is for the city in Chile, off the coast of which Captain David Porter, for whom the county was named, fought the British in the War of 1812.

Van Buren [ˌvæn 'byurən], town in Grant County (E-9).

Settled in 1843 by G. H. Rood and formerly called Rood's Corner, Rood's School House, and Rood's Crossroads. The present name is a local transfer, from Van Buren Township, applied to the town in 1880 when it was laid out.

Vandalia [ˌvæn'dāl¸yə], village in Owen County (K-5).

Laid out in 1839. Possibly the name is a transfer, perhaps from New York or Ohio. The name is found in other states, too, such as Illinois, where it is the name of the former capital.

Vanderburgh ['vændər¸bərg] County (O-3).

Organized in 1818 and named for Judge Henry Vanderburgh, officer in the Revolution and judge of the first court in Indiana Territory.

Veales Creek ['vēlz ¸krēk], stream in Daviess County.

About 12 miles long, it flows west to West Fork White River at the Daviess-Knox county line. Formerly Veal's Creek and Veal Creek, it was named for James C. Veal, who built the first mill in the county around 1808.

Veedersburg ['vēdərz¸bərg], town in Fountain County (G-4).

Platted in 1872 by Peter S. Veeder and others and named for Veeder.

Vera Cruz [ˌverə 'krūz], town in Wells County (E-10).

Laid out in 1848 and named for the Mexican city, taken by American soldiers in 1847.

Vermillion [vər'mil¸yən] County (H-3).

Organized in 1824 and named for the Big Vermillion River, q.v.

Vermont [vər'mant], village in Howard County (F-7).

Laid out in 1849 by Milton Hadley from Ohio. Apparently named for the Green Mountain State.

Vernon ['vərnən], county seat, town in Jennings County (L-8).

Platted in 1815 and named for the home of George Washington.

Versailles [vər'sālz], county seat, town in Ripley County (K-9).

Founded in 1818 and named for the French town and palace.

Vevay ['vēvē], county seat, town in Switzerland County (M-10).

Founded in 1802 by Swiss settlers, platted in 1813, and named for the commune in Switzerland.

Vicksburg ['viks¸bərg], village in Greene County (K-4).

Founded in 1901 and named for Victoria Hanna, whose father owned land here.

Vienna [ˌvaiˈinə; -enə], village in Scott County (M-8).

Platted in 1849 and named for the capital of Austria.

Vigo [ˈvaigō; ˈvē-] County (J-3).

Organized in 1818 and named for Colonel Francis Vigo, a Sardinian merchant who came to Vincennes about 1777 and assisted George Rogers Clark's army.

Vigo [ˈvaigō; ˈvē-], village in Vigo County (K-3).

A post office was located here from 1844 until 1905. Named for Vigo County, in which it is located.

Vilas [ˈvailəs], village in Owen County (K-5).

Established in 1890 and named for William Freeman Vilas, Postmaster-General, 1885–88, and Secretary of the Interior, 1888–89.

Vincennes [ˌvinˈsinz; -senz], county seat, fourth class city in Knox County (M-3).

The capital of the Old Northwest Territory, it is the oldest town in Indiana. Some say a French trading post was established here as early as 1683. Settlers arrived before 1727, and a fort was built about 1732 under the command of François-Marie Bissot, Sieur de Vincennes, for whom it was named about 1736 when he was captured and burned at the stake by Chicka-

saw Indians. Before 1736 it went by several names, including *Au Poste, Post Ouabache,* and Post St. Vincent.

Vine [vain], village in Fountain County (F-4).

Founded about 1896. Allegedly the Post Office Department wanted a short name, and Vine was selected arbitrarily for its shortness.

Virgie [ˈvərjē], village in Jasper County (C-4).

Platted in 1893 and named for a daughter, Virgie Warner, of the founders.

Vistula [ˈvisˌchələ; -ˈchūlə], village in Elkhart County (A-8).

Laid out in 1865 and originally called Middlebury Station, as it was a railroad depot for the town of Middlebury. The name was changed to Vistula when a post office was established here. The present name comes from the river in northern Europe.

Vivalia [ˌvaiˈvālˌyə], village in Putnam County (H-4).

Settled as early as 1828, and a post office was established in 1882.

Volga [ˈvolgə], village in Jefferson County (L-9).

A post office was established here in 1856. Apparently named for the Volga River in Russia.

Voltz [vōlts] (Beardstown), village in Pulaski County (C-6).

See Beardstown.

W

Wabash ['wobæsh] County (D-8).

Organized in 1835 and named for the Wabash River.

Wabash ['wobæsh], county seat, fourth class city in Wabash County (E-8).

Settled in 1827, platted in 1834, and named for the Wabash River, on which it is located.

Wabash River ['wobæsh 'rivər], stream.

Over 500 miles long, it is the principal river in Indiana. It heads in the State of Ohio, enters Indiana in Jay County and flows across the state, first northwest, then west, then southwest, becoming the western boundary just south of Terre Haute, and empties into the Ohio River at the extreme southwestern tip of the state. The name is a contraction of the Miami name for the stream, *Wah-bah-shik-ki,* or *Wah-pah-shik-ki,* "b" and "p" being convertible in most Algonquian languages. The name suggests that the object named is pure white, or bright, inanimate, and natural. It refers to a limestone bed in the upper part of the river. The French spelled the name of the stream *Ouabache.*

Waco ['wākō], village in Daviess County (M-4).

A post office was established here in 1891 but discontinued in 1902. Named for the Texas city. Ulti-

mately the name comes from *We-ko,* "heron," a subtribe of the Wichita Indians.

Wadena [wə'dēnə], village in Benton County (E-4).

Platted in 1884. Perhaps the name comes from an Ojibwa word meaning "little round hill." A county and town in Minnesota bear this name.

Wadesville ['wādz‚vil], village in Posey County (O-2).

Laid out in 1852 and named for the local Wade family. Formerly called Cross Roads.

Wakarusa [‚wakə'rūsə], town in Elkhart County (B-7).

Founded in 1852 and named for the stream in Kansas. Formerly called Salem, it was renamed in 1859.

Wakefield ['wāk‚fēld], village in Jefferson County (L-8).

A post office was located here from 1899 until 1905. Named for Robert Wakefield, apparently a citizen.

Waldron ['woldrən], village in Shelby County (J-8).

Platted in 1854 by George Stroup and originally called Stroupville. The post office has been called Conn's Creek, for a nearby stream. The name was changed to Waldron by petition of the citizens.

Walesboro ['wālz,bərō], village in Bartholomew County (K-7).

Laid out in 1851 by John P. Wales, and named for him or his family.

Walkerton ['wokər,tən], town in St. Joseph County (B-6).

Laid out in 1856 and named for John Walker, promoter of the railroad through town.

Wallace ['woləs], town in Fountain County (G-4).

Platted in 1832 and named for Governor David Wallace, who was one of the first merchants in Covington.

Wallen ['wolən], village in Allen County (C-10).

Platted in 1870 and named for a railroad superintendent.

Walnut ['wol,nət], village in Marshall County (C-7).

Laid out in 1866 in Walnut Township and called Fredericks-burg, for the founder, Frederick Stair; however, the railroad named it Walnut, for the township.

Walnut Grove ['wol,nət 'grōv], village in Hamilton County (G-7).

Probably the name is commendatory as well as descriptive.

Walton ['woltn], town in Cass County (E-7).

Laid out in 1852 by Gilbert Wall and named for him.

Walton Lake ['woltn 'lāk], lake in Vigo County.

This 83-acre lake is operated by the Izaak Walton League, for which it was named.

Wanamaker ['wanə,mākər], village in Marion County (H-7).

Platted in 1834 and once called New Bethel. The present name honors John Wanamaker, Postmaster-General.

Wanatah ['wanə,ta], town in LaPorte County (B-5).

Established about 1857 and named for an Indian chief, whose name meant "he who charges his enemies."

Warren ['worən] County (F-3).

Organized in 1827 and named for General Joseph Warren, Massachusetts physician and soldier who was killed in the Battle of Bunker Hill in 1775.

Warren ['worən], town in Huntington County (E-9).

Platted in 1836 and originally named Jonesboro, for Samuel Jones who proposed the town site. It is believed that the present name is for Joseph Warren of the Revolution.

Warrenton ['worən,tən; 'war-], village in Gibson County (N-3).

Platted in 1840 and named for General Joseph Warren of the American Revolution.

Warrick ['worik] County (O-4).

Organized in 1813 and named for Captain Jacob Warrick, who was killed in the Battle of Tippecanoe.

Warrington ['woriŋ,tən], village in Hancock County (H-8).

173

Laid out in 1834 by John Oldham. The name is found in England and Pennsylvania and may be a transfer.

Warsaw ['wor͵so], county seat, fifth class city in Kosciusko County (C-8).
Platted in 1836 and named for the capital of Poland.

Washington ['wo(r)shiŋ͵tən] County (M-7).
Organized in 1814 and named in honor of George Washington.

Washington ['wo(r)shiŋ͵tən], county seat, fourth class city in Daviess County (M-4).
Platted in 1815 and apparently named for George Washington. Formerly called Liverpool.

Washington Center ['woshiŋ͵tən 'sentər], village in Whitley County (D-9).
So named because it is located in the center of Washington Township, which was named for George Washington.

Waterford ['wad̪ər͵fərd], village in LaPorte County (A-5).
A post office was established here in 1838. According to local legend, the town is so named because settlers forded a stream here.

Waterford Mills ['wad̪ər͵fərd 'milz], village in Elkhart County (B-8).
Founded in 1833 by Judge Elias Baker, who built a gristmill here near a ford over the Elkhart River; hence, the name is descriptive. Laid out in 1838.

Waterloo ['wad̪ər͵lū], town in Dekalb County (B-10).
Laid out in 1856 and named for the Belgian village, site of the famous battle of 1815. Earlier called Waterloo City to distinguish it from the other town named Waterloo in Indiana.

Waterloo ['wad̪ər͵lū], village in Fayette County (H-10).
Platted in 1841 in Waterloo Township and named for it. According to local legend, two drunks were engaged in a bloody fight in a saloon when someone remarked that it was worse than the Battle of Waterloo, and the town was named for that remark.

Waterman ['wad̪ər͵mən] (Lodi), village in Parke County (G-3).
Originally called Gilderoy. Platted in 1836 as Fullerton, but the name was changed to Lodi in 1837 for nearby artesian springs. In 1857 the name was changed again to Waterman, for Dr. Richard Waterman who settled here in that year and improved commercial interests. Lodi is still more popular among residents. Lodi is an Italian town, site of Napoleon's victory in 1796.

Waveland ['wav͵lənd], town in Montgomery County (H-4).
Platted in 1835 by John Milligan, who supposedly named it for Waveland, Kentucky, but current maps and gazetteers do not show a town of this name in Kentucky. Beckwith says the Indiana town was named for a "Kentucky gentleman's home."

Waverly ['wāvər‚lē], village in Morgan County (J-6).

Established about 1837 and laid out in 1841. The name probably comes from Scott's popular *Waverley* novels.

Wawaka [‚wə'wakə], village in Noble County (B-9).

Laid out in 1857. The name is Indian meaning "Big Heron."

Wawasee [‚wə'wa'sē], village in Kosciusko County (B-8).

A post office established as Cedar Beach in 1879 was changed to Wawasee in 1893. Named for Wawasee Lake.

Wawasee Lake [‚wa‚wa‚sē 'lāk], lake in Kosciusko County.

This 2618-acre lake at Syracuse was named for a Potawatomi chief, *Wah-wę-as-see,* "full moon," or literally, "the round one."

Wawpecong ['wapə'kaŋ], village in Miami County (E-7).

Platted in 1849. The name comes from the Indian name of the place, *Wa-pi-pa-ka-na,* "shell-bark hickories," for the large number of these trees growing here.

Waymansville ['wāmənz‚vil], village in Bartholomew County (K-7).

Laid out in 1849 by Charles L. Wayman and named for him.

Wayne [wān] County (H-10).

Organized in 1811 and named for General Anthony Wayne, officer in the Revolution but noted here mainly for his defeat of Little Turtle

at the Battle of Fallen Timbers in 1794.

Waynesburg ['wānz‚bərg], village in Decatur County (K-8).

Laid out in 1844, and a post office was located here from 1854 until 1902. Probably named for the personal name.

Waynesville ['wānz‚vil], village in Bartholomew County (K-7).

Laid out in 1851. It was built on the railroad about a mile north of the original settlement, Augusta, an unplatted village soon abandoned in favor of Waynesville.

Waynetown ['wān‚taun], town in Montgomery County (G-4).

Laid out in 1829 and named for Wayne Township, which was named for General Anthony Wayne.

Wea Creek ['wē‚ə ‚krēk], stream in Tippecanoe County.

About 17 miles long, it flows northwest to the Wabash River about 4 miles southwest of Lafayette. The name is an abbreviation of *Ouiatanon,* a Miami tribe and a French post on the Wabash named for the tribe. The full name of the tribe was *Wah-we-ah-tun-ong,* the Algonquian name of the Detroit River, from which the tribe probably took its name.

Weasel Creek ['wēzəl ‚krēk], stream in Miami County.

The name of this tributary of Eel River is a corruption of *Wesaw,* the former name of the stream and a reservation named for a Miami

175

chief. *We-saw* is the Miami word for the gall-bladder of an animal.

Weaver ['wēvər], village in Grant County (F-8).

A post office was established in 1880. Named for Henry Weaver, owner of the first store here.

Webster ['web͵stər], village in Wayne County (H-10).

Formerly called Fairfax and Dover, it was laid out about 1858. The present name is for the township in which it is located.

Weisburg ['wais͵bərg], village in Dearborn County (K-10).

Originally called Cork, it became Van Wedding's Station in 1855, Weisburgh in 1859, and Weisburg in 1892. Laid out in 1858.

Wells [welz] County (E-9).

Organized in 1837 and named for Captain William H. Wells, who was killed by Indians in 1812 while escorting a garrison from Fort Dearborn to Fort Wayne.

Wellsboro ['welz͵bərō], village in LaPorte County (B-5).

Founded in 1875 by the Wells brothers, Charles and Theodore, for whom it was named.

Wellsburg ['welz͵bərg], village in Wells County (E-9).

Platted in 1855 and named for Wells County.

West Atherton ['west 'æthər͵tən], village in Parke County (J-3).

A post office was established here in 1872, and the town was platted in 1904. The name is locational, as the village is just west of Atherton in Vigo County.

West Baden Springs ['wes(t) 'bādn 'spriŋz], town in Orange County (M-5).

Dr. John R. Lane, an itinerant medicine peddler, built the first resort here in 1851 and named it West Baden for the famous spa in Germany. It was first known as Mile Lick, since it was one mile from French Lick.

West College Corner ['west 'kalij 'kornər], town in Union County (J-11).

Platted in 1859. The name is locational, as the town was established west of College Corner, Ohio, founded about 1837.

Westfield ['west͵fēld], town in Hamilton County (G-7).

Founded in 1834 by Quakers. The name also is found in St. Joseph County and over a dozen other states, so it probably is a transfer.

West Fork ['west ͵fork], village in Crawford County (N-6).

Named for the West Fork Little Blue River on which it is located. Formerly called West Fork Post Office and Marietta.

West Fork White River [͵west ͵fork 'hwait ͵rivər], stream.

See White River.

West Franklin ['wes(t) 'fræŋklən], village in Posey County (O-2).

Laid out in 1837, although settled

around 1807. "The town was named West Franklin, it is said, to distinguish it from a man living near called East Franklin." Franklin, however, is nearly as popular as Washington as a place name, so the above account seems apocryphal.

West Harrison ['west 'herəsən], town in Dearborn County (K-11).
Established in 1813. Formerly called Harrison, probably for the township it is in.

West Lafayette ['west 'læfē'et; la-; lā-], fourth class city in Tippecanoe County (F-4).
Founded in 1845 as Kingston; in 1866 the name was changed to Chauncey, for a family of that name; and finally, in 1888, the name was changed to West Lafayette, a locational name, as it is west of Lafayette.

Westland ['wes(t)ˌlænd], village in Hancock County (H-8).
Unplatted. The first store, a log house, was built here in 1852.

West Lebanon ['wes(t) 'lebənən], town in Warren County (F-3).
Platted in 1830 and originally called Lebanon, probably for the biblical mountains. In 1869 the name was changed to West Lebanon by a vote of the citizens, apparently to distinguish it from another Lebanon, Indiana, east of here in Boone County.

West Liberty ['west 'libərdē], village in Howard County (F-8).
Founded in 1849. Probably the name is commendatory.

West Liberty ['wes(t) 'libərdē], village in Jay County (E-10).
Formerly called Mill's Corner, for a local flour mill, the village was originally platted in 1851. The present name probably was chosen for its commendatory value.

West Middleton ['wes(t) 'midlˌtən], village in Howard County (F-7).
Established about 1874 and named for William Middleton, landowner who laid out the town.

West Muncie ['west 'mənsē], village in Delaware County (G-9).
Platted in 1892 and named for its location west of Muncie.

West Newton ['wes(t) 'nūtn], village in Marion County (H-6).
Platted in 1851 and first called Easton, then Newton. West was added to the name to distinguish it from other towns named Newton.

West Noblesville ['wes(t) 'nōbəlzˌvil], village in Hamilton County (G-7).
The name is locational. See Noblesville.

Westphalia ['wes(t)'fālˌyə], village in Knox County (L-4).
Platted in 1881 and named for the German region and former province by German settlers.

West Point ['west ˌpoint], village in Tippecanoe County (F-4).
Platted in 1833. Originally called Middletown or Middleton, as it was the middle point between Lafayette and Attica. Postal authorities influenced changing the name to West

Point, as there were other towns named Middletown in the state.

Westport ['west‚pōrt], town in Decatur County (K-8).

First laid out in 1836 and a post office was established in 1839.

West Terre Haute ['wes(t) ‚terə 'hōt], town in Vigo County (J-3).

Platted in 1836 and originally called Macksville, for the founder, Samuel McQuilkin. The present name is locational, as the town is west of Terre Haute.

West Union ['west 'yūnyən], village in Parke County (H-3).

Settled in 1822 and platted in 1837. The first post office name was Union, but it was changed to Delta in 1840. Probably the name is commendatory.

Westville ['west‚vil], town in La-Porte County (B-5).

A post office was established as New Durham in 1842. In 1852, a year after this town was platted, the post office name was changed to Westville.

Westwood ['west‚wud], village in Henry County (H-9).

Platted in 1923.

Wheatfield ['hwēt‚fēld], town in Jasper County (C-4).

Settled in the early 1870's. Apparently so named because of its location in the midst of a productive grain district.

Wheatland ['hwēt‚lənd], town in Knox County (M-3).

Laid out in 1858 and named for the good wheat-growing land here.

Wheeler ['hwēlər], village in Porter County (B-4).

Laid out in 1858 and named for Captain Wheeler, a fur trader who had a trading post here in the 1820's.

Wheeler ['hwēlər] (Smithson), village in White County (E-5).

See Smithson.

Wheeling ['hwēliŋ] (Carroll), village in Carroll County (E-6).

Platted in 1835 and first called Carroll, for Carroll County. The present name supposedly honors an expert wheelwright who had a shop here.

Wheeling ['hwēliŋ], village in Delaware County (F-9).

A post office named Cranberry was established here in 1834. In 1838, a year after the village was laid out, the name was changed to Wheeling.

Wheeling ['hwēliŋ] (Kirksville), village in Gibson County (N-3).

Platted in 1856 and first called Kirksville, apparently for a personal name.

Whitaker ['hwidəkər; -dēkər], village in Morgan County (J-5).

A post office was established here in 1888. Named for a local family, probably for John Whitaker, who built the first store here.

Whitcomb ['hwit‚kəm], village in Franklin County (J-10).

Also called Union, it was platted in 1816. In 1846 a post office called Whitcomb, apparently for the personal name, was established.

White [hwait] County (E-5).
Organized in 1834 and named for Colonel Isaac White, who was killed in the Battle of Tippecanoe.

White Cloud ['hwait 'klaud], village in Harrison County (N-7).
Settled about 1879 in a valley between two ranges of hills; "its name was suggested by a mist that often hangs lazily over the town."

Whitehall ['hwait,hol], village in Owen County (K-5).
Laid out in 1838 by James Brown, who named it for a town in his native state, White Hall, North Carolina.

Whiteland ['hwait,lənd], town in Johnson County (J-7).
Laid out in 1863 by Joel White and others and probably named for White, although the origin is not certain. The first postmaster was Jacob White.

White Lick Creek ['hwait ,lik ,krēk], stream.
Heads in Boone County and flows south through Hendricks County and Morgan County to West Fork White River, about 6 miles north of Martinsville. It was named for a deer lick near its mouth.

White River ['hwait ,rivər], stream.
The largest tributary of the Wabash River. The West Fork heads in Randolph County and flows southwest across the state to the Wabash River in Gibson County. The Miami name was *Wah-pi-kah-me-ki,* "White Waters." The Delawares at first used a variant of the same name, although later they called the stream *Wah-pi-ha-ni,* "White River." For East Fork see Driftwood River.

White Rose ['hwait 'rōz], village in Greene County (L-4).
Established in 1903, when the White Rose Mine started operations here. The mine apparently received its name because a white rosebush was found on the spot where the shaft was sunk.

Whitestown ['hwaits,taun], town in Boone County (G-6).
Laid out in 1851 and first called New Germantown, but because there was difficulty in securing a post office under that name, the name was changed to Whitestown, for Albert S. White, first president of the I. C. and L. Railroad and congressman from this district.

Whitesville ['hwaits,vil], village in Montgomery County (G-5).
Platted in 1862 and named for the first postmaster, Joseph S. White.

Whitewater ['hwait,wadər], town in Wayne County (G-11).
Platted in 1828 and named for Whitewater River.

Whitewater River ['hwait,wadər ,rivər], stream.
The principal stream in south-

eastern Indiana, its West Fork heads in Randolph County and flows south through Wayne and Fayette counties. Near Brookville in Franklin County it is met by the East Fork and then flows southeast through Franklin and Dearborn counties to its confluence with the Miami River in the State of Ohio. The name is a translation of the Indian name, *Wapi-nepay,* "white, clear water," descriptive of its bed of white sand, gravel, and limestone.

Whitfield [ˈhwitˌfēld], village in Martin County (M-5).

A post office was established as Stremler in 1892, but about a month later the name was changed to Whitfield. An oral account says it was named for Whitfield Force, resident.

Whiting [ˈhwaidi̱ŋ], fourth class city in Lake County (A-3).

Laid out in 1889. Settled around a railroad crossing, it was earlier called Whiting's Crossing, Whiting's Station, and Whiting's for a railroad conductor involved in a train wreck here.

Whitley [ˈhwitˌlē] County (C-8).

Organized in 1839 and named for Colonel William Whitley, Kentucky soldier who was killed in the Battle of the Thames in 1813.

Wickliffe [ˈwiklif], village in Crawford County (N-5).

A post office was established here in 1842. Named for John Wickliffe (or Wycliffe), English religious reformer and translator of the Bible.

Wilbur [ˈwilbər], village in Morgan County (J-6).

Founded in the 1830's. A post office was located here from 1873 until 1906. Apparently named for the personal name.

Wildcat Creek [ˈwaild ˌkæt ˌkrēk], stream.

About 75 miles long, it heads in Howard County and flows west through Carroll County to the Wabash River about 4 miles north of Lafayette. The name comes from the Miami name, *Pin-ji-wa-mo-tai,* "Belly of the Wildcat." The French name, *Panse au Pichou,* was a literal translation of the Indian name.

Wilders [ˈwaildərz], village in LaPorte County (C-5).

A post office was established here in 1889. Formerly called Wilder's Crossing, Wilder's Junction, Wilder's Station, Wilder's, and Wilder. According to local anecdote, it was so named because it was located in the wilderness. Probably it was named for a family here.

Wilfred [ˈwulfrəd; ˈwil-], village in Sullivan County (K-3).

Established about 1902 as a coal mining town. The name was coined from the names of two mine operators, Wilford and Fredman.

Wilkinson [ˈwilkənˌsən], town in Hancock County (H-8).

Named for Elnathan and Thomas B. Wilkinson, who surveyed the original plat on January 16, 1883.

Williams ['wil,yəmz], village in Adams County (D-10).

Platted in 1871 and probably named for the personal name.

Williams ['wil,yəmz], village in Lawrence County (L-5).

Platted in 1889 and named for the Williams family here.

Williamsburg ['wil,yəmz,bərg], village in Wayne County (G-10).

Laid out in 1830 and apparently named for William Johnson, who platted the town.

Williamsport ['wil,yəmz,pōrt], county seat, town in Warren County (F-3).

Platted in 1828 and named for the proprietor, William Harrison.

Williamstown ['wil,yəmz,taun], village in Rush County (J-9).

A railroad station, Earl City, was established here in 1881. It assumed its present name when the older Williamstown Post Office, allegedly named for an early trader, was transferred here.

Willow Branch ['wilə 'brænch], village in Hancock County (H-8).

A post office called Willow Branch was established here in 1854, and the town was platted in 1882. The name comes from the stream, Willow Branch, on which the town is located.

Willow Valley ['wilə 'vælē], village in Martin County (M-5).

Originally named Proctor, probably for County Agent George R. Proctor. The present name was adopted as a post office name in 1858 and is descriptive of the willows that were abundant in a valley here.

Wilmington ['wilmiŋ,tən], village in Dearborn County (K-10).

Laid out in 1815. Apparently the name is a transfer from an eastern state.

Wilmot ['wil,mat], village in Noble County (C-8).

Originally called Ryders Mill, for John Ryder, who had a sawmill here in 1848. The present name honors early settlers named Wilmot.

Wilson ['wilsən], village in Shelby County (J-8).

Commonly called Wilson Corner, the unplatted community was established around a country store owned by the Wilson family, for whom it was named. A post office was established in 1883.

Winamac ['winə,mæk], county seat, town in Pulaski County (D-6).

Founded in 1835, laid out in 1839 and named for the Potawatomi chief *Wi-na-mak,* literally "mudfish," i.e., "catfish."

Winchester ['win,chestər], county seat, fifth class city in Randolph County (G-10).

Established as the county seat in 1818. Perhaps named for the English town via an eastern state.

Windfall ['win,fol], town in Tipton County (F-7).
Laid out in 1853.

Windom ['windəm], village in Martin County (M-5).
A post office was established here in 1892. Named for William Windom, Secretary of the Treasury under Garfield and Benjamin Harrison.

Windsor ['winzər], village in Randolph County (G-9).
Laid out in 1832 and named for the castle in England.

Winfield ['win,fēld], village in Lake County (B-4).
Established around 1888 and formerly called Bibler. The present name is for Winfield Township, which was named for General Winfield Scott by the first settler, Jeremy Hixson.

Wingate ['win,gāt], town in Montgomery County (G-4).
Laid out around 1831 and originally called Pleasant Hill, subjectively descriptive of its location. The present name honors an early and prominent citizen, John Wingate, who helped get a railway through town.

Winona [wə'nōnə; wi-], village in Starke County (C-6).
Laid out in 1891. The name was picked from several suggested names because there was no other post office of that name in Indiana.

Winona Lake [wə'nōnə 'lāk], lake in Kosciusko County.

This 478-acre lake is located 1 mile southeast of Warsaw. The name comes from *Wi-no-nah*, a Sioux proper name given to a first-born child if it is female. Wenonah of Longfellow's "Hiawatha" is the same name.

Winona Lake [wə'nōnə 'lāk], town in Kosciusko County (C-8).
A post office was established as Eagle Lake in 1889. In 1898 the name was changed to Winona Lake, for the lake of the same name.

Winslow ['winz,lō], town in Pike County (N-4).
Laid out in 1837 and a post office was established in 1839. Probably named for the personal name.

Winthrop ['win,thrəp], village in Warren County (F-4).
Platted in 1884. It had its beginning as a railroad town and post office in 1883. Apparently the name comes from a personal name.

Wirt [wərt], village in Jefferson County (L-9).
Laid out in 1837 and named for an early settler, William Wirt.

Witts Station ['wit(s) 'stāshən], village in Union County (H-11).
Probably named for the Witt family, early settlers and prominent citizens.

Wolcott ['wolkət; 'wul-], town in White County (E-4).
Laid out in 1861 by Ebenezer and Maria Wolcott and named for the Wolcott family.

Wolcottville ['wulkət͵vil; 'wol-], town in Lagrange and Noble counties (B-9).

Named for George Wolcott, who settled here in 1837 and established a gristmill, sawmill, carding mill, and distillery.

Wolf Creek ['wulf 'krēk], stream in Marshall County.

This tributary of Yellow River flows northwest and was called *Katam-wah-see-te-wah*, "Black Wolf," by the Indians, hence the name.

Wolf Lake ['wulf 'lāk], village in Noble County (C-9).

Laid out in 1836 on Wolf Lake, for which it was named.

Wolf Run ['wulf 'rən], stream in Clark County.

This small stream in northwestern Clark County allegedly was so named for "the great rendezvous it furnished wolves" in the first decade of the nineteenth century. Wolf is a fairly common specific of stream names in Indiana, as there are streams called Wolf Creek in Boone, Jay, and Marshall counties. Run is a relatively familiar generic applied to small streams in Clark County, as it is in the middle Atlantic states, although throughout Indiana creek is far more common.

Woodburn ['wud͵bərn], fifth class city in Allen County (C-11).

Platted in 1865 as Woodburn, probably for John Woodburn, although a variant name has been

Shirley City, for Indiana Senator Robert B. Shirley.

Woodbury ['wud͵berē], village in Hancock County (H-7).

Francis Ellingwood laid out the town in 1857, and apparently the name was coined from part of his name.

Woodland ['wud͵lənd], village in St. Joseph County (B-7).

Founded as early as 1860 but not platted until 1899. Probably named for the extensive forests and lumber business once here.

Woodruff ['wudrəf], village in Lagrange County (B-9).

Formerly called Wright's Corners, in 1880 it was renamed for a local merchant named Woodruff when the post office name was changed from Marcy, which was established as the post office in 1835. Allen Woodruff was postmaster in 1875.

Worthington ['wərthiŋ͵tən], town in Greene County (K-4).

Laid out in 1849 and named for Worthington, Ohio, home of one of the founders.

Wright Corner ['rait 'kornər], village in Dearborn County (K-10).

Named for Washington Wright, who had a store here about 1825 and became the first postmaster.

Wyalusing Creek [͵wai͵ə'lūsiŋ ͵krēk; ͵wai͵ə'nūsiŋ], stream in Jennings County.

This tributary of Sand Creek was

183

named for the Pennsylvania tributary of the Susquehanna.

Wyandotte ['wain‚dat], village in Crawford County (N-6).

A post office was established here in 1884. Named for the Indian tribe; the name probably means "People of One Speech."

Wyatt ['wai‚ət], village in St. Joseph County (B-7).

Originally called Littleton, it was platted in 1894 and renamed Wyatt, allegedly for a place in Pennsylvania, although current sources do not give this name in that state. Perhaps the name comes from Wyatt, West Virginia, located about 20 miles from Pennsylvania.

Wynn [win] (Palestine), village in Franklin County (J-10).

Platted in 1847 and originally called Palestine, for the biblical region. Apparently renamed Wynn, for a personal name, to distinguish it from another Hoosier town named Palestine. A post office was located here from 1848 until 1906.

Y

Yankeetown ['yæŋkē‚taun], village in Warrick County (O-3).

Platted in 1858 and probably named for Yankee settlers from New England, although one account says for Union sympathizers from Kentucky.

Yeddo ['yedō], village in Fountain County (G-3).

Platted in 1881 and named by the Post Office Department because it wanted a short, uncommon name. Yeddo, or Jeddo, was the former name of Tokyo.

Yellow River ['yelō ‚rivər; 'yelə-], stream.

About 60 miles long, it heads in Kosciusko County and flows west through Marshall and Starke counties to the Kankakee River near English Lake. The name is from the Potawatomi name of the stream, *Way-thow-kah-mik,* "yellow waters."

Yenne ['yenē], village in Martin County (M-5).

A post office was established here in 1860. Named for Peter Yenne, postmaster at Shoals.

Yeoman ['yōmən], town in Carroll County (E-5).

Platted in 1880 and named for Colonel Yeoman, a railroad official.

Yorktown ['york‚taun], town in Delaware County (G-9).

Platted in 1836 and named for the York tribe of the Delaware Indians.

Yorkville ['york‚vil], village in Dearborn County (K-10).

Formerly called York Ridge, it became Yorkville in 1845. Named for York Township, in which it is located.

Young America ['yəŋ ə'merəkə], village in Cass County (E-6).

Platted in 1863. The name preserves a phrase that was a political catchword of expansionists. According to local anecdote, Thomas Henry bought a steam boiler for his sawmill about 1855. Someone wrote "Young America," indicating enterprise, on the boiler, and Henry named the place Young America.

Youngs Creek ['yəŋz ˌkrēk], stream in Johnson County.

Formerly called Lick Creek, for the deer licks along it, it flows southeast to Sugar Creek. The present name is for Joseph Young, who purchased 160 acres near its mouth in 1821.

Youngs Creek ['yəŋz ˌkrēk], village in Orange County (M-6).

Laid out about 1864 and formerly known as Unionville, allegedly as a result of two political parties uniting. The present name comes from the post office here, so named for Youngs Creek, on which it is located, named for an early settler.

Youngstown ['yəŋzˌtaun], village in Vigo County (J-3).

Laid out in 1868 and named for Samuel Young, early settler.

Yountsville ['yantsˌvil], village in Montgomery County (G-4).

Named for the Younts family, early settlers who established a woolen mill here about 1840.

Z

Zanesville ['zānzˌvil], village in Wells County (D-9).

Platted in 1848 and named for Zanesville, Ohio, by early settlers from Ohio.

Zelma ['zelmə], village in Lawrence County (L-6).

Platted in 1889 by Stephen Fountain and named for one of his daughters.

Zenas ['zēnəs], village in Jennings County (K-9).

Founded in 1826. A post office was established as Ely in 1830, but changed to Zenas in 1839.

Zionsville ['zaiˌənzˌvil], town in Boone County (G-6).

Settled in 1830 and platted in 1852, it was named for one of its founders, William Zion.

Zipp [zip], village in Vanderburgh County (O-3).

Formerly called Mechanicsville and locally called Stringtown because the houses here were strung along the road. When a post office was established in 1881, the name became Zipp's, for Frank Zipp, Jr., a senior resident of the town who served as the first postmaster. The name was changed to Zipp in 1894.

Zulu ['zūlū], village in Allen County (D-10).

A post office was established here in 1880. Allegedly the name had to be changed from Four Corners when a post office was established, and the present name was selected from a geography book. A pin stuck in the book fell on the word Zulu on a page about Africa.

Bibliography

Alvord, Samuel E. *History of Noble County, Indiana.* Logansport, Indiana, 1902.

Baber, Jack. *The Early History of Greene County, Indiana.* Worthington, Indiana, 1875.

Bailey, John C. W., and Co. *Floyd County Gazetteer.* Chicago, 1868.

Baird, Lewis C. *Baird's History of Clark County, Indiana.* Indianapolis, 1909.

Baker, Ronald L. "County Names in Indiana," *Indiana Names,* 2 (Fall 1971), 39–54.

Ball, T. H. *Lake County, Indiana, 1834–1872.* Chicago, 1873.

Banta, David Demaree. *A Historical Sketch of Johnson County, Indiana.* Chicago, 1881.

Bash, Frank Sumner, ed. *History of Huntington County, Indiana.* Chicago, 1914. 2 vols.

Beckwith, Hiram Williams. *History of Fountain County, together with Historic Notes on the Wabash Valley.* Chicago, 1881.

Beckwith, Hiram Williams. *History of Montgomery County, together with Historic Notes on the Wabash Valley.* Chicago, 1881.

Beckwith, Hiram Williams. *History of Vigo and Parke Counties, together with Historic Notes on the Wabash Valley.* Chicago, 1880.

Beckwith, H. W. "Indian Names of Water Courses in the State of Indiana," *Annual Report of the Indiana Department of Geography and Natural History.* Indianapolis, 1883 .

Beers, J. H., and Co. *Atlas of Bartholomew County, Indiana.* Chicago, 1879.

Beers, J. H., and Co. *Atlas of Decatur County, Indiana.* Chicago, 1882.

Beers, J. H., and Co. *Atlas of DeKalb County, Indiana.* Chicago, 1880.

Beers, J. H., and Co. *Atlas of Franklin County, Indiana.* Chicago, 1882.

Beers, J. H., and Co. *Atlas of Hendricks County, Indiana.* Chicago, 1878.

Beers, J. H., and Co. *Atlas of Johnson County, Indiana.* Chicago, 1881.

Beers, J. H., and Co. *Atlas of Montgomery County, Indiana.* Chicago, 1878.

Beers, J. H., and Co. *Atlas of Putnam County, Indiana.* Chicago, 1879.

Beers, J. H., and Co. *Atlas of Shelby County, Indiana.* Chicago, 1880.

Beers, J. H., and Co. *Atlas of Steuben County, Indiana.* Chicago, 1880.

Beers, J. H., and Co. *Atlas of Union County, Indiana.* Chicago, 1884.

Binford, John H. *History of Hancock County, Indiana.* Greenfield, Indiana, 1882.

Bibliography

Biographical and Historical Souvenir for the Counties of Clark, Crawford, Harrison, Floyd, Jefferson, Jennings, Scott and Washington, Indiana. Chicago, 1889.

Birch, Jesse S. *History of Benton County and Historic Oxford.* Oxford, Indiana, 1928.

Blair, Don. *Harmonist Construction.* Indianapolis, 1964.

Blanchard, Charles, ed. *Counties of Clay and Owen, Indiana.* Chicago, 1884.

Blanchard, Charles, ed. *Counties of Howard and Tipton, Indiana.* Chicago, 1883.

Blanchard, Charles, ed. *Counties of Morgan, Monroe and Brown, Indiana.* Chicago, 1884.

Bodurtha, Arthur Lawrence. *History of Miami County, Indiana.* Chicago and New York, 1914. 2 vols.

Bogardus, Carl R. *The Centennial History of Austin, Scott County, Indiana.* Paoli, Indiana, 1953.

Bradsby, Henry C. *History of Vigo County, Indiana.* Chicago, 1891.

Branigin, Elba L. *History of Johnson County, Indiana.* Indianapolis, 1913.

Brewster, Paul G. "Additional Observations of Indiana Place-Names," *Hoosier Folklore Bulletin,* 3 (December, 1944), 74–76.

Brewster, Paul G. "A Glance at Some Indiana Place Names," *Hoosier Folklore Bulletin,* 2 (June 1943), 14–16.

Brunvand, Jan H. "Some Indiana Place Name Legends," *Midwest Folklore,* 9 (Winter 1959), 245–48.

Campbell, Frank S. *The Story of Hamilton County, Indiana.* n.p., 1962.

Chadwick, Edward H. *Chadwick's History of Shelby County, Indiana.* Indianapolis, 1909.

Chamberlain, E. *The Indiana Gazetteer, or Topographical Dictionary of the State of Indiana.* Indianapolis, 1849.

Chambers, Doris M. *Ghost Towns of Huntington County.* Huntington, Indiana, 1971.

Clifton, Thomas A., ed. *Past and Present of Fountain and Warren Counties, Indiana.* Indianapolis, 1913.

Counties of LaGrange and Noble, Indiana. Chicago, 1883.

Counties of Warren, Benton, Jasper and Newton, Indiana. Chicago, 1883.

Counties of White and Pulaski, Indiana. Chicago, 1883.

Crist, L. M. *History of Boone County, Indiana.* Indianapolis, 1914. 2 vols.

Daggett, Rowan K. "The Place-Names of Chester Township, Wabash County, Indiana," *Indiana Names,* 4 (Spring 1973), 4–30.

De Hart, Richard P., ed. *Past and Present of Tippecanoe County, Indiana.* Indianapolis, 1909. 2 vols.

De la Hunt, Thomas James. "History Lessons from Indiana Names," *Indiana History Bulletin,* 3 (March 1926), 43–49.

De la Hunt, Thomas James. *Perry County: a History.* Indianapolis, 1916.

Dunn, Jacob Piatt. "Glossary of Indian Names and Supposed Indian Names, in Indiana," *Indiana and Indianans.* Chicago, 1919. Vol. I, 86–97.

188

Bibliography

Dunn, Jacob Piatt. "Indiana Geographical Nomenclature." *Indiana Magazine of History,* 8 (September 1912), 109–14.

Dunn, Jacob Piatt. Notes on Indiana place names in the Indiana Historical Society Library, Indianapolis, Indiana.

Dunn, Jacob Piatt. *True Indian Stories with Glossary of Indiana Indian Names.* Indianapolis, 1909.

Esarey, Logan. *History of Indiana . . . an Account of Fulton County,* ed. H. A. Barnhart. Dayton, 1923. Vol. 3.

Esarey, Logan. *History of Indiana . . . an Account of St. Joseph County,* ed. John B. Stoll. Dayton, 1922. Vol. 3.

Forkner, John La Rue. *Historical Sketches and Reminiscences of Madison County, Indiana.* Anderson. 1897.

Goodspeed, Weston A., and Charles Blanchard, eds. *Counties of Porter and Lake, Indiana.* Chicago, 1882.

Goodspeed, Weston A., and Charles Blanchard, eds. *Counties of Whitley and Noble, Indiana.* Chicago, 1882.

Gratzer, Florence Elise. "A Study of the Place Names in Lawrence County, Indiana." M.A. thesis, Indiana State University, 1957.

Green, George E. *History of Old Vincennes and Knox County, Indiana.* Chicago, 1911. 2 vols.

Griffing, B. N. *Atlas of Daviess County, Indiana.* Philadelphia, 1888.

Griffing, B. N. *Atlas of Jay County, Indiana.* Philadelphia, 1887.

Griffing, Gordon, and Co. *An Atlas of Hancock County, Indiana.* Philadelphia, 1887.

Guthrie, James M. *Thirty-three Years in the History of Lawrence County, 1884–1917.* Greenfield, Indiana, 1958.

Hadley, John V., ed. *History of Hendricks County, Indiana.* Indianapolis, 1914.

Hahn, Holly Jane. "The Place-Names of Brown Township, Montgomery County, Indiana," *Indiana Names,* 5 (Spring 1974), 19–36.

Haimbaugh, Frank D. *History of Delaware County, Indiana.* Indianapolis, 1924. 2 vols.

Hamilton, Louis H. and William Darroch. *A Standard History of Jasper and Newton Counties, Indiana.* Chicago and New York, 1916.

Harden, Samual, comp. *Early Life and Times in Boone County, Indiana.* Indianapolis, 1887.

Harden, Samual, comp. *History of Madison County, Indiana.* Markleville, Indiana, 1874.

Hardesty, A. C. *Illustrated Historical Atlas of Porter County.* Valparaiso, 1876.

Harding, Lewis Albert, ed. *History of Decatur County, Indiana.* Indianapolis, 1915.

Hazzard, George. *History of Henry County, Indiana.* New Castle, Indiana, 1906. 2 vols.

Helm, Thomas B., ed. *History of Allen County, Indiana.* Chicago, 1880.

Helm, Thomas B., ed. *History of Carroll County, Indiana.* Chicago, 1882.

189

Helm, Thomas B., ed. *History of Cass County, Indiana.* Chicago, 1886.

Helm, Thomas B., ed. *History of Delaware County, Indiana.* Chicago, 1881.

Helm, Thomas B., ed. *History of Hamilton County, Indiana.* Chicago, 1880.

Helm, Thomas B., ed. *History of Wabash County, Indiana.* Chicago, 1884.

Historical Sketch of Huntington County, Indiana. Huntington, 1877.

History of Bartholomew County, Indiana. Chicago, 1888.

History of Clinton County, Indiana. Chicago, 1886.

History of Dearborn and Ohio Counties, Indiana. Chicago, 1885.

History of Dekalb County, Indiana. Indianapolis, 1914.

History of Elkhart County, Indiana. Chicago, 1881.

History of Fayette County, Indiana. Chicago, 1885.

History of Gibson County, Indiana. Edwardsville, Indiana, 1884.

History of Grant County, Indiana. Chicago, 1886.

History of Greene and Sullivan Counties, State of Indiana. Chicago, 1884.

History of Hendricks County, Indiana. Chicago, 1885.

History of Henry County, Indiana. Chicago, 1884.

History of Huntington County, Indiana. Chicago, 1887.

History of Jackson County, Indiana. Chicago, 1886.

History of Johnson County, Indiana. Chicago, 1888.

History of Knox and Daviess Counties, Indiana. Chicago, 1886.

History of LaPorte County, Indiana. Chicago, 1880.

History of Lawrence and Monroe Counties, Indiana. Indianapolis, 1914.

History of Lawrence, Orange and Washington Counties, Indiana. Chicago, 1884.

History of Madison County, Indiana. Chicago, 1880.

History of Miami County, Indiana. Chicago, 1887.

History of Montgomery County, Indiana. Indianapolis, 1913. 2 vols.

History of Parke and Vermillion Counties, Indiana. Indianapolis, 1913.

History of Pike and Dubois Counties, Indiana. Chicago, 1885.

History of Posey County, Indiana. Chicago, 1886.

History of Rush County, Indiana. Chicago, 1888.

History of St. Joseph County, Indiana. Chicago, 1880.

History of Shelby County, Indiana. Chicago, 1887.

History of Steuben County, Indiana. Chicago, 1885.

History of the Ohio Falls Cities and Their Counties. Cleveland, 1882. 2 vols.

History of the Town of Remington and Vicinity of Jasper County, Indiana. Logansport, Indiana, 1894.

History of Vanderburgh County, Indiana. Madison, Wisconsin, 1889.

History of Warrick, Spencer, Perry Counties, Indiana. Chicago, 1885.

History of Wayne County, Indiana. Chicago, 1884. 2 vols.

Hixson, Jerome C. "Some Approaches to Indiana Place Names," *Indiana Names,* 1 (Spring 1970), 11–19.

Hoffman, Frank A. "Place Names in Brown County," *Midwest Folklore,* 11 (Spring 1961), 57–62.

Hollar, Jean. "Place-Names of Fayette County, Indiana," *Indiana Names,* 5 (Fall 1974), 43–70.

Hovey, Alvin P. *Centennial Historical Sketch of Posey County, Indiana.* n.p., 1876.

Howard, Timothy Edward. *A History of St. Joseph County, Indiana.* Chicago, 1907. 2 vols.

Howat, William Frederick., ed. *A Standard History of Lake County, Indiana.* Chicago, 1915. 2 vols.

Illustrated Historical Atlas of the State of Indiana. Chicago, 1876.

Indiana Board on Geographic Names. *Findings* (May 1961–June 1965). 3 vols.

"Indiana Geographical Nomenclature," *Indiana Magazine of History,* 8 (June 1912), 70–83.

Indiana Historical Society Library, Indianapolis. Indiana place-names card file.

Indiana State Chamber of Commerce. *Here is Your Indiana Government.* Indianapolis, 1973.

Indiana State Library, Indiana Section, Indianapolis. Card file of Indiana post offices.

Indiana State Library, Indiana Section, Indianapolis. Place-name files, mainly from newspapers.

Indiana State University Folklore Archives. Manuscript files.

Jay, Milton T. *History of Jay County, Indiana.* Indianapolis, 1922. 2 vols.

Kemper, General William Harrison, ed. *A Twentieth Century History of Delaware County, Indiana.* Chicago, 1908. 2 vols.

Kingman, A. L. *Combination Atlas Map of Fulton County, Indiana.* n.p., 1883.

Kingman Brothers. *Combination Atlas Map of Boone County, Indiana.* Chicago, 1878.

Kingman Brothers. *Combination Atlas Map of Howard County, Indiana.* Chicago, 1877.

Kreitzer, Alves John. *A History of Northeast Dubois County.* Dubois, 1970.

Lagrange and Noble Counties, Indiana. Chicago, 1882.

McDonald, Daniel. *A Twentieth Century History of Marshall County, Indiana.* Chicago, 1908. 2 vols.

McDonald, Daniel. *History of Marshall County, Indiana.* Chicago, 1881.

Montgomery, M. W. *History of Jay County, Indiana.* Chicago, 1864.

Morrow, Jackson. *History of Howard County, Indiana.* Indianapolis, 1870.

O'Donnell, Harold L. *Newport and Vermillion Township: the First 100 Years, 1824–1924.* Danville, Illinois, 1969.

Ogle, George A., and Co. *Standard Atlas of St. Joseph County, Indiana.* Chicago, 1895.

Bibliography

Packard, Jasper. *History of LaPorte County, Indiana.* LaPorte, Indiana, 1876.

Paul, Hosea. *Atlas of Wabash County, Indiana.* Philadelphia, 1875.

Pegee, O. W. *Atlas of Ripley County, Indiana.* New York, 1900.

Pleas, Elwood. *Henry County . . . a Brief History of the County from 1821 to 1871.* New Castle, 1871.

Powell, Jehu Z., ed. *History of Cass County, Indiana.* Chicago and New York, 1913. 2 vols.

Pulaski County Centennial Association. *Souvenir Program and History, Pulaski County, Indiana.* Winamac, Indiana, 1939.

Putnam County Sesquicentennial Committee. *A Journey through Putnam County History.* n.p., 1966.

Quinn, French. *A Short, Short Story of Adams County, Indiana.* Berne, Indiana, n.d.

Reifel, August J. *History of Franklin County, Indiana.* Indianapolis, 1915.

Rennick, Robert. "Place-Name Derivations Are Not Always What They Seem," *Indiana Names,* 2 (Spring 1971), 19–28.

Rennick, Robert M. "The Folklore of Place-Naming in Indiana," *Indiana Folklore,* 3, No. 1 (1970), 35–94.

Richman, George J. *History of Hancock County, Indiana.* Indianapolis, 1916.

Roose, William H. *Indiana's Birthplace: A History of Harrison County, Indiana.* New Albany, Indiana, 1911.

Seits, Laurence E. "Place Names of Parke County, Indiana," M.A. thesis, Indiana State University, 1970.

Smith, John L. and Lee L. Driver. *Past and Present of Randolph County, Indiana.* Indianapolis, 1914.

Stewart, George S. *American Place-Names.* New York, 1970.

Travis, William. *A History of Clay County, Indiana.* New York and Chicago, 1909. 2 vols.

Tucker, E. *History of Randolph County, Indiana.* Chicago, 1882.

Warren County Historical Society. *A History of Warren County, Indiana.* n.p., 1966.

Wolfe, Thomas Jefferson, ed. *A History of Sullivan County, Indiana.* New York and Chicago, 1909. 2 vols.

Works Progress Administration. *Indiana: A Guide to the Hoosier State.* American Guide Series. New York, 1941.

Works Progress Administration. Indiana files of the Federal Writers' Project, Cunningham Memorial Library, Indiana State University, Terre Haute, Indiana.

Pronunciation Informants

Adams County: 68-year-old retired auto dealer; born Berne, resides Geneva.

Bartholomew County: 54-year-old electronic technician; born Augusta, resides Columbus.

Benton County: 54-year-old farmer; born Iroquois, Illinois; resides Earl Park.

Blackford County: 34-year-old teacher; born Bluffton, resides Montpelier.

Boone County: 32-year-old electrical engineer; born Richmond, resides Zionsville.

Brown County: 29-year-old computer science student; born Chicago, Illinois; resides Nashville.

Carroll County: 43-year-old farmer; born, resides Logansport.

Cass County: 51-year-old corporation executive; born, resides Logansport.

Clark County: 57-year-old optical technician; born Floyd County, resides Jeffersonville.

Clay County: 33-year-old communications technician; born Indianapolis, resides Brazil.

Clinton County: 50-year-old oil jobber; born Hillisburg, resides Frankfort.

Crawford County: 41-year-old public health sanitarian; born Huntington, long-time Crawford County resident now resides Wadesville.

Daviess County: 56-year-old retired supervisory engineering technician; born, resides Odon.

Dearborn County: 59-year-old maintenance and electricians' foreman; born, resides Milan.

Decatur County: 47-year-old inspector for automotive manufacturing plant; born Martinsville, Illinois; resides Greensburg.

Dekalb County: 26-year-old electronics technician; born Scott County, resides Waterloo.

Delaware County: (a) 52-year-old supervisor at automotive plant; born Lilly Dale, Tennessee; resides Muncie. (b) 57-year-old TV and radio serviceman; born Anderson, resides Muncie.

Dubois County: 58-year-old convent chaplain; born Evansville, resides Ferdinand.

Elkhart County: 62-year-old electronic technician; born, resides New Paris.

Fayette County: 68-year-old retired appliance service manager; born, resides Connersville.

Floyd County: 37-year-old electronic technician; born New Albany, resides Owensburg.

Franklin County: 43-year-old chemist; born Cincinnati, Ohio; resides Brookville.

Fulton County: 49-year-old campground owner; born Macy, resides Akron.

Gibson County: 59-year-old homemaker; born Gibson County, resides Princeton.

Grant County: 79-year-old retired machinist; born Indianapolis, resides Gas City.

Green County: 49-year-old electrician; born Dugger, resides Linton.

Hancock County: 68-year-old retired department store assistant manager; born Rush County, resides Greenfield.

Harrison County: 32-year-old electronics technician; born New Albany, resides Lanesville.

Hendricks County: 49-year-old software engineer; born South Bend, resides Brownsburg.

Henry County: 14-year-old student; born Marion, resides New Castle.

Howard County: 42-year-old retiree; born Royal Center, resides Kokomo.

Huntington County: 69-year-old retired electrical manufacturing plant employee; born Richmond, resides Roanoke.

Jackson County: 68-year-old retired telephone company employee; born Eden, resides Seymour.

Jasper County: (a) 66-year-old retired farm implement employee; born Chicago, Illinois; resident of De Motte for 61 years. (b) 63-year-old retired radio operator; born Francesville, resides Rensselaer. (c) 40-year-old housewife; born Monon, resides Rensselaer. (d) 53-year-old county assessor; born Monon, resides Rensselaer.

Jay County: 59-year-old retired inspector for automotive manufacturer; born, resides Dunkirk.

Jefferson County: 63-year-old retired electronic engineer; born, resides Madison.

Jennings County: 30-year-old manufacturing engineer; born Alexandria, resides Scipio.

Johnson County: 38-year-old school principal; born Shelbyville, resides Franklin.

Knox County: 45-year-old electronics technician; born Decker, resides Vincennes.

Kosciusko County: (a) 66-year-old retired supervisor of maintenance at automotive plant; born Greenfield, resides Syracuse. (b) 68-year-old retired science teacher; born Peru, resides Silver Lake.

LaGrange County: (a) 45-year-old math and physics teacher; born Sheridan, resides Shipshewana. (b) 37-year-old tool maker; born Chicago, Illinois; resides Wolcottville.

Lake County: 29-year-old elementary school principal; born Gary, resides Crown Point.

Pronunciation Informants

LaPorte County: 48-year-old salesman; born Laketon, resides LaPorte.

Lawrence County: (a) 47-year-old engineer; born Lawrence County, resides Bedford. (b) 64-year-old electronics mechanics instructor; born Chicago, Illinois; resides Bedford.

Madison County: 49-year-old machinist; born, resides Anderson.

Marion County: 29-year-old engineer; born Indianapolis, resides Beech Grove.

Marshall County: (a) 60-year-old retired government administrator; born Greencastle, resides Jonesboro. (b) 56-year-old piano tuner; born, resides Culver.

Monroe County: 48-year-old math teacher; born Livingston, Tennessee; resides Bloomington.

Morgan County: 58-year-old electrical engineer; born Hancock County, Ohio; resides Martinsville.

Newton County: (a) 63-year-old attorney; born Brook, resides Kentland. (b) 35-year-old waitress and housewife; born Watseka, Illinois; resides Kentland.

Noble County: 65-year-old deputy auditor; born Albion, resides Wawaka.

Orange County: 36-year-old prosecuting attorney; born New Albany, resides Paoli.

Owen County: 43-year-old county deputy recorder; born Owen County, resides Spencer.

Parke County: 68-year-old retired utility company employee; born, Shelbyville, resides Rockville.

Perry County: 72-year-old mechanical engineer; born Carrington, North Dakota; resides Troy.

Pike County: (a) 51-year-old retired postmaster; born, resides Stendal. (b) 51-year-old supermarket owner; born Washington, resides Petersburg.

Porter County: 54-year-old radio engineer; born Goodland, resides Porter.

Posey County: 49-year-old steelworker; born Louisville, Kentucky; resides Mt. Vernon.

Pulaski County: 49-year-old farmer; born Bourbon, resides Star City.

Putnam County: 35-year-old county auditor; born Rensselaer, resides Greencastle.

Randolph County: 67-year-old TV serviceman and farmer; born Dark County, Ohio; resides Lynn.

Ripley County: 59-year-old maintenance and electricians' foreman; born, resides Milan.

Rush County: 66-year-old retiree; born Morristown, resides Arlington.

St. Joseph County: 76-year-old retired commercial photographer, born Etna Green, resides South Bend.

Scott County: 59-year-old process control technician; born St. Helens, Kentucky; resides Austin.

Shelby County: (a) 59-year-old housewife; born Shelby County, resides Morristown. (b) 69-year-old farmer; born Morristown, resides Gwynneville.

Starke County: 34-year-old minister; born Crawfordsville, resides Knox.

195

Steuben County: 62-year-old retired electrical engineering professor; born West Elizabeth, Pennsylvania; resides Angola.

Sullivan County: (a) 48-year-old tool and die maker; born Sullivan County, resides Merom. (b) 59-year-old utility company serviceman; born Logansport, resides Sullivan. (c) 64-year-old police radio technician; born Montgomery City, Missouri; resides Farmersburg.

Switzerland County: 58-year-old mechanical engineer; born Switzerland County, resides Vevay.

Tippecanoe County: 57-year-old research and development technician; born, resides Lafayette.

Tipton County: 51-year-old die maker; born Anderson, resides Atlanta.

Union County: 59-year-old electrician; born, resides Liberty.

Vanderburgh County: 75-year-old retired schoolteacher; born Velpen, resides Evansville.

Vermillion County: 61-year-old electrician; born, resides Cayuga.

Vigo County: (a) 53-year-old university administrator; born, resides Terre Haute. (b) 51-year-old dental laboratory technician; born, resides Terre Haute.

Wabash County: 25-year-old drainage contractor; born Wabash, resides North Manchester.

Warren County: 74-year-old restaurant operator; born Marshfield, resides West Lebanon.

Warrick County: 32-year-old appliance serviceman; born, resides Boonville.

Washington County: (a) 46-year-old salesman; born, resides Pekin. (b) 76-year-old retired assistant postmaster; born Washington County, resides Salem.

Wayne County: 75-year-old retired heavy machinery salesman; born Chicago, Illinois; resides Richmond.

Wells County: 77-year-old retired banker; born, resides Bluffton.

White County: 57-year-old farmer; born White County, resides Monon.

Whitley County: 70-year-old electrical contractor; born Napoleon, Ohio; resides Columbia City.